by Tom Wolfe

THE KANDY-KOLORED
TANGERINE-FLAKE
STREAMLINE BABY

by Tom Wolfe

FARRAR, STRAUS
AND GIROUX
New York

THE KANDY-KOLORED TANGERINE-FLAKE STREAMLINE BABY

ACKNOWLEDGMENTS

The following chapters were first published in *Esquire* Magazine: "Las Vegas (What?) Las Vegas (Can't Hear You! Too Noisy) Las Vegas!!!!," "The Kandy-Kolored Tangerine-Flake Streamline Baby" (under the title, "There Goes [Varoom! Varoom!] That Kandy-Kolored Tangerine-Flake Streamline Baby"), "The Marvelous Mouth," "The Last American Hero" (under the title, "The Last American Hero is Junior Johnson. Yes!"), and "Purveyor of the Public Life" (under the title, "Public Lives: *Confidential* Magazine; Reflection in Tranquility by the Former Owner, Robert Harrison"); "The New Art Gallery Society" first appeared in *Harper's Bazaar;* all the other essays first appeared in the New York *Herald Tribune*'s Sunday magazine, *New York.* "The Big League Complex" is reprinted from the book, *New York, New York,* © 1964 by the New York *Herald Tribune,* with the permission of the publishers, The Dial Press, Inc.

The drawings for "Teen-Age Male Hairdos" first appeared in the Springfield (Mass.) *Sunday Republican,* those for "New York's Beautiful People" first appeared in *Venture* Magazine, and the other drawings first appeared in the New York *Herald Tribune's New York.*

CONTENTS

o

Introduction

I don't mean for this to sound like "I had a vision" or anything, but there was a specific starting point for practically all of these stories. I wrote them in a fifteen-month period, and the whole thing started with the afternoon I went to a Hot Rod & Custom Car show at the Coliseum in New York. Strange afternoon! I was sent up there to cover the Hot Rod & Custom Car show by the New York *Herald Tribune*, and I brought back exactly the kind of story any of the somnambulistic totem newspapers in America would have come up with. A totem newspaper is the kind people don't really buy to read but just to *have*, physically, because they know it supports their own outlook on life. They're just like the buffalo tongues the Omaha

Indians used to carry around or the dog ears the Mahili clan carried around in Bengal. There are two kinds of totem newspapers in the country. One is the symbol of the frightened chair-arm-doilie Vicks Vapo-Rub *Weltanschauung* that lies there in the solar plexus of all good gray burghers. All those nice stories on the first page of the second section about eighty-seven-year-old ladies on Gramercy Park who have one-hundred-and-two-year-old turtles or about the colorful street vendors of Havana. Mommy! This fellow Castro is in there, and revolutions may come and go, but the picturesque poor will endure, padding around in the streets selling their chestnuts and salt pretzels the world over, even in Havana, Cuba, assuring a paradise, after all, full of respect and obeisance, for all us Vicks Vapo-Rub chair-arm-doilie burghers. After all. Or another totem group buys the kind of paper they can put under their arms and have the totem for the tough-but-wholesome outlook, the Mom's Pie view of life. Everybody can go off to the bar and drink a few "brews" and retail some cynical remarks about Zora Folley and how the fight game is these days and round it off, though, with how George Chuvalo has "a lot of heart," which he got, one understands, by eating mom's pie. Anyway, I went to the Hot Rod & Custom Car show and wrote a story that would have suited any of the totem newspapers. All the totem newspapers would regard one of these shows as a sideshow, a panopticon, for creeps and kooks; not even wealthy, eccentric creeps and kooks, which would be all right, but lower class creeps and nutballs with dermatitic skin and ratty hair. The totem story usually makes what is known as "gentle fun" of this, which is a way of saying, don't worry, these people are nothing.

So I wrote a story about a kid who had built a golden motorcycle, which he called "The Golden Alligator." The seat was made of some kind of gold-painted leather that kept going back, on and on, as long as an alligator's tail, and had scales embossed on it, like an alligator's. The kid had made a whole golden suit for himself, like a space suit, that also looked as if it were covered with scales and he would lie down on his stomach on this long seat, stretched out full length, so that he appeared to be made into the motorcycle or something, and roar around Greenwich Village on Saturday nights, down Macdougal Street, down there in Nut Heaven, looking like a golden alligator on wheels. Nutty! He seemed like a Gentle Nut when I got through. It was a shame I wrote that sort of story, the usual totem story, because I was working for the *Herald Tribune,* and the *Herald Tribune* was the only experimental paper in town, breaking out of the totem formula. The thing was, I knew I had another story all the time, a bona fide story, the real story of the Hot Rod & Custom Car show, but I didn't know what to do with it. It was outside the system of ideas I was used to working with, even though I had been through the whole Ph.D. route at Yale, in American Studies and everything.

Here were all these . . . *weird* . . . nutty-looking, crazy baroque custom cars, sitting in little nests of pink angora angel's hair for the purpose of "glamorous" display—but then I got to talking to one of the men who make them, a fellow named Dale Alexander. He was a very serious and soft-spoken man, about thirty, completely serious about the whole thing, in fact, and pretty soon it became clear, as I talked to this man for a while, that he had been living like the *complete artist* for years. He had starved, suffered—the whole thing—so he could sit inside a garage and create these cars which more than 99 per cent of the American people would consider ridiculous, vulgar and lower-class-awful beyond comment almost. He had started off with a garage that fixed banged-up cars and everything, to pay the rent, but gradually he couldn't stand it any more. Creativity—his own custom car art—became an obsession with him. So he became the complete custom car artist.

And he said he wasn't the only one. All the great custom car designers had gone through it. It was the *only way*. *Holy beasts!* Starving artists! Inspiration! Only instead of garrets, they had these garages.

So I went over to *Esquire* magazine after a while and talked to them about this phenomenon, and they sent me out to California to take a look at the custom car world. Dale Alexander was from Detroit or some place, but the real center of the thing was in California, around Los Angeles. I started talking to a lot of these people, like George Barris and Ed Roth, and seeing what they were doing, and—well, eventually it became the story from which the title of this book was taken, "The Kandy-Kolored Tangerine-Flake Streamline Baby." But at first I couldn't even write the story. I came back to New York and just sat around worrying over the thing. I had a lot of trouble analyzing exactly what I had on my hands. By this time *Esquire* practically had a gun at my head because they had a two-page-wide color picture for the story locked into the printing presses and no story. Finally, I told Byron Dobell, the managing editor at *Esquire*, that I couldn't pull the thing together. O.K., he tells me, just type out my notes and send them over and he will get somebody else to write it. So about 8 o'clock that night I started typing the notes out in the form of a memorandum that began, "Dear Byron." I started typing away, starting right with the first time I saw any custom cars in California. I just started recording it all, and inside of a couple of hours, typing along like a madman, I could tell that something was beginning to happen. By midnight this memorandum to Byron was twenty pages long and I was still typing like a maniac. About 2 A.M. or something like that I turned on WABC, a radio station that plays rock and roll music all night long, and got a little more manic. I wrapped up the memorandum about 6:15 A.M., and by this time it was 49 pages long. I took it over to *Esquire* as soon as they opened up, about 9:30

A.M. About 4 P.M. I got a call from Byron Dobell. He told me they were striking out the "Dear Byron" at the top of the memorandum and running the rest of it in the magazine. That was the story, "The Kandy-Kolored Tangerine-Flake Stream-line Baby."

What had happened was that I started writing down everything I had seen the first place I went in California, this incredible event, a "Teen Fair." The details themselves, when I wrote them down, suddenly made me see what was happening. Here was this incredible combination of form plus money in a place nobody ever thought about finding it, namely, among teen-agers. Practically every style recorded in art history is the result of the same thing—a lot of attention to form, plus the money to make monuments to it. The "classic" English style of Inigo Jones, for example, places like the Covent Garden and the royal banquet hall at Whitehall, were the result of a worship of Italian Palladian grandeur . . . form . . . plus the money that began pouring in under James I and Charles I from colonial possessions. These were the kind of forms, styles, symbols . . . Palladian classicism . . . that influence a whole society. But throughout history, everywhere this kind of thing took place, China, Egypt, France under the Bourbons, every place, it has been something the aristocracy has been responsible for. What has happened in the United States since World War II, however, has broken that pattern. The war created money. It made massive infusions of money into every level of society. Suddenly classes of people whose styles of life had been practically invisible had the money to build monuments to their own styles. Among teen-agers, this took the form of custom cars, the twist, the jerk, the monkey, the shake, rock music generally, stretch pants, decal eyes—and all these things, these teen-age styles of life, like Inigo Jones' classicism, have started having an influence on the life of the whole country. It is not merely teen-agers. In the South, for example, all the proles, peasants, and petty burghers suddenly got enough money to start up their incredible car world. In fifteen years stock car racing has replaced baseball as the number one sport in the South. It doesn't make much difference what happens to baseball or stock car racing, actually, but this shift, from a fixed land sport, modeled on cricket, to this wild car sport, with standard, or standard-looking, cars that go 180 miles an hour or so—this symbolizes a radical change in the people as a whole. Practically nobody has bothered to see what these changes are all about. People have been looking at the new money since the war in economic terms only. Nobody will even take a look at our incredible new national pastimes, things like stock car racing, drag racing, demolition derbies, sports that attract five to ten million more spectators than football, baseball and basketball each year. Part of it is a built-in class bias. The educated classes in this country, as in every country, the people who grow up to control visual and printed communication media, are all plugged into what is, when one gets down to it, an ancient, aristocratic aesthetic. Stock car racing, custom cars—and, for that matter, the jerk, the monkey, rock music—still seem beneath serious consideration, still the preserve of ratty people with ratty hair and dermatitis and corroded thoracic boxes and so forth. Yet all these rancid people are creating new styles all the time and changing the life of the whole country in ways that nobody even seems to bother to record, much less analyze.

A curious example of what is happening is Society, in the sense of High Society, in New York City today. Only it isn't called High Society or even Café Society anymore. Nobody seems to know quite what to call it, but the term that is catching on is Pop Society. This is because socialites in New York today seem to have no natural, aristocratic styles of their own —they are taking all their styles from "pop" groups, which stands for popular, or "vulgar" or "bohemian" groups. They dance the Jerk, the Monkey, the Shake, they listen to rock music, the women wear teen-age and even "sub-teen" styles, such as stretch pants and decal eyes, they draw their taste in art, such as "underground" movies and "pop" painting, from various bohos and camp culturati, mainly. New York's "Girl of the Year"—Baby Jane Holzer—is the most incredible socialite in history. Here in this one girl is a living embodiment of almost pure "pop" sensation, a kind of corn-haired essence of the new styles of life. I never had written a story that seemed to touch so many nerves in so many people. Television and the movies all of a sudden went crazy over her, but that was just one side of it. A lot of readers were enraged. They wrote letters to the publisher of the *Herald Tribune,* to the *Herald Tribune* magazine, *New York,* where it appeared, they made phone calls, they would confront me with it in restaurants, all sorts of things—and in all of it I kept noticing the same thing. Nobody ever seemed to be able to put his finger on what he was enraged about. Most of them took the line that the *Herald Tribune* had no business paying that much attention to such a person and such a life as she was leading. Refreshing! Moral Outrage! But it was all based on the idea that Jane Holzer was some kind of freak they didn't like. Jane Holzer—and the Baby Jane syndrome—there's nothing freakish about it. Baby Jane is the hyper-version of a whole new style of life in America. I think she is a very profound symbol. But she is not the super-hyper-version. The super-hyper-version is Las Vegas. I call Las Vegas the Versailles of America, and for specific reasons. Las Vegas happened to be created after the war, with war money, by gangsters. Gangsters happened to be the first uneducated . . . but more to the point, unaristocratic, *outside* of the aristocratic tradition . . . the first uneducated, prole-petty-burgher Americans to have enough money to build a monument to their style of life. They built it in an isolated spot, Las Vegas, out in the desert, just like Louis XIV, the Sun King, who purposely went outside of Paris, into the countryside, to create a fantastic baroque environment to celebrate his rule. It is no accident that Las Vegas and Versailles are the only two architecturally uniform cities in Western history. The important thing about the building of Las Vegas is not that the builders were gangsters but that they were proles. They celebrated, very early, the new style of life of America—using the money pumped in by the war to show a prole vision . . . *Glamor!* . . . of style. The usual thing has happened, of course. Because it is prole, it gets ignored, except on the most sensational level. Yet long after Las Vegas' influence as a gambling heaven has gone, Las Vegas' forms and symbols will be influencing American life. That fantastic skyline! Las Vegas' neon sculpture, its fantastic fifteen-story-high display signs, parabolas, boomerangs, rhomboids, trapezoids and all the rest of it, are already the staple design of the American landscape outside of the oldest parts of the oldest cities. They are all over every suburb, every subdivision, every highway . . . every *hamlet,* as it were, the new crossroads, spiraling Servicenter signs. They are the new landmarks of America, the new guideposts, the new way Americans get their bearings. And yet what do we know about these signs, these incredible pieces of neon sculpture, and what kind of impact they have on people? Nobody seems to know the first thing about it, not even the men who design them. I hunted out some of the great sign makers of Las Vegas, men who design for the Young Electric Sign Co., and the Federal Sign and Signal Corporation—and marvelous! —they come from completely outside the art history tradition of the design schools of the Eastern universities. I remember talking with this one designer, Ted Blaney, from Federal, their chief designer, in the cocktail lounge of the Dunes Hotel on "The Strip." I showed him a shape, a boomerang shape, that one sees all over Las Vegas, in small signs, huge signs, huge things like the archway entrance to the Desert Inn—it is not an arch, really, but this huge boomerang shape—and I asked him what they, the men who design these things, call it.

Ted was a stocky little guy, very sunburnt, with a pencil mustache and a Texas string tie, the kind that has strings sticking through some kind of silver dollar or something situated at the throat. He talked slowly and he had a way of furling his eyebrows around his nose when he did mental calculations such as figuring out this boomerang shape.

He stared at the shape, which he and his brothers in the art have created over and over and over, over, over and over and over in Las Vegas, and finally he said,

"Well, that's what we call—what we sort of call—'free form.'"

Free form! Marvelous! No hung-up old art history words for these guys. America's first unconscious avant-garde! The hell with Mondrian, whoever the hell he is. The hell with Moholy-Nagy, if anybody ever heard of him. Artists for the new age, sculptors for the new style and new money of the . . . Yah! lower orders. The new sensibility—*Baby baby baby where did our love go?*—the new world, submerged so long, invisible, and now arising, slippy, shiny, electric—Super Scuba-man!—out of the vinyl deeps.

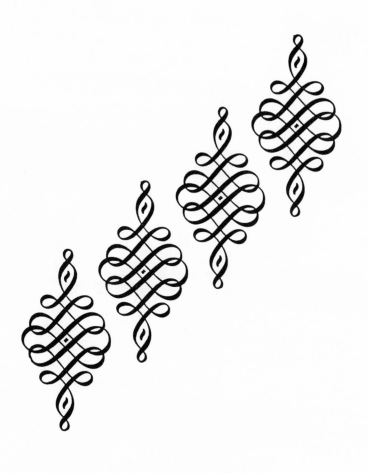

1

THE NEW
CULTURE-MAKERS

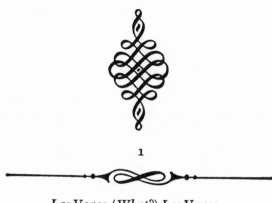

1

Las Vegas (What?) Las Vegas
(Can't hear you! Too noisy)
Las Vegas! ! ! !

Hernia, hernia, hernia, hernia, hernia, hernia, hernia, hernia, hernia, hernia, hernia, hernia, hernia, HERNia; hernia, HERNia, hernia, hernia, hernia, hernia, HERNia, HERNia, HERNia; hernia, hernia, hernia, hernia, hernia, hernia, hernia, eight is the point, the point is eight; hernia, hernia, HERNia; hernia, hernia, hernia, hernia, all right, hernia, hernia, hernia, hernia, hard eight, hernia, hernia, hernia, HERNia, hernia,

3

hernia, hernia, HERNia, hernia, hernia, hernia, HERNia, hernia, hernia, hernia, hernia

"What is all this *hernia hernia* stuff?"

This was Raymond talking to the wavy-haired fellow with the stick, the dealer, at the craps table about 3:45 Sunday morning. The stickman had no idea what this big wiseacre was talking about, but he resented the tone. He gave Raymond that patient arch of the eyebrows known as a Red Hook brush-off, which is supposed to convey some such thought as, I am a very tough but cool guy, as you can tell by the way I carry my eyeballs low in the pouches, and if this wasn't such a high-class joint we would take wiseacres like you out back and beat you into jellied madrilene.

At this point, however, Raymond was immune to subtle looks.

The stickman tried to get the game going again, but every time he would start up his singsong, by easing the words out through the nose, which seems to be the style among craps dealers in Las Vegas—"All right, a new shooter . . . eight is the point, the point is eight" and so on—Raymond would start droning along with him in exactly the same tone of voice, "Hernia, hernia, hernia; hernia, HERNia, HERNia, hernia; hernia, hernia, hernia."

Everybody at the craps table was staring in consternation to think that anybody would try to needle a tough, hip, elite *soldat* like a Las Vegas craps dealer. The gold-lamé odalisques of Los Angeles were staring. The Western sports, fifty-eight-year-old men who wear Texas string ties, were staring. The old babes at the slot machines, holding Dixie Cups full of nickles, were staring at the craps tables, but cranking away the whole time.

Raymond, who is thirty-four years old and works as an engineer in Phoenix, is big but not terrifying. He has the sort of thatchwork hair that grows so low all along the forehead there is no logical place to part it, but he tries anyway. He has a huge, prognathous jaw, but it is as smooth, soft and round as a melon, so that Raymond's total effect is that of an Episcopal divinity student.

The guards were wonderful. They were dressed in cowboy uniforms like Bruce Cabot in *Sundown* and they wore sheriff's stars.

"Mister, is there something we can do for you?"

"The expression is 'Sir,'" said Raymond. "You said 'Mister.' The expression is 'Sir.' How's your old Cosa Nostra?"

Amazingly, the casino guards were easing Raymond out peaceably, without putting a hand on him. I had never seen the fellow before, but possibly because I had been following his progress for the last five minutes, he turned to me and said, "Hey, do you have a car? This wild stuff is starting again."

The gist of it was that he had left his car somewhere and he wanted to ride up the Strip to the Stardust, one of the big hotel-casinos. I am describing this big goof Raymond not because he is a typical Las Vegas tourist, although he has some typical symptoms, but because he is a good example of the marvelous impact Las Vegas has on the senses. Raymond's senses were at a high pitch of excitation, the only trouble being that he was going off his nut. He had been up since Thursday afternoon, and it was now about 3:45 A.M. Sunday. He had an envelope full of pep pills—amphetamine—in his left coat pocket and an envelope full of Equanils—meprobamate—in his right pocket, or were the Equanils in the left and the pep pills in the right? He could tell by looking, but he wasn't going to look anymore. He didn't care to see how many were left.

He had been rolling up and down the incredible electric-sign gauntlet of Las Vegas' Strip, U.S. Route 91, where the neon and the par lamps—bubbling, spiraling, rocketing, and exploding in sunbursts ten stories high out in the middle of the desert—celebrate one-story casinos. He had been gambling and drinking and eating now and again at the buffet tables the casinos keep heaped with food day and night, but mostly hopping himself up with good old amphetamine, cooling himself down with meprobamate, then hooking down more alcohol, until now, after sixty hours, he was slipping into the symptoms of toxic schizophrenia.

He was also enjoying what the prophets of hallucinogen call "consciousness expansion." The man was psychedelic. He was beginning to isolate the components of Las Vegas' unique bombardment of the senses. He was quite right about this *hernia hernia* stuff. Every casino in Las Vegas is, among the other things, a room full of craps tables with dealers who keep up a running singsong that sounds as though they are saying "hernia, hernia, hernia, hernia, hernia" and so on. There they are day and night, easing a running commentary through their nostrils. What they have to say contains next to no useful instruction. Its underlying message is, We are the initiates, riding the crest of chance. That the accumulated sound comes out "hernia" is merely an unfortunate phonetic coincidence. Actually, it is part of something rare and rather grand: a combination of baroque stimuli that brings to mind the bronze gongs, no larger than a blue plate, that Louis XIV, his ruff collars larded with the lint of the foul Old City of Byzantium, peronally hunted out in the bazaars of Asia Minor to provide exotic acoustics for his new palace outside Paris.

The sounds of the craps dealer will be in, let's say, the middle register. In the lower register will be the sound of the old babes at the slot machines. Men play the slots too, of course, but one of the indelible images of Las Vegas is that of the old babes at the row upon row of slot machines. There they are at six o'clock Sunday morning no less than at three o'clock Tuesday afternoon. Some of them pack their old hummocky shanks into Capri pants, but many of them just put on the old print dress, the same one day after day, and the old hob-heeled shoes, looking like they might be going out to buy eggs in Tupelo, Mississippi. They have a Dixie Cup full of nickles or dimes in the left hand and an Iron Boy work glove on the right hand to keep the callouses from getting sore. Every time they pull the handle, the machine makes a sound much like the sound a cash register makes before the bell rings, then the slot pictures start clattering up from left to right, the oranges, lemons, plums, cherries, bells, bars, bucka-roos—the figure of a cowboy riding a bucking bronco. The whole sound keeps churning up over and over again in eccentric series all over the place, like one of those random-sound radio symphonies by John Cage. You can hear it at any hour of the day or night all over Las Vegas. You can walk down Fremont Street at dawn and hear it without even walking in a door, that and the spins of the wheels of fortune, a boring and not very popular sort of simplified roulette, as the tabs flap to a stop. As an overtone, or at times simply as a loud sound, comes the babble of the casino crowds, with an occasional shriek from the craps tables, or, anywhere from 4 P.M. to 6 A.M., the sound of brass instruments or electrified string instruments from the cocktail-lounge shows.

The crowd and band sounds are not very extraordinary, of course. But Las Vegas' Muzak is. Muzak pervades Las Vagas from the time you walk into the airport upon landing to the last time you leave the casinos. It is piped out to the swimming pool. It is in the drugstores. It is as if there were a communal fear that someone, somewhere in Las Vegas, was going to be left with a totally vacant minute on his hands.

Las Vegas has succeeded in wiring an entire city with this electronic stimulation, day and night, out in the middle of the desert. In the automobile I rented, the radio could not be turned off, no matter which dial you went after. I drove for days in a happy burble of Action Checkpoint News, "Monkey No. 9," "Donna, Donna, the Prima Donna," and picking-and-singing jingles for the Frontier Bank and the Fremont Hotel.

One can see the magnitude of the achievement. Las Vegas

7

takes what in other American towns is but a quixotic inflammation of the senses for some poor salary mule in the brief interval between the flagstone rambler and the automatic elevator downtown and magnifies it, foliates it, embellishes it into an institution.

For example, Las Vegas is the only town in the world whose skyline is made up neither of buildings, like New York, nor of trees, like Wilbraham, Massachusetts, but signs. One can look at Las Vegas from a mile away on Route 91 and see no buildings, no trees, only signs. But such signs! They tower. They revolve, they oscillate, they soar in shapes before which the existing vocabulary of art history is helpless. I can only attempt to supply names—Boomerang Modern, Palette Curvilinear, Flash Gordon Ming-Alert Spiral, McDonald's Hamburger Parabola, Mint Casino Elliptical, Miami Beach Kidney. Las Vegas' sign makers work so far out beyond the frontiers of conventional studio art that they have no names themselves for the forms they create. Vaughan Cannon, one of those tall, blond Westerners, the builders of places like Las Vegas and Los Angeles, whose eyes seem to have been bleached by the sun, is in the back shop of the Young Electric Sign Company out on East Charleston Boulevard with Herman Boernge, one of his designers, looking at the model they have prepared for the Lucky Strike Casino sign, and Cannon points to where the sign's two great curving faces meet to form a narrow vertical face and says:

"Well, here we are again—what do we call that?"

"I don't know," says Boernge. "It's sort of a nose effect. Call it a nose."

Okay, a nose, but it rises sixteen stories high above a two-story building. In Las Vegas no farseeing entrepreneur buys a sign to fit a building he owns. He rebuilds the building to support the biggest sign he can get up the money for and, if necessary, changes the name. The Lucky Strike Casino today is the Lucky Casino, which fits better when recorded in sixteen stories of flaming peach and incandescent yellow in the middle of the Mojave Desert. In the Young Electric Sign Co. era signs have become the architecture of Las Vegas, and the most whimsical, Yale-seminar-frenzied devices of the two late geniuses of Baroque Modern, Frank Lloyd Wright and Eero Saarinen, seem rather stuffy business, like a jest at a faculty meeting, compared to it. Men like Boernge, Kermit Wayne, Ben Mitchem and Jack Larsen, formerly an artist for Walt Disney, are the designer-sculptor geniuses of Las Vegas, but their motifs have been carried faithfully throughout the town by lesser men, for gasoline stations, motels, funeral parlors, churches, public buildings, flophouses and sauna baths.

Then there is a stimulus that is both visual and sexual—the Las Vegas buttocks décolletage. This is a form of sexually provocative dress seen more and more in the United States, but avoided like Broadway message-embroidered ("Kiss Me, I'm Cold") underwear in the fashion pages, so that the euphemisms have not been established and I have no choice but clinical terms. To achieve buttocks décolletage a woman wears bikini-style shorts that cut across the round fatty masses of the buttocks rather than cupping them from below, so that the outer-lower edges of these fatty masses, or "cheeks," are exposed. I am in the cocktail lounge of the Hacienda Hotel, talking to managing director Dick Taylor about the great success his place has had in attracting family and tour groups, and all around me the waitresses are bobbing on their high heels, bare legs and décolletage-bare backsides, set off by pelvis-length lingerie of an uncertain denomination. I stare, but I am new here. At the White Cross Rexall drugstore on the Strip a pregnant brunette walks in off the street wearing black shorts with buttocks décolletage aft and illusion-of-cloth nylon lingerie hanging fore, and not even the old mom's-pie pensioners up near the door are staring. They just crank away at the slot machines. On the streets of Las Vegas, not only the show girls, of which the town has about two hundred fifty, bona fide, in residence, but girls of every sort, including, especially, Las Vegas' little high-school buds, who adorn what locals seeking roots in the sand call "our city of churches and schools," have taken up the chic of wearing buttocks décolletage step-ins under flesh-tight slacks, with the outline of the undergarment showing through fashionably. Others go them one better. They achieve the effect of having been dipped once, briefly, in Helenca stretch nylon. More and more they look like those wonderful old girls out of Flash Gordon who were wrapped just once over in Baghdad pantaloons of clear polyethylene with only Flash Gordon between them and the insane red-eyed assaults of the minions of Ming. It is as if all the hip young suburban gals of America named Lana, Deborah and Sandra, who gather wherever the arc lights shine and the studs steady their coiffures in the plate-glass reflection, have convened in Las Vegas with their bouffant hair above and anatomically stretch-pant-swathed little bottoms below, here on the new American frontier. But exactly!

None of it would have been possible, however, without one of those historic combinations of nature and art that creates an epoch. In this case, the Mojave Desert plus the father of Las Vegas, the late Benjamin "Bugsy" Siegel.

Bugsy was an inspired man. Back in 1944 the city fathers of Las Vegas, their Protestant rectitude alloyed only by the giddy prospect of gambling revenues, were considering the sort of ordinance that would have preserved the town with a kind of Colonial Williamsburg dinkiness in the motif of the Wild West. All new buildings would have to have at least the façade of the sort of place where piano players used to wear garters on their sleeves in Virginia City around 1880. In Las Vegas in 1944, it should be noted, there was nothing more stimulating in the entire town than a Fremont Street bar where the composer of "Deep in the Heart of Texas" held forth and the regulars downed fifteen-cent beer.

Bugsy pulled into Las Vegas in 1945 with several million dollars that, after his assassination, was traced back in the general direction of gangster-financiers. Siegel put up a hotel-casino such as Las Vegas had never seen and called it the Flamingo—all Miami Modern, and the hell with piano players with garters and whatever that was all about. Everybody drove out Route 91 just to gape. Such shapes! Boomerang Modern supports, Palette Curvilinear bars, Hot Shoppe Cantilever roofs and a scalloped swimming pool. Such colors! All the new electrochemical pastels of the Florida littoral: tangerine, broiling magenta, livid pink, incarnadine, fuchsia demure, Congo ruby, methyl green, viridine, aquamarine, phenosafranine, incandescent orange, scarlet-fever purple, cyanic blue, tessellated bronze, hospital-fruit-basket orange. And such signs! Two cylinders rose at either end of the Flamingo—eight stories high and covered from top to bottom with neon rings in the shape of bubbles that fizzed all eight stories up into the desert sky all night long like an illuminated whisky-soda tumbler filled to the brim with pink champagne.

The business history of the Flamingo, on the other hand, was not such a smashing success. For one thing, the gambling operation was losing money at a rate that rather gloriously refuted all the recorded odds of the gaming science. Siegel's backers apparently suspected that he was playing both ends against the middle in collusion with professional gamblers who hung out at the Flamingo as though they had liens on it. What with one thing and another, someone decided by the night of June 20, 1947, that Benny Siegel, lord of the Flamingo, had had it. He was shot to death in Los Angeles.

Yet Siegel's aesthetic, psychological and cultural insights, like Cézanne's, Freud's and Max Weber's, could not die. The

Siegel vision and the Siegel aesthetic were already sweeping Las Vegas like gold fever. And there were builders of the West equal to the opportunity. All over Las Vegas the incredible electric pastels were repeated. Overnight the Baroque Modern forms made Las Vegas one of the few architecturally unified cities of the world—the style was Late American Rich—and without the bother and bad humor of a City Council ordinance. No enterprise was too small, too pedestrian or too solemn for The Look. The Supersonic Carwash, the Mercury Jetaway, Gas Vegas Village and Terrible Herbst gasoline stations, the Par-a-Dice Motel, the Palm Mortuary, the Orbit Inn, the Desert Moon, the Blue Onion Drive-In—on it went, like Wildwood, New Jersey, entering Heaven.

The atmosphere of the six-mile-long Strip of hotel-casinos grips even those segments of the population who rarely go near it. Barely twenty-five-hundred feet off the Strip, over by the Convention Center, stands Landmark Towers, a shaft thirty stories high, full of apartments, supporting a huge circular structure shaped like a space observation platform, which was to have contained the restaurant and casino. Somewhere along the way Landmark Towers went bankrupt, probably at that point in the last of the many crises when the construction workers *still* insisted on spending half the day flat on their bellies with their heads, tongues and eyeballs hanging over the edge of the tower, looking down into the swimming pool of the Playboy Apartments below, which has a "nudes only" section for show girls whose work calls for a tan all over.

Elsewhere, Las Vegas' beautiful little high-school buds in their buttocks-décolletage stretch pants are back on the foam-rubber upholstery of luxury broughams peeling off the entire chick ensemble long enough to establish the highest venereal-disease rate among high-school students anywhere north of the yaws-rotting shanty jungles of the Eighth Parallel. The Negroes who have done much of the construction work in Las

Vegas' sixteen-year boom are off in their ghetto on the west side of town, and some of them are smoking marijuana, eating peyote buttons and taking horse (heroin), which they get from Tijuana, I mean it's simple, baby, right through the mails, and old Raymond, the Phoenix engineer, does not have the high life to himself.

I am on the third floor of the Clark County Courthouse talking to Sheriff Captain Ray Gubser, another of these strong, pale-eyed Western-builder types, who is obligingly explaining to me law enforcement on the Strip, where the problem is not so much the drunks, crooks or roughhousers, but these nuts on pills who don't want to ever go to bed, and they have hallucinations and try to bring down the casinos like Samson. The county has two padded cells for them. They cool down after three or four days and they turn out to be somebody's earnest breadwinner back in Denver or Minneapolis, loaded with the right credentials and pouring soul and apologiae all over the county cops before finally pulling out of never-never land for good by plane. Captain Gubser is telling me about life and eccentric times in Las Vegas, but I am distracted. The captain's office has windows out on the corridor. Coming down the corridor is a covey of girls, skipping and screaming, giggling along, their heads exploding in platinum-and-neon-yellow bouffants or beehives or raspberry-silk scarves, their eyes appliquéd in black like mail-order decals, their breasts aimed up under their jerseys at the angle of anti-aircraft automatic weapons, and, as they swing around the corner toward the elevator, their glutei maximi are bobbing up and down with their pumps in the inevitable buttocks décolletage pressed out against black, beige and incarnadine stretch pants. This is part of the latest shipment of show girls to Las Vegas, seventy in all, for the "Lido de Paris" revue at the Stardust, to be entitled *Bravo!*, replacing the old show, entitled *Voilà*. The girls are in the county courthouse getting their working papers, and fifteen days from now these little glutei maximi and ack-ack breasts with stars pasted on the tips will be swinging out over the slack jaws and cocked-up noses of patrons sitting at stageside at the Stardust. I am still listening to Gubser, but somehow it is a courthouse where mere words are beaten back like old atonal Arturo Toscanini trying to sing along with the NBC Symphony. There he would be, flapping his little toy arms like Tony Galento shadowboxing with fate, bawling away in the face of union musicians who drowned him without a bubble. I sat in on three trials in the courthouse, and it was wonderful, because the courtrooms are all blond-wood modern and look like sets for TV panel discussions on marriage and the teenager. What the judge has to say is no less formal and no more fatuous than what judges say everywhere, but inside of forty seconds it is all meaningless because the atmosphere is precisely like a news broadcast over Las Vegas' finest radio station, KORK. The newscast, as it is called, begins with a series of electronic wheeps out on that far edge of sound where only quadrupeds can hear. A voice then announces that this is Action Checkpoint News. "The news—all the news—flows first through Action Checkpoint!—then reaches You! at the speed of Sound!" More electronic wheeps, beeps and lulus, and then an item: "Cuban Premier Fidel Castro nearly drowned yesterday." Urp! Wheep! Lulu! No news a KORK announcer has ever brought to Las Vegas at the speed of sound, or could possibly bring, short of word of the annihilation of Los Angeles, could conceivably compete within the brain with the giddiness of this electronic jollification.

The wheeps, beeps, freeps, electronic lulus, Boomerang Modern and Flash Gordon sunbursts soar on through the night over the billowing hernia–hernia sounds and the old babes at the slots—until it is 7:30 A.M. and I am watching five men at a green-topped card table playing poker. They are sliding their

Bee-brand cards into their hands and squinting at the pips
with a set to the lips like Conrad Veidt in a tunic collar studying a code message from S.S. headquarters. Big Sid Wyman,
the old Big-Time gambler from St. Louis, is there, with his
eyes looking like two poached eggs engraved with a road map
of West Virginia after all night at the poker table. Sixty-year-
old Chicago Tommy Hargan is there with his topknot of white
hair pulled back over his little pink skull and a mountain of
chips in front of his old caved-in sternum. Sixty-two-year-old
Dallas Maxie Welch is there, fat and phlegmatic as an Indian
Ocean potentate. Two Los Angeles biggies are there exhaling
smoke from candela-green cigars into the gloom. It looks like
the perfect vignette of every Big Time back room, "athletic
club," snooker house and floating poker game in the history of
the guys-and-dolls lumpen-bourgeoisie. But what is all this?
Off to the side, at a rostrum, sits a flawless little creature with
bouffant hair and Stridex-pure skin who looks like she is polished each morning with a rotary buffer. Before her on the
rostrum is a globe of coffee on a hot coil. Her sole job is to
keep the poker players warmed up with coffee. Meantime,
numberless uniformed lackeys are cocked and aimed about the
edges to bring the five Big Timers whatever else they might
desire, cigarettes, drinks, napkins, eyeglass-cleaning tissues,
plug-in telephones. All around the poker table, at a respectful
distance of ten feet, is a fence with the most delicate golden
pickets. Upon it, even at this narcoleptic hour, lean men and
women in their best clothes watching the combat of the titans.
The scene is the charmed circle of the casino of the Dunes
Hotel. As everyone there knows, or believes, these fabulous
men are playing for table stakes of fifteen or twenty thousand
dollars. One hundred dollars rides on a chip. Mandibles gape
at the progress of the battle. And now Sid Wyman, who is also
a vice-president of the Dunes, is at a small escritoire just inside
the golden fence signing a stack of vouchers for such sums as

$4500, all printed in the heavy Mondrianesque digits of a Burroughs business check-making machine. It is as if America's guys-and-dolls gamblers have somehow been tapped upon the shoulders, knighted, initiated into a new aristocracy.

Las Vegas has become, just as Bugsy Siegel dreamed, the American Monte Carlo—without any of the inevitable upper-class baggage of the Riviera casinos. At Monte Carlo there is still the plush mustiness of the 19th century noble lions—of Baron Bleichroden, a big winner at roulette who always said, "My dear friends, it is so easy on Black." Of Lord Jersey, who won seventeen maximum bets in a row—on black, as a matter of fact—nodded to the croupier, and said, "Much obliged, old sport, old sport," took his winnings to England, retired to the country and never gambled again in his life. Or of the old Duc de Dinc who said he could win only in the high-toned Club Privé, and who won very heavily one night, saw two Englishmen gaping at his good fortune, threw them every mille-franc note he had in his hands and said, "Here. Englishmen without money are altogether odious." Thousands of Europeans from the lower orders now have the money to go to the Riviera, but they remain under the century-old status pall of the aristocracy. At Monte Carlo there are still Wrong Forks, Deficient Accents, Poor Tailoring, Gauche Displays, Nouveau Richness, Cultural Aridity—concepts unknown in Las Vegas. For the grand debut of Monte Carlo as a resort in 1879 the architect Charles Garnier designed an opera house for the Place du Casino; and Sarah Bernhardt read a symbolic poem. For the debut of Las Vegas as a resort in 1946 Bugsy Siegel hired Abbott and Costello, and there, in a way, you have it all.

I am in the office of Major A. Riddle—Major is his name— the president of the Dunes Hotel. He combs his hair straight back and wears a heavy gold band on his little finger with a diamond sunk into it. As everywhere else in Las Vegas, some-

16

one has turned on the air conditioning to the point where it will be remembered, all right, as Las Vegas-style air conditioning. Riddle has an appointment to see a doctor at 4:30 about a crimp in his neck. His secretary, Maude McBride, has her head down and is rubbing the back of her neck. Lee Fisher, the P.R. man, and I are turning ours from time to time to keep the pivots from freezing up. Riddle is telling me about "the French war" and moving his neck gingerly. The Stardust bought and imported a version of the Lido de Paris spectacular, and the sight of all those sequined giblets pooning around on flamingo legs inflamed the tourists. The Tropicana fought back with the Folies Bergère, the New Frontier installed "Paree Ooh La La," the Hacienda reached for the puppets "Les Poupées de Paris," and the Silver Slipper called in Lili St. Cyr, the stripper, which was going French after a fashion. So the Dunes has bought up the third and last of the great Paris girlie shows, the Casino de Paris. Lee Fisher says, "And we're going to do things they *can't* top. In this town you've got to move ahead in quantum jumps."

Quantum? But exactly! The beauty of the Dunes' Casino de Paris show is that it will be beyond art, beyond dance, beyond spectacle, even beyond the titillations of the winking crotch. The Casino de Paris will be a behemoth piece of American calculus, like Project Mercury.

"This show alone will cost us two and a half million a year to operate and one and a half million to produce," Major A. Riddle is saying. "The costumes alone will be fantastic. There'll be more than five hundred costumes and—well, they'll be fantastic.

"And this machine—by the time we get through expanding the stage, this machine will cost us $250,000."

"Machine?"

"Yes. Sean Kenny is doing the staging. The whole set moves

electronically right in front of your eyes. He used to work with this fellow Lloyd Wright."

"Frank Lloyd Wright?"

"Yes. Kenny did the staging for *Blitz*. Did you see it? Fantastic. Well, it's all done electronically. They built this machine for us in Glasgow, Scotland, and it's being shipped here right now. It moves all over the place and creates smoke and special effects. We'll have everything. You can stage a bombardment with it. You'll think the whole theatre is blowing up.

"You'll have to program it. They had to use the same mechanism that's in the Skybolt Missile to build it. It's called a 'Celson' or something like that. That's how complicated this thing is. They have to have the same thing as the Skybolt Missile."

As Riddle speaks, one gets a wonderful picture of sex riding the crest of the future. Whole tableaux of bare-bottomed Cosmonaughties will be hurtling around the Casino de Paris Room of the Dunes Hotel at fantastic speed in elliptical orbits, a flash of the sequined giblets here, a blur of the black-rimmed decal eyes there, a wink of the crotch here and there, until, with one vast Project Climax for our times, Sean Kenny, who used to work with this fellow Frank Lloyd Wright, presses the red button and the whole yahooing harem, shrieking ooh-la-la amid the din, exits in a mushroom cloud.

The allure is most irresistible not to the young but the old. No one in Las Vegas will admit it—it is not the modern, glamorous notion—but Las Vegas is a resort for old people. In those last years, before the tissue deteriorates and the wires of the cerebral cortex hang in the skull like a clump of dried seaweed, they are seeking liberation.

At eight o'clock Sunday morning it is another almost boringly sunny day in the desert, and Clara and Abby, both about sixty, and their husbands, Earl, sixty-three, and Ernest, sixty-four, come squinting out of the Mint Casino onto Fremont Street.

"I don't know what's wrong with me," Abby says. "Those last three drinks, I couldn't even feel them. It was just like drinking fizz. You know what I mean?"

"Hey," says Ernest, "how about that place back 'ere? We ain't been back 'ere. Come on."

The others are standing there on the corner, squinting and looking doubtful. Abby and Clara have both entered old babehood. They have that fleshy, humped-over shape across the back of the shoulders. Their torsos are hunched up into fat little loaves supported by bony, atrophied leg stems sticking up into their hummocky hips. Their hair has been fried and dyed into improbable designs.

"You know what I mean? After a while it just gives me gas," says Abby. "I don't even feel it."

"Did you see me over there?" says Earl. "I was just going along, nice and easy, not too much, just riding along real nice. You know? And then, boy, I don't know what happened to me. First thing I know I'm laying down fifty dollars. . . . "

Abby lets out a great belch. Clara giggles.

"Gives me gas," Abby says mechanically.

"Hey, how about that place back 'ere?" says Ernest.

". . . Just nice and easy as you please. . . ."

". . . get me all fizzed up. . . ."

"Aw, come on. . . ."

And there at eight o'clock Sunday morning stand four old parties from Albuquerque, New Mexico, up all night, squinting at the sun, belching from a surfeit of tall drinks at eight o'clock Sunday morning, and—marvelous!—there is no one around to snigger at what an old babe with decaying haunches looks like in Capri pants with her heels jacked up on decorated wedgies.

"Where do we *come* from?" Clara said to me, speaking for the first time since I approached them on Fremont Street. "He

19

wants to know where we come from. I think it's past your bedtime, sweets."

"Climb the stairs and go to bed," said Abby.

Laughter all around.

"Climb the stairs" was Abby's finest line. At present there are almost no stairs to climb in Las Vegas. Avalon homes are soon to go up, advertising "Two-Story Homes!" as though this were an incredibly lavish and exotic concept. As I talked to Clara, Abby, Earl and Ernest, it came out that "climb the stairs" was a phrase they brought along to Albuquerque with them from Marshalltown, Iowa, those many years ago, along with a lot of other baggage, such as the entire cupboard of Protestant taboos against drinking, lusting, gambling, staying out late, getting up late, loafing, idling, lollygagging around the streets and wearing Capri pants—all designed to deny a person short-term pleasures so he will center his energies on bigger, long-term goals.

"We was in 'ere"—the Mint—"a couple of hours ago, and that old boy was playing the guitar, you know, 'Walk right in, set right down,' and I kept hearing an old song I haven't heard for twenty years. It has this little boy and his folks keep telling him it's late and he has to go to bed. He keeps saying, 'Don't make me go to bed and I'll be good.' Am I *good*, Earl? Am I *good?*"

The liberated cortex in all its glory is none other than the old babes at the slot machines. Some of them are tourists whose husbands said, *Here is fifty bucks, go play the slot machines,* while they themselves went off to more complex pleasures. But most of these old babes are part of the permanent landscape of Las Vegas. In they go to the Golden Nugget or the Mint, with their Social Security check or their pension check from the Ohio telephone company, cash it at the casino cashier's, pull out the Dixie Cup and the Iron Boy work glove, disappear down a row of slots and get on with it. I remember particularly talking to another Abby—a widow, sixty-two years old, built short and up from the bottom like a fire hydrant. After living alone for twelve years in Canton, Ohio, she had moved out to Las Vegas to live with her daughter and her husband, who worked for the Army.

"They were wonderful about it," she said. "Perfect hypocrites. She kept saying, you know, 'Mother, we'd be delighted to have you, only we don't think you'll *like* it. It's practically a fron*tier* town,' she says. 'It's so *ga*rish,' she says. So I said, I told her, 'Well, if you'd rather I didn't come. . . .' 'Oh, no!' she says. I wish I could have heard what her husband was saying. He calls me 'Mother.' '*Mo*ther,' he says. Well, once I was here, they figured, well, I *might* make a good baby-sitter and dishwasher and duster and mopper. The children are nasty little things. So one day I was in town for something or other and I just played a slot machine. It's fun—I can't describe it to you. I suppose I lose. I lose a little. And *they* have fits about it. 'For God's sake, Grandmother,' and so forth. They always say '*Grand*mother' when I am supposed to 'act my age' or crawl through a crack in the floor. Well, I'll tell you, the slot machines are a *whole lot* better than sitting in that little house all day. They kind of get you; I can't explain it."

The childlike megalomania of gambling is, of course, from the same cloth as the megalomania of the town. And, as the children of the liberated cortex, the old guys and babes are running up and down the Strip around the clock like everybody else. It is not by chance that much of the entertainment in Las Vegas, especially the second-stringers who perform in the cocktail lounges, will recall for an aging man what was glamorous twenty-five years ago when he had neither the money nor the freedom of spirit to indulge himself in it. In the big theatre-dining room at the Desert Inn, The Painted Desert Room, Eddie Fisher's act is on and he is saying cozily to a florid guy at a table right next to the stage, "Manny, you know you shouldn'a sat this close—you know you're in for it now, Manny, baby," while Manny beams with fright. But in the cocktail lounge, where the idea is chiefly just to keep the razzle-dazzle going, there is Hugh Farr, one of the stars of another era in the West, composer of two of the five Western songs the Library of Congress has taped for posterity, "Cool Water" and "Tumbling Tumbleweed," when he played the violin for the Sons of the Pioneers. And now around the eyes he looks like an aging Chinese savant, but he is wearing a white tuxedo and powder-blue leather boots and playing his sad old Western violin with an electric cord plugged in it for a group called The Country Gentlemen. And there is Ben Blue, looking like a waxwork exhibit of vaudeville, doffing his straw skimmer to reveal the sculptural qualities of his skull. And down at the Flamingo cocktail lounge—Ella Fitzgerald is in the main room —there is Harry James, looking old and pudgy in one of those toy Italian-style show-biz suits. And the Ink Spots are at the New Frontier and Louis Prima is at the Sahara, and the old parties are seeing it all, roaring through the dawn into the next day, until the sun seems like a par lamp fading in and out. The casinos, the bars, the liquor stores are open every minute of every day, like a sempiternal wading pool for the childhood ego. ". . . Don't make me go to bed. . . ."

Finally the casualties start piling up. I am in the manager's office of a hotel on the Strip. A man and his wife, each about sixty, are in there, raging. Someone got into their room and stole seventy dollars from her purse, and they want the hotel to make it up to them. The man pops up and down from a chair and ricochets back and forth across the room, flailing his great pig's-knuckle elbows about.

"What kind of security you call that? Walk right in the god-dern room and just help themselves. And where do you think I found your security man? Back around the corner reading a god-dern detective magazine!"

He had scored a point there, but he was wearing a striped polo shirt with a hip Hollywood solid-color collar, and she had on Capri pants, and hooked across their wrinkly old faces they both had rimless, wraparound French sunglasses of the sort young-punk heroes in *nouvelle vague* movies wear, and it was impossible to give any earnest contemplation to a word they said. They seemed to have the great shiny popeyes of a praying mantis.

"Listen, Mister," she is saying, "I don't care about the seventy bucks. I'd lose seventy bucks at your craps table and I wouldn't think nothing of it. I'd play seventy bucks just like that, and it wouldn't mean nothing. I wouldn't regret it. But when they can just walk in—and you don't give a damn—for Christ's sake!"

They are both zeroing in on the manager with their great insect corneas. The manager is a cool number in a white-on-white shirt and silver tie.

"This happened three days ago. Why didn't you tell us about it then?"

"Well, I was gonna be a nice guy about it. Seventy dollars," he said, as if it would be difficult for the brain to grasp a sum much smaller. "But then I found your man back there reading a god-dern detective magazine. *True Detectives* it was. Had a picture on the front of some floozie with one leg up on a chair and her garter showing. Looked like a god-derned athlete's-foot ad. Boy, I went into a slow burn. But when I am burned up, I am *burned up!* You get me, Mister? There he was, reading the god-derned *True Detectives*."

"Any decent hotel would have insurance," she says.

The manager says, "I don't know a hotel in the world that offers insurance against theft."

"Hold on, Mister," he says, "are you calling my wife a liar?

You just get smart, and I'm gonna pop you one! I'll pop you one right now if you call my wife a liar."

At this point the manager lowers his head to one side and looks up at the old guy from under his eyebrows with a version of the Red Hook brush-off, and the old guy begins to cool off.

But others are beyond cooling off. Hornette Reilly, a buttery hipped whore from New York City, is lying in bed with a bald-headed guy from some place who has skin like oatmeal. He is asleep or passed out or something. Hornette is relating all this to the doctor over the Princess telephone by the bed.

"Look," she says, "I'm breaking up. I can't tell you how much I've drunk. About a bottle of brandy since four o'clock, I'm not kidding. I'm in bed with a guy. Right this minute. I'm talking on the telephone to you and this slob is lying here like an animal. He's all fat and his skin looks like oatmeal—what's happening to me? I'm going to take some more pills. I'm not kidding, I'm breaking up. I'm going to kill myself. You've got to put me in Rose de Lima. I'm breaking up, and I don't even know what's happening to me."

"So naturally you want to go to Rose de Lima."

"Well, yeah."

"You can come by the office, but I'm not sending you to Rose de Lima."

"Doctor, I'm not kidding."

"I don't doubt that you're sick, old girl, but I'm not sending you to Rose de Lima to sober up."

The girls do not want to go to the County Hospital. They want to go to Rose de Lima, where the psychiatric cases receive milieu therapy. The patients dress in street clothes, socialize and play games with the staff, eat well and relax in the sun, all paid for by the State. One of the folk heroines of the Las Vegas floozies, apparently, is the call girl who last year was spending Monday through Friday at Rose de Lima and "turning out," as they call it, Saturdays and Sundays on the Strip, to the tune of $200 to $300 a weekend. She looks upon herself not as a whore, or even a call girl, but as a lady of assignation. When some guy comes to the Strip and unveils the little art-nouveau curves in his psyche and calls for two girls to perform arts upon one another, this one consents to be the passive member of the team only. A Rose de Lima girl, she draws the line.

At the County Hospital the psychiatric ward is latched, bolted, wired up and jammed with patients who are edging along the walls in the inner hall, the only place they have to take a walk other than the courtyard.

A big brunette with the remnants of a beehive hairdo and decal eyes and an obvious pregnancy is the liveliest of the lot. She is making eyes at everyone who walks in. She also nods gaily toward vacant place places along the wall.

"Mrs. —— is refusing medication," a nurse tells one of the psychiatrists. "She won't even open her mouth."

Presently the woman, in a white hospital tunic, is led up the hall. She looks about fifty, but she has extraordinary lines on her face.

"Welcome home," says Dr. ——.

"This is not my home," she says.

"Well, as I told you before, it has to be for the time being."

"Listen, you didn't analyze me."

"Oh, yes. Two psychiatrists examined you—all over again."

"You mean that time in jail."

"Exactly."

"You can't tell anything from that. I was excited. I had been out on the Strip, and then all that stupid—"

Three-fourths of the 640 patients who clustered into the ward last year were casualties of the Strip or the Strip milieu of Las Vegas, the psychiatrist tells me. He is a bright and energetic man in a shawl-collared black silk suit with brass buttons.

"I'm not even her doctor," he says. "I don't know her case. There's nothing I can do for her."

Here, securely out of sight in this little warren, are all those who have taken the loop-the-loop and could not stand the centripety. Some, like Raymond, who has been rocketing for days on pills and liquor, who has gone without sleep to the point of anoxia, might pull out of the toxic reaction in two or three days, or eight or ten. Others have conflicts to add to the chemical wackiness. A man who has thrown all his cash to the flabby homunculus who sits at every craps table stuffing the take down an almost hidden chute so it won't pile up in front of the customers' eyes; a man who has sold the family car for next to nothing at a car lot advertising "Cash for your car—*right now*" and then thrown that to the homunculus, too, but also still has the family waiting guiltlessly, guilelessly back home; well, he has troubles.

". . . After I came here and began doing personal studies," the doctor is saying, "I recognized extreme aggressiveness continually. It's not merely what Las Vegas can do to a person, it's the type of person it attracts. Gambling is a very aggressive pastime, and Las Vegas attracts aggressive people. They have an amazing capacity to louse up a normal situation."

The girl, probably a looker in more favorable moments, is pressed face into the wall, cutting glances at the doctor. The nurse tells her something and she puts her face in her hands, convulsing but not making a sound. She retreats to her room, and then the sounds come shrieking out. The doctor rushes back. Other patients are sticking their heads out of their rooms along the hall.

"The young girl?" a quiet guy says to a nurse. "The young girl," he says to somebody in the room.

But the big brunette just keeps rolling her decal eyes.

Out in the courtyard—all bare sand—the light is a kind of light-bulb twilight. An old babe is rocking herself back and forth on a straight chair and putting one hand out in front from time to time and pulling it in toward her bosom.

It seems clear enough to me. "A slot machine?" I say to the nurse, but she says there is no telling.

". . . and yet the same aggressive types are necessary to build a frontier town, and Las Vegas is a frontier town, certainly by any psychological standard," Dr. ———— is saying. "They'll undertake anything and they'll accomplish it. The building here has been incredible. They don't seem to care what they're up against, so they do it."

I go out to the parking lot in back of the County Hospital and it doesn't take a second; as soon as I turn on the motor I'm swinging again with Action Checkpoint News, "Monkey No. 9," "Donna, Donna, the Prima Donna," and friendly picking and swinging for the Fremont Hotel and Frontier Federal. Me and my big white car are sailing down the Strip and the Boomerang Modern, Palette Curvilinear, Flash Gordon Ming-Alert Spiral, McDonald's Hamburger Parabola, Mint Casino Elliptical and Miami Beach Kidney sunbursts are exploding in the Young Electric Sign Company's Grand Gallery for all the sun kings. At the airport there was that bad interval between the rental-car stall and the terminal entrance, but once through the automatic door the Muzak came bubbling up with "Song of India." On the upper level around the ramps the slots were cranking away. They are placed like "traps," a word Las Vegas picked up from golf. And an old guy is walking up the ramp, just off the plane from Denver, with a huge plastic bag of clothes slung over the left shoulder and a two-suiter suitcase in his right hand. He has to put the suitcase down on the floor and jostle the plastic bag all up around his neck to keep it from falling, but he manages to dig into his pocket for a couple of coins and get going on the slot machines. All seems right, but walking out to my plane I sense that something is missing. Then I recall sitting in the cocktail lounge of the Dunes at 3 P.M. with Jack Heskett, district manager of the Federal Sign and Signal Corporation, and Marty Steinman, the sales manager, and Ted Blaney, a designer. They are telling me about the sign they are building for the Dunes to put up at the airport. It will be five thousand square feet of free-standing sign, done in flaming-lake red on burning-desert gold. The d—the D—alone in the word Dunes, written in Cyrillic modern, will be practically two stories high. An inset plexiglas display, the largest revolving, trivision plexiglas sign in the world, will turn and show first the Dunes, with its twenty-two-story addition, then the seahorse swimming pool, then the new golf course. The scimitar curves of the sign will soar to a huge roaring diamond at the very top. "You'll be able to see it from an airplane fifteen miles away," says Jack Heskett. "Fifty miles," says Lee Fisher. And it will be sixty-five feet up in the air—because the thing was, somebody was out at the airport and they noticed there was only one display to be topped. That was that shaft about sixty feet high with the lit-up globe and the beacon lights, which is to say, the control tower. Hell, you can only see that forty miles away. But exactly!

2

Clean Fun at Riverhead

The inspiration for the demolition derby came to Lawrence Mendelsohn one night in 1958 when he was nothing but a spare-ribbed twenty-eight-year-old stock-car driver halfway through his 10th lap around the Islip, L.I., Speedway and taking a curve too wide. A lubberly young man with a Chicago boxcar haircut came up on the inside in a 1949 Ford and caromed him 12 rows up into the grandstand, but Lawrence Mendelsohn and his entire car did not hit one spectator.

"That was what got me," he said, "I remember I was hanging upside down from my seat belt like a side of Jersey bacon and wondering why no one was sitting where I hit. 'Lousy promotion,' I said to myself.

29

"Not only that, but everybody who *was* in the stands forgot about the race and came running over to look at me gift-wrapped upside down in a fresh pile of junk."

At that moment occurred the transformation of Lawrence Mendelsohn, racing driver, into Lawrence Mendelsohn, promoter, and, a few transactions later, owner of the Islip Speedway, where he kept seeing more of this same underside of stock car racing that everyone in the industry avoids putting into words. Namely, that for every purist who comes to see the fine points of the race, such as who is going to win, there are probably five waiting for the wrecks to which stock car racing is so gloriously prone.

The pack will be going into a curve when suddenly two cars, three cars, four cars tangle, spinning and splattering all over each other and the retaining walls, upside down, right side up, inside out and in pieces, with the seams bursting open and discs, rods, wires and gasoline spewing out and yards of sheet metal shearing off like Reynolds Wrap and crumpling into the most baroque shapes, after which an ash-blue smoke starts seeping up from the ruins and a thrill begins to spread over the stands like Newburg sauce.

So why put up with the monotony between crashes?

Such, in brief, is the early history of what is culturally the most important sport ever originated in the United States, a sport that ranks with the gladiatorial games of Rome as a piece of national symbolism. Lawrence Mendelsohn had a vision of an automobile sport that would be all crashes. Not two cars, not three cars, not four cars, but 100 cars would be out in an arena doing nothing but smashing each other into shrapnel. The car that outrammed and outdodged all the rest, the last car that could still move amid the smoking heap, would take the prize money.

So at 8:15 at night at the Riverhead Raceway, just west of Riverhead, L.I., on Route 25, amid the quaint tranquility of the duck and turkey farm flatlands of eastern Long Island, Lawrence Mendelsohn stood up on the back of a flat truck in his red neon warmup jacket and lectured his 100 drivers on the rules and niceties of the new game, the "demolition derby." And so at 8:30 the first 25 cars moved out onto the raceway's quarter-mile stock car track. There was not enough room for 100 cars to mangle each other. Lawrence Mendelsohn's dream would require four heats. Now the 25 cars were placed at intervals all about the circumference of the track, making flatulent revving noises, all headed not around the track but toward a point in the center of the infield.

Then the entire crowd, about 4,000, started chanting a countdown, "Ten, nine, eight, seven, six, five, four, three, two," but it was impossible to hear the rest, because right after "two" half the crowd went into a strange whinnying wail. The starter's flag went up, and the 25 cars took off, roaring into second gear with no mufflers, all headed toward that same point in the center of the infield, converging nose on nose.

The effect was exactly what one expects that many simultaneous crashes to produce: the unmistakable tympany of automobiles colliding and cheap-gauge sheet metal buckling; front ends folding together at the same cockeyed angles police photographs of night-time wreck scenes capture so well on grainy paper; smoke pouring from under the hoods and hanging over the infield like a howitzer cloud; a few of the surviving cars lurching eccentrically on bent axles. At last, after four heats, there were only two cars moving through the junk, a 1953 Chrysler and a 1958 Cadillac. In the Chrysler a small fascia of muscles named Spider Ligon, who smoked a cigar while he drove, had the Cadillac cornered up against a guard rail in front of the main grandstand. He dispatched it by swinging around and backing full throttle through the left side of its grille and radiator.

By now the crowd was quite beside itself. Spectators broke

through a gate in the retaining screen. Some rushed to Spider Ligon's car, hoisted him to their shoulders and marched off the field, howling. Others clambered over the stricken cars of the defeated, enjoying the details of their ruin, and howling. The good, full cry of triumph and annihilation rose from Riverhead Raceway, and the demolition derby was over.

That was the 154th demolition derby in two years. Since Lawrence Mendelsohn staged the first one at Islip Speedway in 1961, they have been held throughout the United States at the rate of one every five days, resulting in the destruction of about 15,000 cars. The figures alone indicate a gluttonous appetite for the sport. Sports writers, of course, have managed to ignore demolition derbies even more successfully than they have ignored stock car racing and drag racing. All in all, the new automobile sports have shown that the sports pages, which on the surface appear to hum with life and earthiness, are at bottom pillars of gentility. This drag racing and demolition derbies and things, well, there are too many kids in it with sideburns, tight Levis and winkle-picker boots.

Yet the demolition derbies keep growing on word-of-mouth publicity. The "nationals" were held last month at Langhorne, Pa., with 50 cars in the finals, and demolition derby fans everywhere know that Don McTavish, of Dover, Mass., is the new world's champion. About 1,250,000 spectators have come to the 154 contests held so far. More than 75 per cent of the derbies have drawn full houses.

The nature of their appeal is clear enough. Since the onset of the Christian era, i.e., since about 500 A.D., no game has come along to fill the gap left by the abolition of the purest of all sports, gladiatorial combat. As late as 300 A.D. these bloody duels, usually between men but sometimes between women and dwarfs, were enormously popular not only in Rome but throughout the Roman Empire. Since then no game, not even boxing, has successfully acted out the underlying motifs of most sport, that is, aggression and destruction.

Boxing, of course, is an aggressive sport, but one contestant has actually destroyed the other in a relatively small percentage of matches. Other games are progressively more sublimated forms of sport. Often, as in the case of football, they are encrusted with oddments of passive theology and metaphysics to the effect that the real purpose of the game is to foster character, teamwork, stamina, physical fitness and the ability to "give-and-take."

But not even those wonderful clergymen who pray in behalf of Congress, expressway ribbon-cuttings, urban renewal projects and testimonial dinners for ethnic aldermen would pray for a demolition derby. The demolition derby is, pure and simple, a form of gladiatorial combat for our times.

As hand-to-hand combat has gradually disappeared from our civilization, even in wartime, and competition has become more and more sophisticated and abstract, Americans have turned to the automobile to satisfy their love of direct aggression. The mild-mannered man who turns into a bear behind the wheel of a car—i.e., who finds in the power of the automobile a vehicle for the release of his inhibitions—is part of American folklore. Among teen-agers the automobile has become the symbol, and in part the physical means, of triumph over family and community restrictions. Seventy-five per cent of all car thefts in the United States are by teen-agers out for "joy rides."

The symbolic meaning of the automobile tones down but by no means vanishes in adulthood. Police traffic investigators have long been convinced that far more accidents are purposeful crashes by belligerent drivers than they could ever prove. One of the heroes of the era was the Middle Eastern diplomat who rammed a magazine writer's car from behind in the Kalorama embassy district of Washington two years ago. When the

American bellowed out the window at him, he backed up and smashed his car again. When the fellow leaped out of his car to pick a fight, he backed up and smashed his car a third time, then drove off. He was recalled home for having "gone native."

The unabashed, undisguised, quite purposeful sense of destruction of the demolition derby is its unique contribution. The aggression, the battering, the ruination are there to be enjoyed. The crowd at a demolition derby seldom gasps and often laughs. It enjoys the same full-throated participation as Romans at the Colosseum. After each trial or heat at a demolition derby, two drivers go into the finals. One is the driver whose car was still going at the end. The other is the driver the crowd selects from among the 24 vanquished on the basis of his courage, showmanship or simply the awesomeness of his crashes. The numbers of the cars are read over loudspeakers, and the crowd chooses one with its cheers. By the same token, the crowd may force a driver out of competition if he appears cowardly or merely cunning. This is the sort of driver who drifts around the edge of the battle avoiding crashes with the hope that the other cars will eliminate one another. The umpire waves a yellow flag at him and he must crash into someone within 30 seconds or run the risk of being booed off the field in dishonor and disgrace.

The frank relish of the crowd is nothing, however, compared to the kick the contestants get out of the game. It costs a man an average of $50 to retrieve a car from a junk yard and get it running for a derby. He will only get his money back—$50—for winning a heat. The chance of being smashed up in the madhouse first 30 seconds of a round are so great, even the best of drivers faces long odds in his shot at the $500 first prize. None of that matters to them.

Tommy Fox, who is nineteen, said he entered the demolition derby because, "You know, it's fun. I like it. You know what I mean?" What was fun about it? Tommy Fox had a way of speaking that was much like the early Marlon Brando. Much of what he had to say came from the trapezii, which he rolled quite a bit, and the forehead, which he cocked, and the eyebrows, which he could bring together expressively from time to time. "Well," he said, "you know, like when you hit 'em, and all that. It's fun."

Tommy Fox had a lot of fun in the first heat. Nobody was bashing around quite like he was in his old green Hudson. He did not win, chiefly because he took too many chances, but the crowd voted him into the finals as the best showman.

"I got my brother," said Tommy. "I came in from the side and he didn't even see me."

His brother is Don Fox, thirty-two, who owns the junk yard where they both got their cars. Don likes to hit them, too, only he likes it almost too much. Don drives with such abandon, smashing into the first car he can get a shot at and leaving himself wide open, he does not stand much chance of finishing the first three minutes.

For years now sociologists have been calling upon one another to undertake a serious study of America's "car culture." No small part of it is the way the automobile has, for one very large segment of the population, become the focus of the same sort of quasi-religious dedication as art is currently for another large segment of a higher social order. Tommy Fox is unemployed, Don Fox runs a junk yard, Spider Ligon is a maintenance man for Brookhaven Naval Laboratory, but to categorize them as such is getting no closer to the truth than to have categorized William Faulkner in 1926 as a clerk at Lord & Taylor, although he was.

Tommy Fox, Don Fox and Spider Ligon are acolytes of the car culture, an often esoteric world of arts and sciences that came into its own after World War II and now has believers of two generations. Charlie Turbush, thirty-five, and his son, Buddy, seventeen, were two more contestants, and by no stretch of the imagination can they be characterized as bizarre figures or cultists of the death wish. As for the dangers of driving in a demolition derby, they are quite real by all physical laws. The drivers are protected only by crash helmets, seat belts and the fact that all glass, interior handles, knobs and fixtures have been removed. Yet Lawrence Mendelsohn claims that there have been no serious injuries in 154 demolition derbies and now gets his insurance at a rate below that of stock car racing.

The sport's future may depend in part on word getting around about its relative safety. Already it is beginning to draw contestants here and there from social levels that could give the demolition derby the cachet of respectability. In eastern derbies so far two doctors and three young men of more than passable connections in eastern society have entered under whimsical *noms de combat* and emerged neither scarred nor victorious. Bull fighting had to win the same social combat.

All of which brings to mind that fine afternoon when some high-born Roman women were out in Nero's box at the Colosseum watching this sexy Thracian carve an ugly little Samnite up into prime cuts, and one said, darling, she had an inspiration, and Nero, needless to say, was all for it. Thus began the new vogue of Roman socialites fighting as gladiators themselves, for kicks. By the second century A.D. even the Emperor Commodus was out there with a tiger's head as a helmet hacking away at some poor dazed fall guy. He did a lot for the sport. Arenas sprang up all over the empire like shopping center bowling alleys.

The future of the demolition derby, then, stretches out over the face of America. The sport draws no lines of gender, and post-debs may reach Lawrence Mendelsohn at his office in Deer Park.

3

The Fifth Beatle

John, Paul, George, Ringo and—Murray the K!—the Fifth
Beatle! Does anybody out there really under*stand* what it
means that Murray the K is the Fifth Beatle? Does anybody
comprehend what something like that *took?* Does anybody
comprehend what a victory it was to become George the
Beatle's roommate in the hotel in Miami and do things like
tape record conversations with George during those magic
bloomings of the soul just before a man goes to sleep and bring
back to the kids the sound of a pure universe with nothing but
George, Murray the K and Fedders Miami air-conditioning in
it? No; practically nobody out there comprehends. Not even
Murray the K's fellow disc jockey William B. Williams, of

WNEW, who likes singers like Frank Sinatra, all that corny nostalgia of the New Jersey roadhouses, and says, "I like Murray, but if that's what he has to do to make a buck, he can have it."

You can imagine how Murray the K feels! He not only makes a buck, he makes about $150,000 a year, he is the king of the Hysterical Disc Jockeys, and people *still* look at him and think he is some kind of amok gnome. Do they know what's happening? Here in the studio, close up, inside the glass panels, amid the microphone grilles, cue sheets and commercials in capital letters, Murray the K sits on the edge of his seat, a solidly built man, thirty-eight years old, with the normal adult worried look on his face, looking through the glass at an engineer in a sport shirt. Granted, there are Murray the K's clothes. He has on a Stingy Brim straw hat, a shirt with wide lavender stripes on it, a pair of black pants so tight they have to have three-inch Chinese slits on the sides at the bottom so they will fit over the gussets of his boots. Murray the K has 62 outfits like this, elf boots, Russian hats, flipnik jerseys, but isn't that part of it? Murray the K is sitting on the vinyl upholstery on the edge of a chair, which makes it tip forward, and his legs are pumping up and down, but all the time he has to be thinking. He has to concentrate under all these layers of noise, such as the Barbasol commercial.

"Men, listen as we rub a microphone against an ordinary beard . . ."

What comes out of the speaker is a sound like a garbage man dragging a can up the cellar stairs of the Union Square Automat.

". . . and now listen to the Barbasol sound . . ."

This sounds like an otter turned loose in a bin full of immies. And through the whole thing, while all these odd sounds come over the speaker, Murray the K has to sit there in a glass box in the techni-blue of the fluorescent lights and think ahead. He presses down the lever on the intercom box and says to the engineer, "Give me Ringo and me—'You're what's happening.'" Then he wheels around to where Earl, from a British record magazine, is sitting, right behind him in the studio, and Earl gets his word in:

"Look, Murray, when can we sit down and talk?"

"Wait a minute," says Murray, "I got a whole tumultuous opening here and I don't know whether I'm coming or going. I can't do a show tonight—look at those commercials!"

"You sound like you've got troubles!"

Murray the K eyes the Englishman for a second and then says, "Yeah, I've got troubles and I'm creating troubles."

"What do you mean?"

Old Barbasol is scraping and rumbling away overhead.

"The Animals," says Murray.

"Murray!" says the Englishman. "The Animals are *very big!*"

"Yeah, but they're trying to do me in," says Murray.

What a sixth sense the man has! In the very same moment the red light is going on, before he can even see it, Murray is wheeling around, putting his face up to the microphone, starting his legs pumping and throwing body English into his delivery—and out comes the incredible cascade of words:

"All right, baby, that's Barbasol, baby, and this is the boss sound, 1010 WINS in New York, and that's what's happening, babe, John, Paul, George, Ringo and yours truly, Murray the K, the Fifth Beatle, seven minutes before seven o'clock, Beatle time, Beyezeatle Teyezime, and you ask Ringo what's happening, baby——"

All this starts out in a Southern accent ground out from way back in the throat like a Bible Way preacher and then turns into hippodrome circuit showbiz, and all the while Murray the K is wrenching his body this way and that and the words are barreling out on top of one another, piling up hysteria until he points at the engineer and—pow—the tape of Ringo and him is on, and the voice of Murray the K is heard shouting;

"What's happening, baby?"

And the curious black-water adenoid of Ringo Starr the Beatle is heard shouting:

"You're what's happening, baby!"

And Murray shouts, "You're happening, too, baby!"

And Ringo shouts, "O.K., we're both happening, baby!"

And—what is happening?

What is happening is radio in the modern age. It is a curious thing, psychologically. Radio is back strong after its early losses to television, but in an altogether different form. The radio is now something people listen to while they are doing something else. They're getting dressed in the morning, driving to work, sorting mail, painting a building, working in a manhole and listening to the radio. Then comes nightfall, and all the adults in New York and New Jersey and Long Island and Connecticut, like everywhere else, are stroked out, catatonic, in front of the television set. The kids, however, are more active. They are outside, all over the place, tooling around in automobiles, lollygagging around with transistors plugged into their skulls, listening to the radio. Listening is not exactly the word. They use the radio as a background, the aural prop for whatever kind of life they want to imagine they're leading. They don't want any messages at all, they want an atmosphere. Half the time, as soon as they get a message—namely, a commercial or a news spot—they start turning the dial, looking for the atmosphere they lost. So there are all those kids out there somewhere, roaming all over the dial, looking for something that will hook not the minds, but the psyche.

That was the problem for which Murray the K, at Station WINS, was the solution. Given the problem, this man was a genius. He was probably the original hysterical disc jockey and in any case he was the first big hysterical disc jockey. Murray the K doesn't operate on Aristotelian logic. He operates on symbolic logic. He builds up an atmosphere of breathless jollification, comic hysteria, and turns it up to a pitch so high it can hypnotize kids and keep them frozen to WINS through the commercials and everything else. The name Murray the K itself is an example of what he does. His real name is Murray Kaufman, but who cares if they're listening to somebody named Murray Kaufman? Murray the K is different. It doesn't mean anything, but it signifies something, a kind of nutty hipsterism. Symbolic logic. He does the same thing with sound effects. The sound effects come on cartridges. He can ask the engineer for No. 39 and wham, when he gives the signal, the biggest crash in the history of the world comes over the air. There are freight trains, cavalry charges, the screams of men plunging down an abyss, nutty macaw laughter from the jungle, anything, and it all goes off like rockets in an on-going lunacy, all spliced together only by the hysterical apostrophes —"All right, baby!"—of Murray the K.

For a while, after discovering hysteria and symbolic logic, Murray the K was murdering the competition. His rating was 29, he says, against 9 for the next best disc jockey in New York. Other stations were slow to copy the new technique because— well, it was too damned nutty. It sounded kind of *demented* or something. But they got over that, and pretty soon two stations, WABC and WMCA, had set up teams of disc jockeys who were working the rock and roll and hysteria gimmick practically around the clock. WABC called its group the All Americans and WMCA called theirs the Good Guys. Some of them, like Bruce Morrow of WABC, "Cousin Brucie" he is called, could even keep up with Murray the K in sheer pace. It got wild on the airways. There was a great manic competition going on, shrieks, giggles, falsettos, heaving buffoonery, laughing gargles, high school beat talk, shouts, gasps, sighs, yuks, loony laughs, nonsense rhymes, puns, crazy accents, anything that came spinning off the mind. And by last February 7, Murray the K was losing. He was behind both the All Americans and the Good Guys in the ratings.

"For one thing," says Murray the K, "I was boxed in. The station made some changes in the format and there was a half-hour news bloc in front of me and a talk show behind me."

Sure, Murray the K may have been boxed in, but a lot of times radio stations don't show much appreciation for the esoterica of disc jockey competition, just as nobody else out there does. Murray the K had put in four years at WINS, which was some kind of a record, but historically that doesn't mean much. There are about 25,000 or more disc jockeys in the country, and the turnover is ferocious; they are all the time quitting or getting fired, and about 95 per cent of them, employed or unemployed, have their jaws open and their eyes set on the 16 big disc jockey jobs in New York, the minimum expectation here being $20,000 a year for a no-talent disc jockey who works regularly.

Actually, Murray the K has done a great deal to diversify his work. About half his income comes from things like pop music shows he puts on at the Fox Theater in Brooklyn, his personal appearances at places like Freedomland, the Murray the K T shirts he sells, the record albums he "hosts," such as "Murray the K's Golden Gassers" and "Murray the K and Jackie the K's Golden Gassers." Jackie is his wife. Jackie's father, Hilary Hayes, runs Murray the K's office over at Station WINS, upstairs in a two-story building on Central Park West right where it hits Columbus Circle. And one of the finer points of Hilary Hayes' approach is that Murray the K is not merely WINS' outstanding disc jockey, he is a showman and personality in his own right. Hayes is a white-haired man who sits up there in the office at a desk underneath a poster reading, "Kongratulations to Murray the K, You're What's Happening, Baby." On the other side of the desk are a bunch of girls, volunteers, who answer Murray the K's mail, 150 or so letters a day. The girls being volunteers, there are always a lot of new girls, and he has to keep going over the instructions for answering the letters.

"Now remember," he tells them, "end the note with 'Murray sends his love' before 'Sincerely,' and remember to say, 'Listen to the boss show'—don't name it, if they don't know which it is, too bad. Also, remember, we're not happy because they listen to WINS—we're just happy they listen to Murray the K. If he was on any other station, we'd be just as happy."

The truth is, however, that for Murray the K, like every other disc jockey, all of it would evaporate, the T shirts, the albums, everything, if he ever found himself without a top radio show. That was what he had to think over when the All Americans and the Good Guys made their big surge. And then came February 7, 1964, the day of the biggest coup in Murray the K's life.

That was the day the Beatles first arrived in the United States, out at Kennedy Airport. The scene out there was the expected madhouse, 4,000 kids ricocheting all over the place, hurling themselves at plate glass to try to break through into the customs area when the Beatles got off the plane and came through, things like that. Every newspaper, television station, network, all the wire services, all the radio stations, everybody who could get somebody out there was covering it, and they were all angling for something exclusive. At WINS they had been trying to figure out which of their regular news reporters to send out to Kennedy to do a live broadcast of the Beatles' arrival, and they couldn't think of anybody suitable, and then Joel Chaseman, the station's manager, got the idea of why not send Murray the K.

The trouble was, the press was only going to get one shot at the Beatles, and that was when they were led into a steaming little press room and put up on a platform with literally about a hundred reporters, photographers and interviewers packed into the room around them in overcoats, it being February. To make it worse, all the photographers were yelling at once, and it was bedlam generally, but this was Murray the K's finest hour. Murray the K must have looked odd even to the Beatles. Here he was with a straw hat on in February, hunched up practically in a ball at the foot of the platform, looking up at them with his best manic look on and sticking a stick microphone up to about the level of their knees. Murray the K was copping an interview. The photographers were supposed to have first crack at the Beatles, but Murray the K was copping an interview by shooting questions up to them from somewhere in the general area of their feet, so they could answer into the microphone at their knees. Some photographer would be yelling something like, "Hey, how about you guys getting in a little closer there!" but all the time Murray the K would be singling out one Beatle like George Harrison and saying something like, "Hey, George, baby, hey, hey, George, George, baby, yeah, hey down here, how did this reception compare with the reception you got in Stockholm, baby?" Murray knew their whole history. And George, a literal-minded boy, would look down and see this odd friendly face under a straw hat and say, "Well, we were worried at first. Everywhere else we couldn't hear the plane for the screams, you know. But here we could hear the screams but we could also hear the planes—you know?—it worried us. It didn't seem big, you know, sort-of-thing."

All right! Cuba, de Gaulle, unilateral disarmament, Lyndon B. Johnson, South Viet Nam, it wasn't the sweep of history, but in the league of disc jockeys covering the first moments the Beatles set foot on the earth of America, it was a historic scoop. The whole press conference went that way. Even after the questions started from everybody, Murray the K kept copping exclusive interviews. Some reporter would yell out a question like, "What do you think of Beethoven?" John Lennon, the Beatle, would answer most of these random questions, saying things like, "Beethoven? He's crazy, especially the poems," and all the while Murray the K would be sticking the stick microphone up and asking, say, Ringo Starr, something like, "Ringo, what's the first thing you want to see in New York?" and Ringo would look down and see this odd little character balled up at his feet and say, "Oh, I dunno, some of the historic buildings, like the Peppermint Lounge." Finally somebody in the back, some reporter, yelled out, "Hey, somebody tell Murray the K to cut out the crap!" So Paul McCartney, the Beatle, stepped forward and looked down at Murray the K and said, "Murray the K, cut out the crap!" Paradise! "Crazy, Paul, baby," Murray the K said into the microphone, "You're what's happening, Paul, baby, and remember, you heard it first on 1010 WINS!" Cut out the crap! From Paul himself! This was the perfect note, for by now it seemed like this was Murray the K's press conference and the rest of these hundred or so guys around here were just some kind of a chorus. Murray the K's fortunes started skyrocketing from that very moment.

Somehow, the next night, it was Murray the K who was taking the Beatles twisting at the Peppermint Lounge and from then on he was the Beatles' guide, Boswell, buffer, playmate throughout their American tour, and he even went to England with them. Maybe it was his magic hat, he doesn't know, he had never had any communication with the Beatles at all before the moment he turned up stationed at their feet at Kennedy. "It was involuntary," says Murray, not necessarily choosing the precise word. By the end of a week there were reporters who were getting mad because to get anything out of the Beatles they had to go through Murray the K, and who the hell was he anyway. In Miami, Murray the K roomed with one of the Beatles, George Harrison, and there and everywhere else Murray the K was making tape recordings a mile a minute. He had all the Beatles, one by one, saying anything he wanted into the tape recorder—plugs for WINS, plugs for Murray the K, plugs for the "Swinging Soiree," which is the name of his nightly show from 6:30 to 10.

The impact of all this was great for Murray the K. Every station, practically every disc jockey in town, was trying to capitalize on the Beatles, who were probably the biggest single popular music phenomenon ever. WABC, for example, was calling itself WABeatleC, and so forth, but nobody could match Murray the K. He was the Fifth Beatle!

Susan Tyrer, a seventeen-year-old girl, is now sitting in Murray the K's studio. She is up there for something called the "Miss Swinging Soiree" contest, and there are 25 finalists, none of whom seems to have the faintest notion of what happens if she wins. Susan tells how it was with her: "I started listening to Murray the K when he started getting popular, you know, with the Beatles and the English groups." Murray the K also plays a lot of the other English groups, such as the Dave Clark Five and The Animals, groups like that. "Murray the K—well, you know," says Susan, "like, he's what's happening!"

So Murray the K's rating shot back up, and now his program is almost entirely Murray the K and the Beatles. He not only plays Beatle records all the time, the whole show sort of moves in the medium of the Beatles.

One evening there is a story in the newspapers that Ringo Starr, the Beatle, is going to get married.

"I'm here to deny, baby," Murray the K says into the microphone, "I mean I'm here to deny that Ringo's marrying anyone. You know if he was you'd hear it first on the boss show, 1010 WINS, New York. And now, baby, listen, baby, it's the Beyezeatlesingbooees!"

Murray the K even has tapes denying Beatle marriages. He'll say something like, "Paul, baby, we're glad you called us about that marriage bit, baby." And Paul says, "Well, Murray, I was glad to get it cleared up sort-of-thing."

He runs in Beatle dialogues all night long. Sometimes they have a wacky jumpy quality about them, something on the order of Murray the K saying, "Hey, Paul, baby, what's happening, baby?"

"I dunno, Murray, everything's happening sort-of-thing."

"Paul, somebody asked me to ask you—I mean, they asked me, some of your fans, they asked me to ask you, so I'm going to go ahead and ask you, What is your favorite color?"

"Well, uh, it's kind of, you know, black."

"Black."

"Yeah, you know, black. John is going to jump off the ladder now."

There is a sound of applause.

"They applaud," says Paul. "Sounds like a cricket match."

"You're what's happening, Paul, baby!"

Symbolic logic, baby! Who cares what's happening? The Beatles are there, and Murray the K is in there with them, tight.

One minute he feels like he is a showman who is playing the role of "Murray the K" at this particular stage in his career, which is a way of saying that Murray the K is not the real him. Then the next minute he has a very jealous regard for his Murray the K role and all the unique skills that have gone into it. The symbol of his pride about this is his hat. He keeps his straw hat on all the time when he is being Murray the K and he is ready to fight over it. One time he was MC'ing a show at the Fox Theater in Brooklyn and some singer, one of the parade of them that come and go, got playful and grabbed Murray the K's hat off his head and threw it out into the audience. Murray the K blew up. He made the fellow stop everything, right in the middle of the show, and go out in the audience, out among a lot of screaming kids, and retrieve the hat. There was something about the look in his eyes, and the fellow didn't have to think twice about whether he was going to obey or not. He just went after the hat.

The same goes for the music he plays, which is generally called rock and roll, a term that Murray the K considers out of date. He argues that it is *the* popular music now, not just a teenage deviation, just as swing was the popular music of the 1930's. He really blows up when someone like William B. Williams starts panning rock and roll as infra dig, such as the way Williams used to introduce the Beatles' first hit record, "I Want to Hold Your Hand," as "I Want to Hold My Nose" and just play 12 seconds of it. The same people, says Murray the K, will then start going on and on about Glenn Miller, Tommy Dorsey, Artie Shaw and all that bunch as if they were classics, all those mushy woodwinds, mushy ballads, all that stupid roadhouse glamor of the "Big Band" and some aging smoothie leading the band with a moon face and his hair combed straight back. The Glenn Miller business really gets him. Pop music today has a vitality and an intricacy that Glenn Miller couldn't have come up with in a hundred years.

"When I hear people start going about Glenn Miller," says Murray the K, "well, that's too much."

Ironically, rock and roll, or whatever you want to call what the hysterical disc jockeys play, is very much in vogue now among intellectuals in New York and Paris and London. They revere it like primitive art. They play the Shirelles, the Jellybeans, the Beach Boys, Shirley Ellis, Dionne Warwick, Johnny Rivers, musicians like that, on the record player at parties. Jazz, especially jazz as played by people like Miles Davis and Thelonius Monk, is considered a hopelessly bourgeois taste, the kind you might expect from a Williams College boy with a lie-down crewcut on a big weekend in New York.

Yet the vogue has never included the disc jockeys themselves, although you hear some of them, Murray the K and

Cousin Brucie, particularly, mentioned as sort of pop art phe-
nomena. So the disc jockeys themselves remain about the only
people who appreciate the art. Does anybody truly realize
what it amounted to when Murray the K took over the
Beatles?

"When the Beatles came here," he says, "I believed that this
was the test. This was the biggest thing in the history of popular music. Presley was never this big, neither was Sinatra. The
fact that I was able to be associated with the Beatles the way I
was, living with them, having George as my roommate—well,
it caused such jealousy as I have never seen in my life."

Murray the K stands up and paces around in his gusseted
boots. When he says something with conviction, his southern
accent breaks through. He was born in Virginia.

"But I'm not riding on the Beatles' coat tails," he says. "Actually, I think the Beatles are going to last a lot longer than
everybody believes. I think they are natural wits and come-
dians, they're the coolest, they're too much, they're the greatest. But I'm not riding the Beatles' coat tails, and if they go,
I'm going to be ready for the next person who comes along.

"I've done everything you have to do in this business, I've
made every move you have to make, I've put cash on the line,
and I came out a winner, and now I want everything that goes
with it, all the goodies and all the respect, because I earned
it."

Murray the K winds up his show a couple of minutes before
10 o'clock, and as soon as he leaves his glass cubicle, in walks a
young man wearing a crease-top hat, of the genre known as
the Madison Avenue crash helmet, and carrying an attaché
case. He looks like an account executive on the 5:25. He sits at
a table studying a script. His name is Pete Myers. Suddenly he
leans into the microphone and says, "It's 10 P.M. and now, from
Sponge Rubber Hall—it's Mad Daddy."

Down on the street, on Central Park West, three girls are

waiting to get Murray the K's autograph as he comes out the door. One of them is squeezed into a pair of short shorts that come up to about her ilial crest. Coming down over her left breast she has a row of buttons. The top one says, "We Love the Beatles." The next one says, "We Love Ringo," the next one, "We Love Paul," the next, "We Love John," the next "We Love George," and the next—well, the next one, the bottom one, is kind of rough in execution. It is made of paper wrapped around an old button with the letters penciled on, saying, "We Love Murray the K." But so what? The letters are big, and her little mary poppins tremble honestly.

4

The Peppermint Lounge
Revisited

All right, girls, into your stretch nylon denims! You know the ones—the ones that look like they were designed by some leering, knuckle-rubbing old tailor with a case of workbench back who spent five years, like Da Vinci, studying nothing but the ischia, the gemelli and the glutei maximi. Next, hoist up those bras, up to the angle of a Nike missile launcher. Then get into the cable-knit mohair sweaters, the ones that fluff out like a cat by a project heating duct. And then unroll the rollers and explode the hair a couple of feet up in the air into bouffants, beehives and Passaic pompadours. Stroke in the black makeup all around the eyelids, so that the eyes look as though Chester

Gould, who does Dick Tracy, drew them on. And then put those patient curls in your lips and tell Mother—you have to spell it out for her like a kid—that yes, you're going out with some of your girlfriends, and no, you don't know where you're going, and yes, you won't be out late, and for God's sake, like don't panic all the time, and then, with an I-give-up groan, tell her that "for God's sake" is *not* cursing.

At least that is the way it always seemed, as if some invisible force were out there. It was as though all these girls, all these flaming little Jersey Teen-agers, had their transistors plugged into their skulls and were taking orders, simultaneously, from somebody like the Ringleader Deejay.

Simultaneously, all over Plainfield, Scotch Plains, Ridgefield, Union City, Weehawken, Elizabeth, Hoboken and all the stretches of the Jersey asphalt, there they went, the Jersey Teen-agers, out of the house, off to New York, every week, for the on-going Jersey Teen-agers' weekend rebellion.

They headed off up Front Street if it was, say, Plainfield, and caught the Somerset Line bus at the stop across the street from the Public Service building around 7:30 P.M. Their bouffant heads would be bouncing up and down like dandelions until the bus hit the Turnpike and those crazy blue lights out there on the toothpaste factories started streaming by. They went through the Lincoln Tunnel, up the spiral ramps into the Port Authority Terminal and disembarked at some platform with an incredible number like 155. One hundred and fifty-five bus platforms; this was New York.

The first time people in Manhattan noticed the Jersey Teen-agers was when they would come bobbing out of the Port Authority and move into Times Square. No one ever really figured out what they were up to. They were generally written off as Times Square punks. Besides the bouffant babies in their stretch pants, furry sweaters and Dick Tracy eyes, there would be the boys in Presley, Big Bopper, Tony Curtis and Chicago boxcar hairdos. They would be steadying their hairdos in the reflections in the plate glass of clothing stores on 42nd Street that featured Nehru coats, Stingy-Brim hats, tab-collar shirts and winkle-picker elf boots. No one ever seemed to notice how maniacally serious they were about their hairdos, their flesh-tight pants, puffy sweaters, about the way they walked, idled, ogled or acted cool; in short, how serious they were about anything that had to do with form and each other. They had a Jersey Teen-age netherworld going in the middle of Manhattan. Their presence may not have been understood, but it was not ignored. There were nightspots that catered to them with rock and roll music. And when the Jersey Teen-agers started dancing in Times Square nightspots, they were serious about that, too. The Lindy, which was the name the kids had for what an older generation called jitterbugging, was already out. The kids were doing a dance called the Mashed Potatoes and another called the Puppet. Curiously, they were like the dances at a Lebanese maharajan. There was a lot of hip movement, but the boy and girl never touched. Then a new variation caught on, the Twist. There would be the Jersey Teen-agers, every weekend, doing the Mashed Potatoes, the Puppet and the Twist, studying each other's legs and feet through the entire number, never smiling, serious as always about form. One of these places was the Wagon Wheel. Another one was the Peppermint Lounge, 128 West 45th Street, half a block east of Times Square.

The Peppermint Lounge! You know about the Peppermint Lounge. One week in October, 1961, a few socialites, riding hard under the crop of a couple of New York columnists, discovered the Peppermint Lounge and by the next week all of Jet Set New York was discovering the Twist, after the manner of the first 900 decorators who ever laid hands on an African mask. Great Garbo, Elsa Maxwell, Countess Bernadotte, Noel

Coward, Tennessee Williams and the Duke of Bedford—everybody was there, and the hindmost were laying fives, tens and twenty-dollar bills on cops, doormen and a couple of sets of maître d's to get within sight of the bandstand and a dance floor the size of somebody's kitchen. By November, Joey Dee, twenty-two, the bandleader at the Peppermint Lounge, was playing the Twist at the $100-a-plate Party of the Year at the Metropolitan Museum of Art.

That, of course, was two years ago. Everybody knows what has happened to the Jet Set in that time, for the Jet Set is always with us. But whatever became of the Jersey Teen-agers and the Peppermint Lounge?

Marlene Klaire, leader of the club's Twist chorus line, is standing in the hall off the dressing rooms in back, talking about the kind of fall it has been for her. Marlene is a short, lithe, gorgeous brunette. It is right after the second show, and she has on her Twist chorus satin, a pair of net stockings, Cleopatra eye makeup and a Passaic pompadour that brings her up to about six feet four. Yes, there is an institution now called the Twist chorus line, tended by a couple of choreographers named Wakefield Poole and Tom Roba. Marlene arrived at the Peppermint Lounge two years ago via the Jersey Teen-age route, but now her life is full of institutions.

"The Waddle," Marlene is saying, "is one of the dances we were demonstrating the other night over at Sacred Heart. You get in two straight lines sort of like, you know, the Hully Gully."

"Sacred Heart?"

"The Catholic Church. We weren't *in* the church, really, it was the auditorium. They let us wear our costumes. They were all adults there. We were teaching them the Waddle, the Dog, the Monkey—the Monkey is probably the most popular right now."

Well, all that was with the young adults at Sacred Heart.

And then there was the night the educational program took her and the girls over to the Plaza Hotel for the Bourbon Ball, where they showed the Society people the Waddle, the Dog, the Monkey, the Mashed Potatoes and the Slop.

"The society people loved it," Marlene is saying, "but the Mashed Potatoes is hard for some of them, and—"

Marlene came to New York over the Jersey Teen-age route way back in 1961 when the Peppermint Lounge was first getting hot. She was from Trenton, and then she had a job as a secretary in Newark, but then one night she came rolling into the Port Authority like everybody else and headed for the Peppermint Lounge. She worked her way up fast. First she got a job as a waitress, then she got one of the jobs dancing between shows, in street clothes, which is to say, something like stretch pants and a mohair sweater, to encourage customers to come up and dance. Marlene could really dance, and she got a job in the first Twist chorus line.

Now, two years later, the Jet Set has moved on from the Peppermint Lounge, but the Jersey Teen-age cycle is continuing. Inside the club the Younger Brothers and the Epics are on the bandstand, and Janet Gail and Misty More and Louis and Ronnie are in street clothes, dancing between shows, and customers are packed in around them, bouncing. A few leggy kids in red satin shorts, waitresses, are standing around the sides miming the Monkey with their hips, shuffling to themselves. And out in the center nine girls from Jersey, all with exploding hair and Dick Tracy eyes, have a table and watch the dancing with that same old dead-serious look. Nobody is doing the Twist anymore. Everybody is doing something like the Monkey, in which you make some motions with your arms like you're climbing the bars of your cage, or the T-Bird, in which there is some complicated business with the hands about opening the front door and going inside and mixing a cocktail. Every now and then Larry Cope, who is one of the Younger Brothers, will introduce a pure Twist number, but he has to use a historical preface, sort of like they do at Roseland or some place when they say, well, now we're going to have a good old-fashioned waltz.

The Jersey Teen-age set has no trouble getting into the place now, although there are always a lot of tourists, especially on the weekends, who have heard of the Twist and the Peppermint Lounge.

"—and we had a lot of little kids in here Saturday, showing them the dances. They were, you know, little kids, four to ten years old, something like that. They catch on pretty fast, or at least they see us, you know, shaking around, and they do that. And then sometimes we get women's groups. They're going to a show or something, and they then drop in here."

On the one hand Marlene sees a limitless future for the Twist as an institution. She figures the tourists coming to the World's Fair will add years to its life, and already she and the dancers are working on an act for the Fair called "Twisting Around the World," in which they will start off doing a native dance from some country when somebody shouts out "Twist!" in the native tongue, which usually comes out "Tweest!" and then the native dance becomes the native twist. Marlene had another idea, which was "Twisting Into Outer Space," but it looks like it will be "Around the World."

In another sense, however, Marlene does not associate the Twist with the future at all. Marlene's goal! Marlene's goal is . . . Marlene's answer should reassure a whole generation of Jersey mothers about where the Jersey Teen-age rebellion is heading, it and all its bouffant babies, nylon stretch denims, Dick Tracy eyes, Nehru coats and Monkey dancers.

Out in the club the Epics, with four electric instruments going, are playing "Doing the Dog," and Misty is doing the Dog, and Janet is doing the Mashed Potatoes, and Jerri Miller is doing the Monkey, with a few baroque emendations, but Marlene reflects a moment, as if upon her busy round of work with the churches, the benefit balls, the women's groups and the youth.

"Well," she says, "I'd like to teach dancing, in my own house, you know, the way it was when I took lessons from my teacher. Or maybe be a psychologist. I used to want to, and I may still do that. Anyway, I don't want to live in New York. I want some place more like where we used to live in New Jersey. I don't like living here. There aren't any trees."

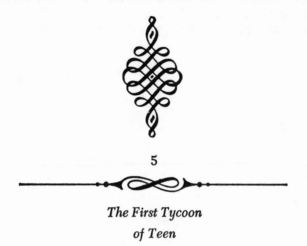

5

The First Tycoon
of Teen

All these raindrops are *high* or something. They don't roll down the window, they come straight back, toward the tail, wobbling, like all those Mr. Cool snow heads walking on mattresses. The plane is taxiing out toward the runway to take off, and this stupid infarcted water wobbles, sideways, across the window. Phil Spector, twenty-three years old, the rock and roll magnate, producer of Philles Records, America's first teen-age tycoon watches . . . this watery pathology. . . . It is *sick*, *fatal*. He tightens his seat belt over his bowels. . . . A hum rises inside the plane, a shot of air comes shooting through the vent over somebody's seat, some ass turns on a cone of light, there is a sign stuck out by the runway, a mad, cryptic, insane instruction to the pilot—Runway 4, Are Cylinder Lap Mainside DOWN?—and beyond, disoriented crop rows of sulphur blue lights, like the lights on top of a New Jersey toothpaste factory, only spreading on and on in sulphur blue rows over Los Angeles County. It is . . . disoriented. Schizoid raindrops. The plane breaks in two on takeoff and everybody in the front half comes rushing toward Phil Spector in a gush of bodies in a thick orange—*napalm!* No, it happens aloft; there is a long rip in the side of the plane, it just rips, he can see the top ripping, folding back in sick curds, like a sick Dali egg, and Phil Spector goes sailing through the rip, dark, freezing. And the engine, it is *reedy*—

Miss!

A stewardess is walking back to the back to buckle herself in for the takeoff. The plane is moving, the jets are revving. Under a Lifebuoy blue skirt, her fireproof legs are clicking out of her Pinki-Kini-Panty Fantasy—

"Miss!" says Phil Spector.

"Yes?"

"I, like I have to get off the plane."

She stops there beside his seat with her legs bent slightly, at a 25-degree angle to her ischium. She laughs with her mouth, yes yes, but there is no no in her eyes, you little bearded creep, you are not very funny. Her face . . . congeals . . . she looks at his suede jerkin. She says,

"Sir?"

"I, you know, I have to get off," says Phil Spector, "I don't want to *fly* on this plane. Let me—" but she will never figure out about the raindrops. She is standing there hoping this is a joke. "—uh, I'm not putting you on, I'm not putting you down, I'm not anything, all I want is—you know?—just open the door and let me off. I'll walk back. The rest—everybody—I mean, go ahead, *fly*."

"Sir, we're already in a pattern. There are seven aircraft, seven jet aircraft, behind us waiting for the runway—"

By this time Phil Spector's Hollywood friends, in this nutball music business—there is one of them beside him and a couple of them behind him, they are craning around.

"Phil! What's wrong, baby!"

Phil turns around and says in his soft and slightly broken voice: "Man, this plane's not going to make it."

They all look around, they all look like frozen custard in the seat lights.

"You know?" Phil says. "It's not making it."

They all look around, the goddamned *noise* is roaring off the wings, and Phil sits there in that kind of doldrum fury he lives in, his beard, his hair, his suede. O.K., we're in a pattern, seven jets. But this guy Phil Spector has just produced *eight straight hit records*—you know? Eight hits! This kid is practically a baby, twenty-three years old, f'r chrissake, and he has made two million dollars, clear. The first teen-age business magnate—living teen tycoon. Like he is programmed into the Whole Life Bit—you know? He does A & R for Daddy God, he's *lucky*—you know?—and if he's getting off—

So the big chap behind with the moon head and the little Seventh Avenue toy black hat says,

"Yeah, we wanna get off. There's something wiggy or something about this plane."

"Yeah!"

"Yeah!"

The stewardess is looking around, and here is her life being drowned by this little guy—he has a Fu Manchu beard sticking out in front of his hair, his wispy locks are combed back, coming down in back over his shoulders in a kind of pageboy, like Bishop McCullough's, the heir to Daddy Grace. He has on a suede leather shirt, jerkin style. Somebody's cone of light lies in Miami saffron pools on his Italian pants. He looks like— what kind of—

All this commotion. Yeah, says Phil Spector's pals. It's wiggy. Off this flying cretin. Phil Spector broods over the raindrops. The stewardess runs for the cabin.

So they stop the plane, they break up the whole pattern, they knock out everybody's schedule, they turn the plane around, take everybody off. They check Phil Spector's luggage for—*bombs*. Look at this *beatnik's* hair in *back* there, and they stare at Son of Bop in a leather jerkin, ten men in alumicron suits bombarding him with corporate hate rays. But his pals keep up this strange upbeat talk:

"Phil, baby, you saved my life!"

"Phil, if you say it's wiggy, it's wiggy."

"You done it again, Phil, babes, you done it again!"

". . . *You* say it's wiggy, Phil? *I* say it's wiggy . . .'

". . . I hurts, too, D'Artagnan, baby, right here, same as you . . ."

". . . wiggy . . ."

". . . baby . . ."

"So," says Phil Spector, "they grounded me. They took away my credit cards, they suspended the pilot, I don't know."

Spector is sitting in a little cream room in his office suite at 440 East 62nd Street with his back to a window that is practically on top of the East Side Drive. Twenty-three years old— he has a complex of corporations known as Phil Spector Productions. One of them is Mother Bertha productions, named after his mother, Bertha. She works for his office in Los Angeles, but only because she wants to. The main organization is Philles Records. Spector has produced 21 "single" Philles records since October, 1962—and sold more than 13 million copies. All rock and roll. His most recent big hit, "Walking in the Rain," by the Ronettes, went as high No. 20 on the *Cashbox* chart and has sold more than 250,000 copies. His latest record, "You've Lost that Lovin' Feelin'," by the Righteous Brothers, rose from the 70's to No. 37 with a "bullet" beside it—meaning "going up fast." He has produced seven albums. The first teen-age tycoon! He is leaning back in the chair. He has on his suede jerkin, his Italian pants, a pair of pointy British boots with Cuban heels. His hair hangs down to his shoulders in back. The beard is shaved off, however.

Danny Davis, his promotion man, is talking on the phone in the inner office. A fellow sits across from Spector with his legs crossed and a huge chocolate brown Borsalino hat over his bent knee, like he was just trying it on. He says,

"Phil, why do you do—"

"I'm moving the whole thing to California," says Phil Spector. "I can't stand flying anymore."

"—why do you do these things?"

Spector—without his beard, Spector has a small chin, a small head, his face looks at first like all those little kids with bad hair and reedy voices from the Bronx, where he was born. But—an *ordinary* Phil Spector? Phil Spector has the only pure American voice. He was brought up not in the Bronx, but California. It meanders, quietly, shaking, through his doldrum fury, out to somewhere beyond cynical, beyond cool, beyond teen-age world-weary, It is thin, broken and soft. He is only twenty-three years old, for godsake, the first millionaire businessman to rise up out of the teen-age netherworld, king of the rock and roll record producers—

Spector jumps out of the chair.

"Wait a minute," he says. "Just a minute. They're making deals in here."

Spector walks into the inner office, gingerly, like a cowboy, because of the way the English boots lift him up off the floor. He is slight, five feet seven, 130 pounds. His hair shakes faintly behind. It is a big room, like a living room, all beige except for nine gold-plated rock and roll records on the wall, some of Phil Spector's "goldies," one million sales each. "He's a Rebel," by the Crystals, "Zip-a-dee-doo-dah," by Bob B. Soxx and the Blue Jeans. "Be My Baby" by the Ronettes, "Da Do Ron Ron," "Then He Kissed Me," "Uptown," "He's Sure the Boy I Love," all by the Crystals, "Wait Til My Baby Gets Home," by Darlene Love. And beige walls, beige telephones all over the place, a beige upright piano, beige paintings, beige tables, with Danny Davis crowding over a beige desk, talking on the telephone.

"Sure, Sal," says Danny, "I'll ask Phil. Maybe we can work something out on that."

Spector starts motioning thumbs down.

"Just a minute, Sal." Danny puts his hand over the mouthpiece and says,

"We *need* this guy, Phil. He's the biggest distributor out there. He wants the one thousand guarantee."

Phil's hands go up like he is lifting a slaughtered lamb up on top of an ice box.

"I don't care. I'm not interested in the money, I've got millions of dollars of money, I don't care who needs this animal. I'm interested in selling records, O.K.? Why should I give him a guarantee? He orders the records, I guarantee I'll buy a thousand back from him if he can't sell them; he sells them, then after the record dies, he buys up 500 cut rate from somebody, sends them back and cries for his money. Why should we have to be eating his singles later?"

Danny takes his hand away and says into the mouthpiece:

"Look, Sal, there's one thing I forgot. Phil says this record he can't give the guarantee. But you don't have anything to worry about . . . I know what I said, but Phil says . . . look, Sal, don't worry, 'Walking in the Rain,' this is a tremendous record, tremendous, a very big record . . . What? . . . I'm not reading off a paper, Sal . . . Wait a minute, Sal—"

"Who needs these animals?" Phil Spector tells Danny.

"Look, Sal," Danny says, "this man never made a bad record in his life. You tell me one. Nothing but hits."

"Tell him to go to hell," says Spector.

"Sal—"

"Who needs these animals!" says Spector, so loud this time that Danny cups his hand around the receiver and puts his mouth down close.

"Nothing, Sal," says Danny, "that was somebody came in."

"Joan," says Phil, and a girl, Joan Berg, comes in out of another room. "Will you turn the lights off?" he says.

She turns the lights off, and now in the middle of the day the offices of Philles Records and Mother Bertha Productions are all dark except for the light from Danny Davis' lamp. Danny crowds into the pool of light, hunched over the phone, talking to Sal.

Phil puts his fingers between his eyes and wraps his eyebrows around them.

"Phil, it's dark in here," says the fellow with the large hat. "Why do you do these things?"

"I'm paying a doctor $600 a week to find out," says Phil, without looking up.

He sits there in the dark, his fingers buried between his eyes. Just over his head one can make out a painting. The painting is kind of came-with-the-frame surrealist. It shows a single musical note, a half note, suspended over what looks like the desert outside Las Vegas. Danny has to sit there huddled in his own pool of light talking to this animal on the telephone.

"This is a primitive country," says Phil Spector. "I was at Shepheard's, the discotheque, and these guys start saying these things. It's unbelievable. These people are animals."

"What kind of things, Phil?"

"I don't know. They look at, you know, my hair—my wife
and I are dancing, and, I mean, it's unbelievable, I feel somebody yanking on my hair in the back. I turn around, and here's
this guy, a grown man, and he is saying these unbelievable
things to me. So I tell him, like this, 'I'm going to tell you this
one time, that's all—don't ever try that again.' And the guy—
it's unbelievable—he shoves me with the heel of his hand and I
go sprawling back into a table—"

—Spector pauses—

"—I mean, I've studied karate for years. I could literally *kill*
a guy like that. You know? Size means nothing. A couple of
these—" he cocks his elbow in the gloom and brings up the flat
of his forearm—"but what am I going to do, start a fight every
time I go out? Why should I even have to listen to anything
from these animals? I find this country very condemning. I
don't have this kind of trouble in Europe. The people of America are just not born with culture."

Not born with culture! If only David Susskind and William
B. Williams could hear that. Susskind invited Phil Spector to
the *Open End* television program one evening "to talk about
the record business." Suddenly Susskind and "William B.," station WNEW's old-nostalgia disc jockey, were condemning
Spector as some kind of sharpie poisoning American culture,
rotting the minds of Youth and so forth. That was how it all hit
Spector. It was as if he were some kind of old short-armed
fatty in the Brill Building, the music center on Broadway, with
a spread-collar shirt and a bald olive skull with strands of
black hair pulled up over it from above one ear. There was
something very ironic about that. Spector is the one record
producer who wouldn't go near Broadway. His setup is practically out in the East River, up by the Rockefeller Institute.
The Rockefeller Institute, for godsake. Susskind and Williams
kept throwing Spector's songs at him—"He's a Rebel," "Da Do
Ron Ron," "Be My Baby," "Fine Fine Boy," "Breakin' Up"—as

if he were astutely conning millions of the cretins out there with this stuff. Spector didn't know exactly what to tell them. He *likes* the music he produces. He writes it himself. He is something new, the first teen-age millionaire, the first boy to become a millionaire within America's teen-age netherworld. It was never a simple question of him taking a look at the rock and roll universe from the outside and exploiting it. He stayed within it himself. He *liked* the music.

Spector, while still in his teens, seemed to comprehend the prole vitality of rock and roll that has made it the kind of darling holy beast of intellectuals in the United States, England and France. Intellectuals, generally, no longer take jazz seriously. Monk, Mingus, Ferguson—it has all been left to little executive trainees with their first apartment and a mahogany African mask from the free-port shop in Haiti—let me *tell* you!—and a hi-fi. But rock and roll! Poor old arteriosclerotic lawyers with pocky layers of fat over their ribs are out there right now twisting with obscene clumsiness to rock and roll. Their wives wear stretch pants to the seafood shoppe. A style of life! There have been teen-agers who have made a million dollars before, but invariably they are entertainers, they are steered by older people, such as the good Colonel Tom Parker steers Elvis Presley. But Phil Spector is the bona-fide Genius of Teen. Every baroque period has a flowering genius who rises up as the most glorious expression of its style of life—in latter-day Rome, the Emperor Commodus; in Renaissance Italy, Benvenuto Cellini; in late Augustan England, the Earl of Chesterfield; in the sal volatile Victorian age, Dante Gabriel Rossetti; in late-fancy neo-Greek Federal America, Thomas Jefferson; and in Teen America Phil Spector is the bona-fide Genius of Teen. In point of fact, he had turned twenty-one when he made his first clear million. But it was as a teen-ager, working within the teen-age milieu, starting at the age of seventeen, that Phil Spector developed into a great American business man, the greatest of the independent rock and roll record producers. Spector's mother, Bertha, took him from the Bronx to California when he was nine. California! Teen Heaven! By the time he was sixteen he was playing jazz guitar with some group. Then he got interested in rock and roll, which he does not call rock and roll but "pop blues." That is because—well, that is a complicated subject. Anyway, Phil Spector likes this music. He genuinely likes it. He is not a short-armed fatty hustling nutball fads.

"I get a little angry when people say it's bad music," Spector tells the man with the brown hat. "This music has a spontaneity that doesn't exist in any other kind of music, and it's what is here now. It's unfair to classify it as rock and roll and condemn it. It has limited chord changes, and people are always saying the words are banal and why doesn't anybody write lyrics like Cole Porter anymore, but we don't have any presidents like Lincoln anymore, either. You know? Actually, it's more like the blues. It's pop blues. I feel it's very American. It's very *today*. It's what people respond to today. It's not just the kids. I hear cab drivers, everybody, listening to it."

And Susskind sits there on his show reading one of Spector's songs out loud, no music, just reading the words, from the Top Sixty or whatever it is, "Fine Fine Boy," to show how banal rock and roll is. The song just keeps repeating "He's a fine fine boy." So Spector starts drumming on the big coffee table there with the flat of his hands in time to Susskind's voice and says, "What you're missing is the beat." Blam blam.

Everybody is getting a little sore with Susskind reading these simple lyrics and Spector blamming away on the coffee table. Finally, Spector says the hell with it and, being more . . . hip . . . than Susskind or William B. Williams, starts cutting them up. He starts asking Williams how many times he plays Verdi on his show—Monteverdi?—D. Scarlatti?—A. Scarlatti?—that's good music, why don't you play that, you keep saying you play only good music, I don't hear you playing that. Williams doesn't know what to say. Spector tells Susskind he didn't come on the show to listen to somebody tell him he was corrupting the Youth of America—he could be home making money. Susskind—well, ah, all right, Phil. Everybody is testy.

Making money. Yes! At the age of seventeen Spector wrote a rock and roll song called "To Know Him Is To Love Him." He took the title off his father's tombstone. That was what his mother had had engraved on his father's tombstone out in Beth David cemetery in Elmont, L.I. He doesn't say much about his father, just that he was "average lower middle class." Spector wrote the song, sang it and played the guitar in the recording with a group called the Teddy Bears. He made $20,000 on that record, but somebody ran off with $17,000 of it, and, well, no use going into that. Then he was going to UCLA, but he couldn't afford it and became a court reporter, one of the people who sit at the shorthand machine, taking down testimony. He decided to come to New York and get a job as an interpreter at the UN. His mother had taught him French. But he got to New York, and the night before the interview, he fell in with some musicians and never got there. The hell with stenography. He wrote another hit that year, "Spanish Harlem." *There is a rose in Spanish Ha-a-a-a-ar-a-lem.* And then—only nineteen—he became head of A & R, artists and repertoire, for Atlantic Records. By 1961 he was a free-lance producer, producing records for the companies, working with Connie Francis, Elvis Presley, Ray Peterson, the Paris Sisters. All this time, Spector would write a song and run all phases of making records: get the artists, direct the recording sessions, everything. Spector could work with these hairy goslin kids who make these records because he was a kid himself, in one sense. God knows what the music business biggies thought of Phil Spector—he already wore his hair like Salvador

Dali did at that age or like an old mezzotint of Mozart at the Academy or something. And he was somehow *one of them,* the natives, the kids who sang and responded to this . . . music. Phil Spector could get in one of those studios with the heron microphones, a representative of the adult world that makes money from records, and it became all one thing—the kids comprehended him.

Spector had an ideal, Archie Bleyer. Bleyer was a band leader who founded a record company, Cadence Records. Spector formed a partnership with two other people in 1961, then bought them out and went on his own as Philles Records in October of 1962. His first big hit was "He's a Rebel," by the Crystals. Spector had a system. The big record companies put out records like buckshot, 10, maybe 15 rock and roll records a month, and if one of them catches on, they can make money. Spector's system is to put them out one at a time and pour everything into each one. Spector does the whole thing. He writes the words and the music, scouts and signs up the talent. He takes them out to a recording studio in Los Angeles and runs the recording session himself. He puts them through hours and days of recording to get the two or three minutes he wants. Two or three minutes out of the whole struggle. He handles the control dials like an electronic maestro, tuning various instruments or sounds up, down, out, every which way, using things like two pianos, a harpsichord and three guitars on one record; then re-recording the whole thing with esoteric dubbing and over-dubbing effects—reinforcing instruments or voices—coming out with what is known throughout the industry as "the Spector sound."

The only thing he doesn't keep control of is the actual manufacture, the pressing, of the records and the distribution. The only people around to give him any trouble all this time are the distributors—cigar-chewing fatties . . . and—well, to be honest, there is a lot that gives Phil Spector trouble, and not so much any kind of or any group of people as much as his . . . status. A Teen-age Tycoon! It is too wacked out. He is betwixt and between. He identifies with the teen-age netherworld, he defends it, but he is already too mature for it. As a millionaire, a business genius, living in a penthouse 22 stories up over the East River, with his wife, Annette, who is twenty, a student at Hunter College, and with a four-room suite downstairs on the ground floor as his office, and a limousine, and a chauffeur, and a bodyguard, and a staff, Danny and Joan Berg and every- body, and a doorman who directs people to Mr. Spector's office—well, that makes Phil Spector *one of them*, the universe of arteriosclerotic, hypocritical, cigar-chewing, hopeless, larded adults, infarcted vultures, one meets in the music business. And so here in the dark is a twenty-three-year-old man with a Shelley visage, a suede shirt, a kind of page-boy bob and winkle-picker boots, the symbol of the one, sitting in the dark in this great beige office, the symbol of the other, in the middle of the day, in the dark, tamping his frontal lobes with his fingers in the gloom.

One of the beige phones rings and Danny answers. Then he presses the "hold" button and tells Phil Spector, "It's the Roll- ing Stones, they just got in."

Spector comes alive with that. He gets up on his ginger toes and goes to the telephone. He is lively and he spins on the balls of his feet a little as he stands by the phone.

"Hello, Andrew," he says. He is talking with Andrew Old- ham, the manager of the Rolling Stones. And then he puts on a Cockney accent. "Are you all in?" he says.

The Rolling Stones; all right. The Rolling Stones, English group, and Andrew Oldham, are like him. They grew up in the teen-age netherworld and made it, and they all want to have it all, too, the kids' style of life and the adult's . . . money . . . and not cop out on one side or the other, larded and arteriosclerotic. God! Phil Spector's British trip! That was where suddenly he had it all.

Phil Spector is here! The British have the ability to look at all sorts of rebel baddies and alienated thin young fellows and say coo and absorb them like a great soggy lukewarm, mother's poultice. The Beatles, Beatlemania, rock and roll, suddenly it is all absorbed into the center of things as if it could have been there all along if it only asked. Phil Spector arrives at London Airport and, Santa Barranza, there are photographers all over the place, for him, Phil Spector, and the next morning he is all over the center fold of the *London Daily Mirror,* the biggest newspaper in the Western World, five million circulation: "The 23-year-old American rock and roll magnate." He is in the magazines as the "U. S. Recording Tycoon." Invitations go out to come to the receptions to meet "America's outstanding hit maker, Phil Spector." And then he lands back at Idlewild and waiting are, yes, the same bunch of cheese-breath cabbies, and he takes a cab on back to 440 E. 62nd St. and goes into his beige world, the phones are ringing and it is all the same, the same—

"Cigar-smoking sharpies," says Phil Spector. He is in a livelier mood after the talk with Andrew Oldham. "They're a bunch of cigar-smoking sharpies in record distribution. They've all been in the business for years and they resent you if you're young. That's one reason so many kids go broke in this business. They're always starting new record companies, or they used to, the business is very soft right now, they start a company and pour all their money into a record, and it can be successful and they're still broke, because these characters don't even pay you until you've had three or four hit records in a row. They order the records and sell them and don't pay you. They don't pay you because they know they don't have to. You start yelling for the money and they tell you, 'Whattya mean, I have all these records coming back from the retailers and what about my right to return records, and blah-blah.' What are you going to do? Sue twenty guys in twenty different courts in the United States?

"They look at everything as a product. They don't care about the work and sweat you put into a record. They respect me now because I keep turning out hits, and after that they become sort of honest . . . in their own decayed way."

Where does a man find friends, comrades, anything, in a world like that? They resent his youth. They resent his success. But it is no better with the kids. He is so much more mature and more . . . eminent . . . they all want to form "the father thing" with him. Or else they want to fawn over him, cousin him, cajole, fall down before him, whistle, shout, stomp, bang him on the head, anything to get his attention and get "the break," just one chance. Or one more chance. Spector can't go near the Brill Building, the center of the music business, because the place is crawling with kids with winkle-picker shoes cracking in the folds, who made one hit record five years ago and still can't realize that they are now, forever, in oblivion. They crawl all over the place the way the small-time balding fatty promoters and managers used to in the days when A. J. Liebling wrote about the place as the Jollity Building. Phil Spector steps onto an elevator in the Brill Building, the elevator is packed, and suddenly he feels this arm hooking through his in the most hideously cozy way and a mouth is closing in on his ear and saying, "Phil, baby, wait'll you hear this one: 'Ooh-oom-bah-ay,'" and Phil Spector is imprisoned there with the elevator inching up, "vah ump nooby poon fang ooh-ooh ayub bah-ay—you dig that, Phil? You dig that, don't you, Phil? Phil, babes!" He walks down the hall and kids sneak up behind him and slip songs, music, lyrics into his coat pocket. He finds the stuff in there, all this ratty paper, when he gets home. Or he is leaving the Brill Building and he feels a great whack on the back of his head and wheels around and there

are four kids in the singing stance, their heads angled in together, saying, "Just one bar, Phil—Say wohna love boo-uh ay-
yay bubby—" while the guy on the end sings bass with his chin
mashed into a pulpy squash down over his collar bone, *beh-
ungggh, beh-ungggh.*

Status! What is his status? He produces "rock and roll," and,
therefore, he is not a serious person, and he won't join the
Young Presidents or whatever the hell kind of organization
jaycee geniuses would join for their own good.

"Phil," says the man with the hat, "why don't you hire a
press agent, a P. R. man—"

Phil is tamping his frontal lobes in the gloom. Danny Davis
is hunched up in the little pool of light on his desk. Danny is
doing his level best for Phil.

"Jack? Danny Davis . . . Yeah . . . No, I'm with Phil
Spector now . . . Right! It's the best move I ever made. You
know Phil . . . I'm in the best shape of my career . . . Jack,
I just want to tell you we've got—

"A press agent?" Phil says to the man in the hat. "In the first
place, I couldn't stand to hear what he'd say about me."

"——Got two tremendous records going, Jack, 'Walking in
the Rain,' the Ronettes, and—"

"In the second place," Phil says, "there's no way my image
can be bought."

"——And 'You've Lost That Lovin' Feelin'' by the Righteous Brothers," says Danny. ". . . Right, Jack . . . I appreciate that, Jack . . ."

"The only thing I could do—you know what I'd like to do?
I'd like to do a recording session in the office of *Life* or *Esquire*
or *Time,* and then they could see it. That's the only chance I've
got. Because I'm dealing in rock and roll, I'm, like I'm not a
bona-fide human being—"

". . . Absolutely! . . . If there's anything we can do for you on this end, Jack, let us know. O.K.? Great, Jack . . ."

". . . and I even have trouble with people who should never say *any*thing. I go over to Gristede's to get a quart of milk or something and the woman at the cash register has to start in. So I tell her, 'There's a war in Viet Nam, they've fired Khrushchev, the Republican party is falling to pieces, the Ku Klux Klan is running around loose, and you're worrying about my hair. . . .'"

America's first teen-age tycoon, a business genius, a musical genius—and it is as if he were still on the corner on Hoffman Street in the Bronx when the big kids come by in hideous fraternity, the way these people act. What is he now? Who is he in this weird country? Danny talks in the phone in the little pool of light, Joan is typing up whatever it is, Phil is tamping his frontal lobes.

Another airplane! It levels off, and the man in the seat by the window, next to Phil Spector, lights a cigarette, pure as virgin snow. Phil Spector sits there with his kind of page-boy bob pressed down in back and a checked shirt and tight black pants. The man with the cigarette keeps working himself up to something. Finally, he says, "If you don't mind me asking—have I seen you on television or something? What's your name, I mean, if you don't mind me asking?" Phil Spector presses back into the seat but his head won't disappear. Then he says, "I'm Goddard Lieberson."

"Gottfried Lieberman?"

Marvelous! Reassuring! Nobody ever heard of Goddard Lieberson, either. Who the hell is Goddard Lieberson! He is the president of Columbia Records, all those nice straight cookie jar "tunes" William B. Williams would go for, very big—and who the hell knows who he is?

"I'm the president of Columbia Records."

The man sucks on his cigarette a moment. A skinny ash, all limp, hangs out.

"Well—you must be kind of young."

Phil Spector lies back. Then he says,

"I was only kidding. I'm Chubby Checker. That's who I really am."

"Chubby Checker?"

Who the hell is Chubby Checker? Yes! Who the hell has *any*body ever heard of? It's like the last time when he said he was Paul Desmond. Who the hell is Paul Desmond? Or Peter Sellers' cousin. Or Monsieur Fouquet, of the de Gaulle underground. Or . . . who the hell is *any*body? Phil Spector tamps his frontal lobes and closes his eyes and holds his breath. As long as he holds his breath, it will not rain, there will be no raindrops, no schizoid water wobbling, sideways, straight back, it will be an even, even, even, even, even, even, even world.

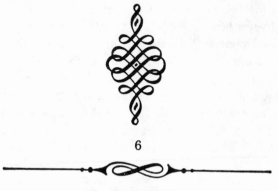

6

The Kandy-Kolored
Tangerine-Flake
Streamline Baby

The first good look I had at customized cars was at an event called a "Teen Fair," held in Burbank, a suburb of Los Angeles beyond Hollywood. This was a wild place to be taking a look at art objects—eventually, I should say, you have to reach the conclusion that these customized cars *are* art objects, at least if you use the standards applied in a civilized society. But I will get to that in a moment. Anyway, about noon you drive up to a place that looks like an outdoor amusement park, and there are three serious-looking kids, like the cafeteria committee in high school, taking tickets, but the scene inside is quite mad.

Inside, two things hit you. The first is a huge platform a good seven feet off the ground with a hully-gully band—everything is electrified, the bass, the guitars, the saxophones—and then behind the band, on the platform, about two hundred kids are doing frantic dances called the hully-gully, the bird, and the shampoo. As I said, it's noontime. The dances the kids are doing are very jerky. The boys and girls don't touch, not even with their hands. They just ricochet around. Then you notice that all the girls are dressed exactly alike. They have bouffant hairdos—all of them—and slacks that are, well, skin-tight does not get the idea across; it's more the conformation than how tight the slacks are. It's as if some lecherous old tailor with a gluteus-maximus fixation designed them, striation by striation. About the time you've managed to focus on this, you notice that out in the middle of the park is a huge, perfectly round swimming pool; really rather enormous. And there is a Chris-Craft cabin cruiser in the pool, going around and around, sending up big waves, with more of these bouffant babies bunched in the back of it. In the water, suspended like plankton, are kids in Scuba-diving outfits; others are tooling around underwater, breathing through a snorkel. And all over the place are booths, put up by shoe companies and guitar companies and God knows who else, and there are kids dancing in all of them—dancing the bird, the hully-gully, and the shampoo—with the music of the hully-gully band piped all over the park through loudspeakers.

All this time, Tex Smith, from *Hot Rod Magazine*, who brought me over to the place, is trying to lead me to the customized-car exhibit—"Tom, I want you to see this car that Bill Cushenberry built, The Silhouette"—which is to say, here are two hundred kids ricocheting over a platform at high noon, and a speedy little boat barreling around and around and around in a round swimming pool, and I seem to be the only person who is distracted. The customized-car exhibit turns out to be the Ford Custom Car Caravan, which Ford is sending all over the country. At first, with the noise and peripheral motion and the inchoate leching you are liable to be doing, what with bouffant nymphets rocketing all over the place, these customized cars do not strike you as anything very special. Obviously they *are* very special, but the first thing you think of is the usual—you know, that the kids who own these cars are probably skinny little hoods who wear T shirts and carry their cigarette packs by winding them around in the T shirt up near the shoulder.

But after a while, I was glad I had seen the cars in this natural setting, which was, after all, a kind of Plato's Republic for teen-agers. Because if you watched anything at this fair very long, you kept noticing the same thing. These kids are absolutely maniacal about form. They are practically religious about it. For example, the dancers: none of them ever smiled. They stared at each other's legs and feet, concentrating. The dances had no grace about them at all, they were more in the nature of a hoedown, but everybody was concentrating to do them exactly *right*. And the bouffant kids all had form, wild form, but form with rigid standards, one gathers. Even the boys. Their dress was prosaic—Levis, Slim Jims, sport shirts, T shirts, polo shirts—but the form was consistent: a stove-pipe silhouette. And they all had the same hairstyle: some wore it long, some short, but none of them had a part; all that hair was brushed back straight from the hairline. I went by one of the guitar booths, and there was a little kid in there, about thirteen, playing the hell out of an electric guitar. The kid was named Cranston something or other. He looked like he ought to be named Kermet or Herschel; all his genes were kind of horribly Okie. Cranston was playing away and a big crowd was watching. But Cranston was slouched back with his spine bent like a sapling up against a table, looking gloriously bored. At thirteen, this kid was being fanatically cool. They all were.

They were all wonderful slaves to form. They have created their own style of life, and they are much more authoritarian about enforcing it than are adults. Not only that, but today these kids—especially in California—have *money*, which, needless to say, is why all these shoe merchants and guitar sellers and the Ford Motor Company were at a Teen Fair in the first place. I don't mind observing that it is this same combination—money plus slavish devotion to form—that accounts for Versailles or St. Mark's Square. Naturally, most of the artifacts that these kids' money-plus-form produce are of a pretty ghastly order. But so was most of the paraphernalia that developed in England during the Regency. I mean, most of it was on the order of starched cravats. A man could walk into Beau Brummel's house at 11 A.M., and here would come the butler with a tray of wilted linen. "These were some of our failures," he confides. But then Brummel comes downstairs wearing one perfect starched cravat. Like one perfect iris, the flower of Mayfair civilization. But the Regency period did see some tremendous formal architecture. And the kids' formal society has also brought at least one substantial thing to a formal development of a high order—the customized cars. I don't have to dwell on the point that cars mean more to these kids than architecture did in Europe's great formal century, say, 1750 to 1850. They are freedom, style, sex, power, motion, color—everything is right there.

Things have been going on in the development of the kids' formal attitude toward cars since 1945, things of great sophistication that adults have not been even remotely aware of, mainly because the kids are so inarticulate about it, especially the ones most hipped on the subject. They are not from the levels of society that produce children who write sensitive analytical prose at age seventeen, or if they do, they soon fall into the hands of English instructors who put them onto Hemingway or a lot of goddamn-and-hungry-breast writers. If they ever write about a highway again, it's a rain-slicked highway and the sound of the automobiles passing over it is like the sound of tearing silk, not that one household in ten thousand has heard the sound of tearing silk since 1945.

Anyway, we are back at the Teen Fair and I am talking to Tex Smith and to Don Beebe, a portly young guy with a white sport shirt and Cuban sunglasses. As they tell me about the Ford Custom Car Caravan, I can see that Ford has begun to comprehend this teen-age style of life and its potential. The way Ford appears to figure it is this: Thousands of kids are getting hold of cars and either hopping them up for speed or customizing them to some extent, usually a little of both. Before they get married they pour *all* their money into this. If Ford can get them hooked on Fords now, after the kids are married they'll buy new Fords. Even the kids who aren't full-time car nuts themselves will be influenced by which car is considered "boss." They use that word a lot, "boss." The kids used to consider Ford the hot car, but then, from 1955 to 1962, Chevrolet became the favorite. They had big engines and were easy to hop up, the styling was simple, and the kids could customize them easily. In 1959, and more so in 1960, Plymouth became a hot car, too. In 1961 and 1962, it was all Chevrolet and Plymouth. Now Ford is making a big push. A lot of the professional hot-rod and custom-car people, adults, will tell you that now Ford is the hot car, but you have to discount some of it, because Ford is laying money on everybody right and left, in one form or another. In the Custom Car Caravan, all the cars have been fashioned out of Ford bodies except the ones that are completely handmade, like the aforementioned Silhouette.

Anyway, Don Beebe is saying, over a loudspeaker, "I hate to break up that dancing, but let's have a little drag racing." He has a phonograph hooked up to the loudspeaker, and he puts on a record, produced by Riverside Records, of Drag-strip sounds, mainly dragsters blasting off and squealing from the starting line. Well, he doesn't really break up the dancing, but a hundred kids come over, when they hear the drag-strip sounds, to where Beebe has a slot racing stand. Slot racing is a model-train-type game in which two model drag racers, each about five inches long, powered by electricity, run down a model drag strip. Beebe takes a microphone and announces that Dick Dale, the singer, is here, and anybody who will race Dick at the slot-racing stand will get one of his records. Dick Dale is pretty popular among the kids out here because he sings a lot of "surfing" songs. The surfers—surfboard riders—are a cult much admired by all the kids. They have their own argot, with adjectives like "hang ten," meaning the best there is. They also go in for one particular brand of customizing: they take old wood-bodied station wagons, which they call "woodies," and fix them up for riding, sleeping and hauling surfing equipment for their weekends at the beach. The surfers also get a hell of a bang out of slot racing for some reason, so with Dick Dale slot racing at the Teen Fair, you have about three areas of the arcane teen world all rolled into one.

Dick Dale, rigged out in Byronic shirt and blue cashmere V-neck sweater and wraparound sunglasses, singer's mufti U.S.A., has one cord with a starter button, while a bouffant nymphet from Newport named Sherma, Sherma of the Capri pants, has the other one. Don Beebe flashes a starting light and Sherma lets out a cry, not a thrilled cry, just nerves, and a model 1963 Ford and a model dragster go running down the slot board, which is about chest high. The slot board is said to be one-twenty-fifth the actual size of a drag strip, which somehow reminds you of those incredible stamp-size pictures in the dictionary with the notation that this is one-hundredth the size of a real elephant. A hundred kids were packed in around the slot racers and did not find it incredible. That is, they were interested in who would win, Dick Dale or Sherma.

I'm sure they had no trouble magnifying the slot racers twenty-five times to the size of the full-blown, esoteric world of hot rods and custom cars.

I met George Barris, one of the celebrities of the custom-car world, at the Teen Fair. Barris is the biggest name in customizing. He is a good example of a kid who grew up completely absorbed in this teen-age world of cars, who pursued the pure flame and its forms with such devotion that he emerged an artist. It was like Tiepolo emerging from the studios of Venice, where the rounded Grecian haunches of the murals on the Palladian domes hung in the atmosphere like clouds. Except that Barris emerged from the auto-body shops of Los Angeles

Barris invited me out to his studio—only he would never think of calling it that, he calls it Kustom City—at 10811 Riverside Drive in North Hollywood. If there is a river within a thousand miles of Riverside Drive, I saw no sign of it. It's like every place else out there: endless scorched boulevards lined with one-story stores, shops, bowling alleys, skating rinks, tacos drive-ins, all of them shaped not like rectangles but like trapezoids, from the way the roofs slant up from the back and the plate-glass fronts slant out as if they're going to pitch forward on the sidewalk and throw up. The signs are great, too. They all stand free on poles outside. They have horribly slick dog-legged shapes that I call boomerang modern. As for Kustom City—Barris grew up at the time when it was considered sharp to change all the C's to K's. He also sells Kandy Lac to paint cars Kandy Kolors with, and I know that sibilant C in City must have bothered the hell out of him at some point. It's interesting, I think, that he still calls the place Kustom City, and still sells Kandy Kolors, because he is an intelligent person. What it means is, he is absolutely untouched by the big amoeba god of Anglo-European sophistication that gets you in the East. You know how it is in the East. One day you notice that the boss's button-down shirt has this sweet percale roll to it, while your own was obviously slapped together by some mass-production graph keepers who are saving an eighth of inch of cloth per shirt, twelve inches per bolt or the like, and this starts eating at you.

Barris, whose family is Greek, is a solid little guy, five feet seven, thirty-seven years old, and he looks just like Picasso. When he's working, which is most of the time, he wears a heavy white T-style shirt, faded off-white pants cut full with pleats in the manner of Picasso walking along in the wind on a bluff at Rapallo, and crepe-sole slipper-style shoes, also off-white. Picasso, I should add, means nothing to Barris, although he knows who he is. It's just that to Barris and the customizers there is no one great universe of form and design called Art. Yet that's the universe he's in. He's not building cars, he's creating forms.

Barris starts taking me through Kustom City, and the place looks like any other body shop at first, but pretty soon you realize you're in a *gallery*. This place is full of cars such as you have never seen before. Half of them will never touch the road. They're put on trucks and trailers and carted all over the country to be exhibited at hot-rod and custom-car shows. They'll run, if it comes to that—they're full of big, powerful, hopped-up chrome-plated motors, because all that speed and power, and all that lovely apparatus, has tremendous emotional meaning to everybody in customizing. But it's like one of these Picasso or Miro rugs. You don't walk on the damn things. You hang them on the wall. It's the same thing with Barris' cars. In effect, they're sculpture.

For example, there is an incredible object he built called the XPAK-400 air car. The customizers love all that X jazz. It runs on a cushion of air, which is beside the point, because it's a pure piece of curvilinear abstract sculpture. If Brancusi is any good, then this thing belongs on a pedestal, too. There is not a straight line in it, and only one true circle, and those countless planes, and tremendous baroque fins, and yet all in all it's a rigid little piece of solid geometrical harmony. As a matter of fact, Brancusi and Barris both developed out of a design concept that we can call Streamlined Modern or Thirties Curvilinear—via utterly different roads, of course—and Barris and most other custom artists are carrying this idea of the abstract curve, which is very tough to handle, on and on and on at a time when your conventional designers—from architects to the guys who lay out magazines—are all Mondrian. Even the young Detroit car stylists are all Mondrian. Only the aircraft designers have done anything more with the Streamline, and they have only because they're forced to by physics, and so on. I want to return to that subject in a minute, but first I want to tell you about another car Barris was showing me.

This was stuck back in a storeroom. Barris wasn't interested in it any more since he did it nine years ago. But this car—this old car, as far as Barris was concerned—was like a dream prefiguration of a very hot sports car, the Quantum, that Saab has come out with this year after a couple of years of consultation with all sorts of aerodynamic experts and advance-guard designers. They're beautiful cars—Saab's and Barris'. They're the same body, practically—with this lovely topology rolling down over the tunneled headlights, with the whole hood curving down very low to the ground in front. I told Barris about the similarity, but he just shrugged; he is quite used to some manufacturer coming up with one of his cars five or six years later.

Anyway, Barris and I were walking around the side of Kustom City, through the parking lot, when I saw an Avanti, the new Studebaker sports model, very expensive. This one had paper mock-ups added to the front and the rear, and so I asked Barris about it. That wasn't much, he said; starting with the paper mock-ups, it brought the hood out a foot with a chic slope to it. He was doing the same sort of thing in the back to eliminate that kind of loaf-of-bread look. It really makes the car. Barris doesn't regard this as a very major project. It may end up in something like a kit you can buy, similar to the old Continental kits, to rig up front and back.

If Barris and the customizers hadn't been buried in the alien and suspect underworld of California youth, I don't think they would seem at all unusual by now. But they've had access to almost nothing but the hot-rod press. They're like Easter Islanders. Suddenly you come upon the astonishing objects, and then you have to figure out how they got there and why they're there.

If you study the work of Barris or Cushenberry, the aforementioned Silhouette, or Ed Roth or Darryl Starbird, can you beat that name?, I think you come up with a fragment of art history. Somewhere back in the thirties, designers, automobile designers among them, came up with the idea of the streamline. It sounded "functional," and on an airplane it is functional, but on a car it's not, unless you're making a Bonneville speed run. Actually, it's baroque. The streamline is baroque abstract or baroque modern or whatever you want to call it. Well, about the time the streamline got going—in the thirties, you may recall, we had curved buildings, like the showpieces later, at the World's Fair—in came the Bauhaus movement, which was blown-up Mondrian, really. Before you knew it, everything was Mondrian—the Kleenex box: Mondrian; the format of the cover of *Life* Magazine: Mondrian; those bled-to-the-edge photograph layouts in *Paris-Match:* Mondrian. Even automobiles: Mondrian. They call Detroit automobiles streamlined, but they're not. If you don't believe it, look down from an airplane at all the cars parked on a shopping-center apron, and except that all the colors are pastel instead of primary, what have you got? A Mondrian painting. The Mondrian principle, those straight edges, is very tight, very Apollonian.

The streamline principle, which really has no function, which curves around and swoops and flows just for the thrill of it, is very free Dionysian. For reasons I don't have to labor over, the kids preferred the Dionysian. And since Detroit blew the thing, the Dionysian principle in cars was left to people in the teen-age netherworld, like George Barris.

Barris was living in Sacramento when he started customizing cars in 1940. As the plot develops, you have the old story of the creative child, the break from the mold of the parents, the garret struggle, the bohemian life, the first success, the accolade of the esoteric following, and finally the money starts pouring in. With this difference: We're out on old Easter Island, in the buried netherworld of teen-age Californians, and those objects, those cars, they have to do with the gods and the spirit and a lot of mystic stuff in the community.

Barris told me his folks were Greeks who owned a restaurant, and "they wanted me to be a restaurant man, like every other typical Greek, I guess," he said. But Barris, even at ten, was wild about cars, carving streamlined cars out of balsa wood. After a few years, he got a car of his own, a 1925 Buick, then a 1932 Ford. Barris established many of the formal conventions of customizing himself. Early in the game he had clients, other kids who paid him to customize their cars. In 1943 he moved to Los Angeles and landed in the middle of the tremendous teen-age culture that developed there during the war. Family life was dislocated, as the phrase goes, but the money was pouring in, and the kids began to work up their own style of life—as they've been doing ever since—and to establish those fanatic forms and conventions I was talking about earlier. Right at the heart of it, of course, was the automobile. Cars were hard to come by, what with the war, so the kids were raiding junkyards for parts, which led to custom-built cars, mostly roadsters by the very nature of it, and also to a lot of radical, hopped-up engines. All teen-age car nuts had elements of both in their work—customizing and hot-rodding, form and power—but tended to concentrate on one or the other. Barris—and Ed Roth later told me it was the same with him—naturally gravitated toward customizing. In high school, and later for a brief time at Sacramento College and the Los Angeles Art Center, he was taking what he described to me as mechanical drawing, shop, and free art.

I liked this term "free art." In Barris' world at the time, and now for that matter, there was no such thing as great big old fructuous Art. There was mechanical drawing and then there was free art, which did not mean that it was liberating in any way, but rather that it was footloose and free and not going anywhere in particular. The kind of art that appealed to Barris, and meant something to the people he hung around with, was the automobile.

Barris gets a wonderful reflective grin on his face when he starts talking about the old days—1944 to 1948. He was a hot-rodder when hot-rodders were hot-rodders, that's the kind of look he gets. They all do. The professional hot-rodders—such as the Petersen magazine syndicate (*Hot Rod Magazine* and many others) and the National Hot Rod Association—have gone to great lengths to obliterate the memory of the gamey hot-rod days, and they try to give everybody in the field transfusions of Halazone so that the public will look at the hot-rodders as nice boys with short-sleeved sport shirts just back from the laundry and a chemistry set, such an interesting hobby.

In point of fact, Barris told me, it was a lurid time. Everybody would meet in drive-ins, the most famous of them being the Piccadilly out near Sepulveda Boulevard. It was a hell of a show, all the weird-looking roadsters and custom cars, with very loud varoom-varoom motors. By this time Barris had a '36 Ford roadster with many exotic features.

"I had just come from Sacramento, and I wasn't supposed to

know anything. I was a tourist, but my car was wilder than anything around. I remember one night this kid comes up with a roadster with no door handles. It looked real sharp, but he had to kick the door from the inside to open it. You should have seen the look on his face when he saw mine—I had the same thing, only with electric buttons."

The real action, though, was the drag racing, which was quite, but quite, illegal.

"We'd all be at the Piccadilly or some place, and guys would start challenging each other. You know, a guy goes up to another guy's car and looks it up and down like it has gangrene or something, and he says: 'You wanna *go?*' Or, if it was a real grudge match for some reason, he'd say, 'You wanna go for pink slips?' The registrations on the cars were pink; in other words, the winner got the other guy's car.

"Well, as soon as a few guys had challenged each other, everybody would ride out onto this stretch of Sepulveda Boulevard or the old divided highway, in Compton, and the guys would start dragging, one car on one side of the center line, the other car on the other. Go a quarter of a mile. It was wild. Some nights there'd be a thousand kids lining the road to watch, boys and girls, all sitting on the sides of their cars with the lights shining across the highway."

But George, what happened if some ordinary motorist happened to be coming down the highway at this point?

"Oh, we'd block off the highway at each end, and if some guy wanted to get through anyway, we'd tell him, 'Well, Mister, there are going to be two cars coming down both sides of the road pretty fast in a minute, and you can go through if you want to, but you'll just have to take your best shot.'

"They always turned around, of course, and after a while the cops would come. Then you *really* saw something. Everybody jumped in their cars and took off, in every direction. Some guys would head right across a field. Of course, all our cars were so hopped up, the cops could never catch anybody.

"Then one night we got raided at the Piccadilly. It was one Friday night. The cops came in and just started loading everybody in the wagons. I was sitting in a car with a cop who was off duty—he was a hot-rodder himself—or they would have picked me up, too. Saturday night everybody came back to the Piccadilly to talk about what happened the night before, and the cops came back again and picked up three hundred fifty that night. That pretty well ended the Piccadilly."

From the very moment he was on his own in Los Angeles, when he was about eighteen, Barris never did anything but customize cars. He never took any other kind of job. At first he worked in a body shop that took him on because so many kids were coming by wanting this and that done to their cars, and the boss really didn't know how to do it, because it was all esoteric teen-age stuff. Barris was making next to nothing at first, but he never remembers feeling hard up, nor does any kid out there today I talked to. They have a magic economy or something. Anyway, in 1945 Barris opened his own shop on Compton Avenue, in Los Angeles, doing nothing but customizing. There was that much demand for it. It was no sweat, he said; pretty soon he was making better than $100 a week.

Most of the work he was doing then was modifying Detroit cars—chopping and channeling. Chopping is lowering the top of the car, bringing it nearer to the hood line. Channeling is lowering the body itself down between the wheels. Also, they'd usually strip off all the chrome and the door handles and cover up the wheel openings in the back. At that time, the look the kids liked was to have the body lowered in the back and slightly jacked up in the front, although today it's just the opposite. The front windshield in those days was divided by a post, and so chopping the top gave the car a very sinister appearance. The front windshield always looked like a couple of narrow, slitty little eyes. And I think this, more than any-thing else, diverted everybody from what Barris and the others were really doing. Hot-rodders had a terrible reputation at that time, and no line was ever drawn between hot-rodders and custom-car owners, because, in truth, they were speed ma-niacs, too.

This was Barris' chopped-and-channeled Mercury period. Mercuries were his favorite. All the kids knew the Barris styl-ing and he was getting a lot of business. What he was really doing, in a formal sense, was trying to achieve the kind of streamlining that Detroit, for all intents and purposes, had abandoned. When modified, some of the old Mercuries were more streamlined than any standard model that Detroit has put out to this day. Many of the coupes he modified had a very sleek slope to the back window that has been picked up just this year in the "fastback" look of the Rivieras, Sting Rays, and a few other cars.

At this point Barris and the other customizers didn't really have enough capital to do many completely original cars, but they were getting more and more radical in modifying Detroit cars. They were doing things Detroit didn't do until years later—tailfins, bubbletops, twin headlights, concealed head-lights, "Frenched" headlights, the low-slung body itself. They lifted some twenty designs from him alone. One, for example, is the way cars now have the exhaust pipes exit through the rear bumper or fender. Another is the bullet-shaped, or breast-shaped if you'd rather, front bumpers on the Cadillac.

Barris says "lifted," because some are exact down to the most minute details. Three years ago when he was in Detroit, Barris met a lot of car designers and, "I was amazed," he told me. "They could tell me about cars I built in 1945. They knew all about the four-door '48 Studebaker I restyled. I chopped the top and dropped the hood and it ended up a pretty good-looking car. And the bubbletop I built in 1954—they knew all about it. And all this time we thought they frowned on us."

Even today—dealing with movie stars and auto manufacturers and all sorts of people on the outside—I think Barris, and certainly the others, still feel psychologically a part of the alien teen-age netherworld in which they grew up. All that while they were carrying the torch for the Dionysian Streamline. They were America's modern baroque designers—and, oddly enough, "serious" designers, Anglo-European-steeped designers, are just coming around to it. Take Saarinen, especially in something like his T.W.A. terminal at Kennedy. The man in his last years came around to baroque modern.

It's interesting that the customizers, like sports-car fans, have always wanted cars minus most of the chrome—but for different ideals. The sports-car owner thinks chrome trim interferes with the "classic" look of his car. In other words, he wants to simplify the thing. The customizer thinks chrome interferes with something else—the luxurious baroque Streamline. The sports-car people snigger at tailfins. The customizers love them and, looked at from a baroque standard of beauty, they are really not so trashy at all. They are an inspiration, if you will, a wonderful fantasy extension of the curved line, and since the car in America is half fantasy anyway, a kind of baroque extention of the ego, you can build up a good argument for them.

Getting back to Easter Island, here were Barris and the others with their blowtorches and hard-rubber mallets, creating their baroque sculpture, cut off from the rest of the world and publicized almost solely via the teen-age grapevine. Barris was making a fairly good living, but others were starving at this thing. The pattern was always the same: a guy would open a body shop and take on enough hack collision work to pay the rent so that he could slam the door shut at 2 P.M. and get in there and do his custom jobs, and pretty soon the guy got so he couldn't even face *any* collision work. Dealing with all those crusty old arteriosclerotic bastards takes up all your *time*, man, and so they're trying to make a living doing nothing but custom work, and they are starving.

The situation is a lot like that today, except that customizing is beginning to be rationalized, in the sense Max Weber used that word. This rationalization, or efficient exploitation, began in the late forties when an $80-a-week movie writer named Robert Petersen noticed all the kids pouring money into cars in a little world they had created for themselves, and he decided to exploit it by starting *Hot Rod Magazine*, which clicked right away and led to a whole chain of hot-rod and custom-car magazines. Petersen, by the way, now has a pot of money and drives Maseratis and other high-status-level sports cars of the Apollonian sort, not the Dionysian custom kind. Which is kind of a shame, because he has the money to commission something really incredible.

Up to that time the only custom-car show in the country was a wild event Barris used to put on bereft of any sort of midwifery by forty-two-year-old promoters with Windsor-knot ties who usually run low-cost productions. This car show was utterly within the teen-age netherworld, with no advertising or coverage of any sort. It took place each spring—during the high-school Easter vacations—when all the kids, as they still do, would converge on the beach at Balboa for their beer-drinking-*Fasching* rites, or whatever the Germans call it. Barris would rent the parking lot of a service station on a corner for a week, and kids from all over California would come with their customized cars. First there would be a parade; the cars, about a hundred fifty of them, would drive all through the streets of Balboa, and the kids would line the sidewalks to watch them; then they'd drive back to the lot and park and be on exhibit for the week.

Barris still goes off to Balboa and places like that. He likes that scene. Last year at Pacific Ocean Park he noticed all these bouffant babies and got the idea of spraying all those great puffed-up dandelion heads with fluorescent water colors, the same Kandy Kolors he uses on the cars. Barris took out an air gun, the girls all lined up and gave him fifty cents per, and he sprayed them with these weird, brilliant color combinations all afternoon until he ran out of colors. Each girl would go skipping and screaming away out onto the sidewalks and the beaches. Barris told me, "It was great that night to take one of the rides, like the Bubble Ride, and look down and see all those fluorescent colors. The kids were bopping [dancing] and running around."

The Bubble is a ride that swings out over the ocean. It is supposed to be like a satellite in orbit.

"But the fellows sky-diving got the best look as they came down by parachute."

In 1948 Petersen put on the first custom-car show in the Los Angeles armory, and this brought customizing out into the open a little. A wild-looking Buick Barris had remodeled was one of the hits of the show, and he was on his way, too.

At some point in the fifties a lot of Hollywood people discovered Barris and the customizers. It was somewhat the way the literary set had discovered the puppeteer, Tony Sarg, during the thirties and deified him in a very arty, in-groupy way, only I think in the case of Hollywood and Barris there was something a lot more in-the-grain about it. The people who end up in Hollywood are mostly Dionysian sorts and they feel alien and resentful when confronted with the Anglo-European ethos. They're a little slow to note the difference between topsides and sneakers, but they appreciate Cuban sunglasses.

In his showroom at Kustom City, down past the XPAK-400 air car, Barris has a corner practically papered with photographs of cars he has customized or handmade for Hollywood people: Harry Karl, Jayne Mansfield, Elvis Presley, Liberace, and even celebrities from the outside like Barry Goldwater (a Jaguar with a lot of airplane-style dials on the dashboard) and quite a few others. In fact, he built most of the wild cars that show-business people come up with for publicity purposes. He did the "diamond-dust" paint job on the Bobby Darin Dream Car, which was designed and built by Andy DiDia of Detroit. That car is an example, par excellence, of baroque streamlining, by the way. It was badly panned when pictures of it were first published, mainly because it looked like Darin was again forcing his ego on the world. But as baroque modern sculpture—again, given the fantasy quotient in cars to begin with—it is pretty good stuff.

As the hot-rod and custom-car-show idea began catching on, and there are really quite a few big ones now, including one at the Coliseum up at Columbus Circle last year, it became like the culture boom in the other arts. The big names, particularly Barris and Roth but also Starbird, began to make a lot of money in the same thing Picasso has made a lot of money in: reproductions. Barris' creations are reproduced by AMT Models as model cars. Roth's are reproduced by Revel. The way people have taken to these models makes it clearer still that what we have here is no longer a car but a design object, an *objet*, as they say.

Of course, it's not an unencumbered art form like oil painting or most conventional modern sculpture. It carries a lot of mental baggage with it, plain old mechanical craftsmanship, the connotations of speed and power and the aforementioned mystique that the teen-age netherworld brings to cars. What you have is something more like sculpture in the era of Benvenuto Cellini, when sculpture was always more tied up with religion and architecture. In a lot of other ways it's like the Renaissance, too. Young customizers have come to Barris' shop, for example, like apprentices coming to the feet of the master. Barris said there were eleven young guys in Los Angeles right now who had worked for him and then gone out on their own, and he doesn't seem to begrudge them that.

"But they take on too much work," he told me. "They want a name, fast, and they take on a lot of work, which they do for practically nothing, just to get a name. They're usually undercapitalized to begin with, and they take on too much work, and then they can't deliver and they go bankrupt."

There's another side to this, too. You have the kid from the small town in the Midwest who's like the kid from Keokuk who wants to go to New York and live in the Village and be an artist and the like—he means, you know, things around home are but *hopelessly*, totally square; home and all that goes with it. Only the kid from the Midwest who wants to be a custom-car artist goes to Los Angeles to do it. He does pretty much the same thing. He lives a kind of suburban bohemian life and takes odd jobs and spends the rest of his time at the feet of somebody like Barris, working on cars.

I ran into a kid like that at Barris'. We were going through his place, back into his interiors—car interiors—department, and we came upon Ronny Camp. Ronny is twenty-two, but he looks about eighteen because he has teen-age posture. Ronny is, in fact, a bright and sensitive kid with an artistic eye, but at first glance he seems always to have his feet propped up on a table or something so you can't walk past, and you have to kind of bat them down, and he then screws up his mouth and withdraws his eyeballs to the optic chiasma and glares at you with his red sulk. That was the misleading first impression.

Ronny was crazy over automobiles and nobody in his home-town, Lafayette, Indiana, knew anything about customizing. So one day Ronny packs up and tells the folks, This is it, I'm striking out for hip territory, Los Angeles, where a customizing artist is an artist. He had no idea where he was going, you understand, all he knew was that he was going to Barris' shop and make it from there. So off he goes in his 1960 Chevrolet.

Ronny got a job at a service station and poured every spare cent into getting the car customized at Barris'. His car was right there while we were talking, a fact I was very aware of, because he never looked at me. He never took his eyes off that car. It's what is called semi-custom. Nothing has been done to it to give it a really sculptural quality, but a lot of streamlining details have been added. The main thing you notice is the color—tangerine flake. This paint—one of Barris' Kandy Kolor concoctions—makes the car look like it has been encrusted with chips of some kind of semi-precious ossified tangerine, all coated with a half-inch of clear lacquer. There used to be very scholarly and abstruse studies of color and color symbolism around the turn of the century, and theorists concluded that preferences for certain colors were closely associated with re-belliousness, and these are the very same colors many of the kids go for—purple, carnal yellow, various violets and lavenders and fuchsias and many other of these Kandy Kolors.

After he got his car fixed up, Ronny made a triumphal progress back home. He won the trophy in his class at the national hot-rod and custom-car show in Indianapolis, and he came tooling into Lafayette, Indiana, and down the main street in his tangerine-flake 1960 Chevrolet. It was like Ezra Pound going back to Hamilton, New York, with his Bollingen plaque and saying, Here I am, Hamilton, New York. The way Ronny and Barris tell it, the homecoming was a big success— all the kids thought Ronny was all right, after all, and he made a big hit at home. I can't believe the part about home. I mean, I can't really believe Ronny made a hit with a tangerine-flake Chevrolet. But I like to conjecture about his parents. I don't know anything about them, really. All I know is, *I* would have had a hell of a lump in my throat if I had seen Ronny coming up to the front door in his tangerine-flake car, bursting so flush and vertical with triumph that no one would ever think of him as a child of the red sulk—Ronny, all the way back from California with his grail.

Along about 1957, Barris started hearing from the Detroit auto manufacturers.

"One day," he said, "I was working in the shop—we were over in Lynwood then—and Chuck Jordan from Cadillac walked in. He just walked in and said he was from Cadillac. I thought he meant the local agency. We had done this Cadillac for Liberace, the interior had his songs, all the notes, done in black and white Moroccan leather, and I thought he wanted to see something about that. But he said he was from the Cadillac styling center in Detroit and they were interested in our colors. Chuck—he's up there pretty good at Cadillac now, I think—said he had read some articles about our colors, so I mixed up some samples for him. I had developed a translucent paint, using six different ingredients, and it had a lot of brilliance and depth. That was what interested them. In this paint you look through a clear surface into the color, which is very brilliant. Anyway, this was the first time we had any idea they even knew who we were."

Since then Barris has made a lot of trips to Detroit. The auto companies, mainly GM and Ford, pump him for ideas about what the kids are going for. He tells them what's wrong with their cars, mainly that they aren't streamlined and sexy enough.

"But, as they told me, they have to design a car they can sell to the farmer in Kansas as well as the hot dog in Hollywood."

For that reason—the inevitable compromise—the customizers do not dream of working as stylists for the Detroit companies, although they deal with them more and more. It would be like René Magritte or somebody going on the payroll of Continental Can to do great ideas of Western man. This is an old story in art, of course, genius vs. the organization. But the customizers don't think of corporate bureaucracy quite the way your conventional artist does, whether he be William Gropper or Larry Rivers, namely, as a lot of small-minded Babbitts, venal enemies of culture, etc. They just think of the big companies as part of that vast mass of *adult* America, sclerotic from years of just being too old, whose rules and ideas weigh down upon Youth like a vast, bloated sac. Both Barris and Roth have met Detroit's Young Stylists, and seem to look upon them as monks from another country. The Young Stylists are designers Detroit recruits from the art schools and sets up in a room with clay and styluses and tells to go to it—start carving models, dream cars, new ideas. Roth especially cannot conceive of anyone having any valid concepts about cars who hasn't come out of the teen-age netherworld. And maybe he's right. While the Young Stylists sit in a north-lit studio smoothing out little Mondrian solids, Barris and Roth carry on in the Dionysian loop-the-loop of streamlined baroque modern.

I've mentioned Ed Roth several times in the course of this without really telling you about him. And I want to, because he, more than any other of the customizers, has kept alive the spirit of alienation and rebellion that is so important to the teen-age ethos that customizing grew up in. He's also the most colorful, and the most intellectual, and the most capricious. Also the most cynical. He's the Salvador Dali of the movement—a surrealist in his designs, a showman by temperament, a prankster. Roth is really too bright to stay within the ethos, but he stays in it with a spirit of luxurious obstinacy. Any style of life is going to produce its celebrities if it sticks to its rigid standards, but in the East a talented guy would most likely be drawn into the Establishment in one way or another. That's not so inevitable in California.

I had been told that Roth was a surly guy who never bathed and was hard to get along with, but from the moment I first talked to him on the telephone he was an easy guy and very articulate. His studio—and he calls it a studio, by the way—is out in Maywood, on the other side of the city from North Hollywood, in what looked to me like a much older and more run-down section. When I walked up, Roth was out on the apron of his place doing complicated drawings and lettering on somebody's ice-cream truck with an airbrush. I knew right away it was Roth from pictures I had seen of him; he has a beatnik-style beard. "Ed Roth?" I said. He said yeah and we started talking and so forth. A little while later we were sitting in a diner having a couple of sandwiches and Roth, who was wearing a short-sleeved T shirt, pointed to this huge tattoo on his left arm that says "Roth" in the lettering style with big serifs that he uses as his signature. "I had that done a couple of years ago because guys keep coming up to me saying, 'Are you Ed Roth?'"

Roth is a big, powerful guy, about six feet four, two hundred seventy pounds, thirty-one years old. He has a constant sort of court attendant named Dirty Doug, a skinny little guy who blew in from out of nowhere, sort of like Ronny Camp over at Barris'. Dirty Doug has a job sweeping up in a steel mill, but what he obviously lives for is the work he does around Roth's. Roth seems to have a lot of sympathy for the Ronny Camp-Dirty Doug syndrome and keeps him around as a permanent fixture. At Roth's behest, apparently, Dirty Doug has dropped his last name, Kinney, altogether, and refers to himself as Dirty Doug—not Doug. The relationship between Roth and Dirty Doug—which is sort of Quixote and Sancho Panza, Holmes and Watson, Lone Ranger and Tonto, Raffles and Bunny—is part of the folklore of the hot-rod and custom-car kids. It even crops up in the hot-rod comic books, which are an interesting phenomenon in themselves. Dirty Doug, in this folklore, is every rejected outcast little kid in the alien nether-world, and Roth is the understanding, if rather overly pranksterish, protective giant or Robin Hood—you know, a good-bad giant, not part of the Establishment.

Dirty Doug drove up in one of his two Cadillacs one Saturday afternoon while I was at Roth's, and he had just gone through another experience of rejection. The police had hounded him out of Newport. He has two Cadillacs, he said, because one is always in the shop. Dirty Doug's cars, like most customizers', are always in the process of becoming. The streaks of "primer" paint on the Cadillac he was driving at the time had led to his rejection in Newport. He had driven to Newport for the weekend. "All the cops have to do is see paint like that and already you're 'one of those hot-rodders,'" he said. "They practically followed me down the street and gave me a ticket every twenty-five feet. I was going to stay the whole weekend, but I came on back."

At custom-car shows, kids are always asking Roth, "Where's Dirty Doug?", and if Dirty Doug couldn't make it for some reason, Roth will recruit any kid around who knows the pitch and install him as Dirty Doug, just to keep the fans happy.

Thus Roth protects the image of Dirty Doug even when the guy's not around, and I think it becomes a very important piece of mythology. The thing is, Roth is not buying the act of the National Hot Rod Association, which for its own reasons, not necessarily the kid's reasons, is trying to assimilate the hot-rod ethos into conventional America. It wants to make all the kids look like candidates for the Peace Corps or something.

The heart of the contretemps between the NHRA Establishment and Roth can be illustrated in their slightly different approach to drag racing on the streets. The Establishment tries to eliminate the practice altogether and restricts drag racing to certified drag strips and, furthermore, lets the people know about that. They encourage the hot-rod clubs to help out little old ladies whose cars are stuck in the snow and then hand them a card reading something like, "You have just been assisted by a member of the Blue Bolt Hot Rod Club, an organization of car enthusiasts dedicated to promoting safety on our highways."

Roth's motto is: "Hell, if a guy wants to go, let him *go*."

Roth's designs are utterly baroque. His air car—the Rotar—is not nearly as good a piece of design as Barris', but his beatnik Bandit is one of the great *objets* of customizing. It's a very Rabelaisian *tour de force*—a twenty-first century version of a '32 Ford hot-rod roadster. And Roth's new car, the Mysterion, which he was working on when I was out there, is another *tour de force*, this time in the hottest new concept in customizing, asymmetrical design. Asymmetrical design, I gather, has grown out of the fact that the driver sits on one side of the car, not in the middle, thereby giving a car an eccentric motif to begin with. In Roth's Mysterion—a bubbletop coupe powered by two 406 -horsepower Thunderbird motors—a thick metal arm sweeps up to the left from the front bumper level, as from the six to the three on a clock, and at the top of it is an elliptical shape housing a bank of three headlights. No headlights on the right side at all; just a small clearance light to orient the oncoming driver. This big arm, by the way, comes up in a spherical geometrical arc, not a flat plane. Balancing this, as far as the design goes, is an arm that comes up over the back of the bubbletop on the right side, like from the nine to the twelve on a clock, also in a spherical arc, if you can picture all this. Anyway, this car takes the streamline and the abstract curve and baroque curvilinear one step further, and I wouldn't be surprised to see it inspiring Detroit designs in the years to come.

Roth is a brilliant designer, but as I was saying, his conduct and his attitude dilutes the Halazone with which the Establishment is trying to transfuse the whole field. For one thing, Roth, a rather thorough-going bohemian, kept turning up at the car shows in a T shirt. That was what he wore at the big

National Show at the New York Coliseum, for example. Roth also insists on sleeping in a car or station wagon while on the road, even though he is making a lot of money now and could travel first class. Things came to a head early this year when Roth was out in Terre Haute, Indiana, for a show. At night Roth would just drive his car out in a cornfield, lie back on the front seat, stick his feet out the window and go to sleep. One morning some kid came by and saw him and took a picture while Roth was still sleeping and sent it to the model company Roth has a contract with, Revel, with a note saying, "Dear Sirs: Here is a picture of the man you say on your boxes is the King of the Customizers." The way Roth tells it, it must have been an extraordinarily good camera, because he says, with considerable pride, "There were a bunch of flies flying around my feet, and this picture showed all of them."

Revel asked Roth if he wouldn't sort of spruce up a little bit for the image and all that, and so Roth entered into a kind of reverse rebellion. He bought a full set of tails, silk hat, boiled shirt, cuff links, studs, the whole apparatus, for $215, also a monocle, and now he comes to all the shows like that. "I bow and kiss all the girls' hands," he told me. "The guys get pretty teed off about that, but what can they do? I'm being a perfect gentleman."

To keep things going at the shows, where he gets $1000 to $2000 per appearance—he's that much of a drawing card—Roth creates and builds one new car a year. This is the Dali pattern, too. Dali usually turns out one huge and (if that's possible any more) shocking painting each year or so and ships it on over to New York, where they install it in Carstairs or hire a hall if the thing is too big, and Dali books in at the St. Regis and appears on television wearing a rhinoceros horn on his forehead. The new car each year also keeps Roth's model-car deal going. But most of Roth's income right now is the heavy business he does in Weirdo and Monster shirts. Roth is very handy with the airbrush—has a very sure hand—and one day at a car show he got the idea of drawing a grotesque cartoon on some guy's sweat shirt with the airbrush, and that started the Weirdo shirts. The typical Weirdo shirt is in a vein of draftsmanship you might call Mad Magazine Bosch, very slickly done for something so grotesque, and will show a guy who looks like Frankenstein, the big square steam-shovel jaw and all, only he has a wacky leer on his face, at the wheel of a hot-rod roadster, and usually he has a round object up in the air in his right hand that looks like it is attached to the dashboard by a cord. This, it turns out, is the gearshift. It doesn't look like a gearshift to me, but every kid knows immediately what it is.

"Kids *love* dragging a car," Roth told me. "I mean they really love it. And what they love the most is when they shift from low to second. They get so they can practically *feel* the r.p.m.'s. They can shift without hardly hitting the clutch at all."

These shirts always have a big caption, and usually something rebellious or at least alienated, something like "Mother Is Wrong" or "Born to Lose."

"A teen-ager always has resentment to adult authority," Roth told me. "These shirts are like a tattoo, only it's a tattoo they can take off if they want to."

I gather Roth doesn't look back on his own childhood with any great relish. Apparently his father was pretty strict and never took any abiding interest in Roth's creative flights, which were mostly in the direction of cars, like Barris'.

"You've got to be real careful when you raise a kid," Roth told me several times. "You've got to spend time with him. If he's working on something, building something, you've got to work with him." Roth's early career was almost exactly like Barris', the hot rods, the drive-ins, the drag racing, the college (East Los Angeles Junior College and UCLA), taking mechanical drawing, the chopped and channeled '32 Ford (a big favorite with all the hot-rodders), purple paint, finally the first custom shop, one stall in a ten-stall body shop.

"They threw me out of there," Roth said, "because I painted a can of Lucky Lager beer on the wall with an airbrush. I mean, it was a perfect can of Lucky Lager beer, all the details, the highlights, the seals, the small print, the whole thing. Somehow this can of Lucky Lager beer really bugged the guy who owned the place. Here was this can of Lucky Lager beer on *his* wall."

The Establishment can't take this side of Roth, just as no Establishment could accommodate Dadaists for very long. Beatniks more easily than Dadaists. The trick has always been to absorb them somehow. So far Roth has resisted absorption.

"We were the real gangsters of the hot-rod field," Roth said. "They keep telling us we have a rotten attitude. We have a different attitude, but that doesn't make us rotten."

Several times, though, Roth would chuckle over something, usually some particularly good gesture he had made, like the Lucky Lager, and say, "I am a real rotten guy."

Roth pointed out, with some insight, I think, that the kids have a revealing vocabulary. They use the words "rotten," "bad" and "tough" in a very fey, ironic way. Often a particularly baroque and sleek custom car will be called a "big, bad Merc" (for Mercury) or something like that. In this case "bad" means "good," but it also retains some of the original meaning of "bad." The kids know that to adults, like their own parents, this car is going to look sinister and somehow like an assault on their style of life. Which it is. It's rebellion, which the parents don't go for—"bad," which the kids *do* go for, "bad" meaning "good."

Roth said that Detroit is beginning to understand that there are just a hell of a lot of these bad kids in the United States and that they are growing up. "And they want a better car. They don't want an old man's car."

Roth has had pretty much the same experience as Barris with the motor companies. He has been taken to Detroit and feted and offered a job as a designer and a consultant. But he never took it seriously.

"I met a lot of the young designers," said Roth. "They were nice guys and they know a lot about design, but none of them has actually done a car. They're just up there working away on those clay models."

I think this was more than the craftsman's scorn of the designer who never actually does the work, like some of the conventional sculptors today who have never chiseled a piece of stone or cast anything. I think it was more that the young Detroit stylists came to the automobile strictly from art school and the abstract world of design—rather than via the teen-age mystique of the automobile and the teen-age ethos of rebellion. This status-group feeling is very important to Roth, and to Barris, for that matter, because it was only because of the existence of this status group—and this style of life—that custom-car sculpture developed at all.

With the Custom Car Caravan on the road—it has already reached Freedomland—the manufacturers may be well on the way to routinizing the charisma, as Max Weber used to say, which is to say, bringing the whole field into a nice, safe, vinyl-glamorous marketable ball of polyethylene. It's probably already happening. The customizers will end up like those poor bastards in Haiti, the artists, who got too much, too soon, from Selden Rodman and the other folk-doters on the subject of primitive genius, so they're all down there at this moment carving African masks out of mahogany—what I mean is, they never *had* an African mask in Haiti before Selden Rodman got there.

I think Roth has a premonition that something like that is

liable to happen, although it will happen to him last, if at all. I couldn't help but get a kick out of what Roth told me about his new house. We had been talking about how much money he was making, and he told me how his taxable income was only about $6200 in 1959, but might hit $15,000 this year, maybe more, and he mentioned he was building a new house for his wife and five kids down at Newport, near the beach. I immediately asked him for details, hoping to hear about an utterly baroque piece of streamlined architecture.

"No, this is going to be my wife's house, the way she wants it, nothing way out; I mean, she has to do the home scene." He has also given her a huge white Cadillac, by the way, unadorned except for his signature—"Roth"—with those big serifs, on the side. I saw the thing, it's huge, and in the back seat were his children, very sweet-looking kids, all drawing away on drawing pads.

But I think Roth was a little embarrassed that he had disappointed me on the house, because he told me his idea of the perfect house—which turned out to be a kind of ironic parable:

"This house would have this big, round living room with a dome over it, you know? Right in the middle of the living room would be a huge television set on a swivel so you could turn it and see it from wherever you are in the room. And you have this huge easy chair for yourself, you know the kind that you can lean back to about ninety-three different positions and it vibrates and massages your back and all that, and this chair is on tracks, like a railroad yard.

"You can take one track into the kitchen, which just shoots off one side of the living room, and you can ride backward if you want to and watch the television all the time, and of course in the meantime you've pressed a lot of buttons so your TV dinner is cooking in the kitchen and all you have to do is go and take it out of the oven.

"Then you can roll right back into the living room, and if somebody rings the doorbell you don't move at all. You just press a button on this big automatic console you have by your chair and the front door opens, and you just yell for the guy to come in, and you can keep watching television.

"At night, if you want to go to bed, you take another track into the bedroom, which shoots off on another side, and you just kind of roll out of the chair into the sack. On the ceiling above your bed you have another TV set, so you can watch all night."

Roth is given, apparently, to spinning out long Jean Shepherd stories like this with a very straight face, and he told me all of this very seriously. I guess I didn't look like I was taking it very seriously, because he said, "I have a TV set over the bed in my house right now—you can ask my wife."

I met his wife, but I didn't ask her. The funny thing is, I did find myself taking the story seriously. To me it was a sort of parable of the Bad Guys, and the Custom Sculpture. The Bad Guys built themselves a little world and got onto something good and then the Establishment, all sorts of Establishments, began closing in, with a lot of cajolery, thievery and hypnosis, and in the end, thrown into a vinyl Petri dish, the only way left to tell the whole bunch of them where to head in was to draw them a huge asinine picture of themselves, which they were sure to like. After all, Roth's dream house is nothing more than his set of boiled shirt and tails expanded into a whole universe. And he is not really very hopeful about that either.

2

HEROES
AND
CELEBRITIES

7

The Marvelous Mouth

One thing that stuck in my mind, for some reason, was the way that Cassius Clay and his brother, Rudy, and their high-school pal, Tuddie King, and Frankie Tucker, the singer who was opening in Brooklyn, and Cassius' pride of "foxes," Sophia Burton, Dottie, Frenchie, Barbara and the others, and Richie Pittman and "Lou" Little, the football player, and everybody else up there in Cassius' suite on the forty-second floor of the Americana Hotel kept telling time by looking out the panorama window and down at the clock on top of the Paramount Building on Times Square. Everybody had a watch. Cassius, for example, is practically a watch fancier. But, every time, somebody would look out the panorama window, across the City Lights scene you get from up high in the Americana and down to the lit-up clock on that whacky Twenties-modern poly-hedron on top of the Paramount Building.

One minute Cassius would be out in the middle of the floor reenacting his "High Noon" encounter with Sonny Liston in a Las Vegas casino. He has a whole act about it, beginning with a pantomime of him shoving open the swinging doors and standing there bowlegged, like a beer delivery man. Then he plays the part of the crowd falling back and whispering, "It's Cassius Clay, Cassius Clay, Cassius Clay, Cassius Clay." Then he plays the part of an effete Las Vegas hipster at the bar with his back turned, suddenly freezing in mid-drink, as the hush falls over the joint, and sliding his eyes around to see the duel. Then he plays the part of Cassius Clay stalking across the floor with his finger pointed at Sonny Liston and saying, "You big ugly bear," "You big ugly bear," about eighteen times, "I ain't gonna fight you on no September thirtieth, I'm gonna fight you right now. Right here. You too ugly to run loose, you big ugly bear. You so ugly, when you cry, the tears run down the back of your head. You so ugly, you have to sneak up on the mirror so it won't run off the wall," and so on, up to the point where Liston says, "Come over here and sit on my knee, little boy, and I'll give you your orange juice," and where Cassius pulls back his right and three guys hold him back and keep him from throwing it at Liston, "And I'm hollering, 'Lemme go,' and I'm telling them out the side of my mouth, 'You better *not* lemme go.'" All this time Frankie Tucker, the singer, is con-torted across one of the Americana's neo-Louis XIV chairs, breaking up and exclaiming, "That's my man!"

The next minute Cassius is fooling around with Rudy's phonograph-and-speaker set and having some fun with the foxes. The foxes are seated around the room at ornamental intervals, all ya-ya length silk sheaths, long legs and slithery knees. Cassius takes one of Rudy's cool jazz records or an Eretha Franklin or something like that off the phonograph and puts on one of the 45-r.p.m. rock-and-roll records that the singers keep sending to him at the hotel.

"Those are Rudy's records, I don't *dig* that mess. I'm just a boy from Louisville"—he turns his eyes up at the foxes—"I dig rock and roll. Isn't that right?"

All the girls are hip, and therefore cool jazz fans currently, so most of them think the whole thing over for a few seconds before saying, "That's right."

Cassius puts a 45–r.p.m. on and says, "This old boy's an alley singer, nobody ever heard of him, he sings about beans and bread and all that old mess."

Cassius starts laughing at that and looking out over the city lights, out the panorama window. The girls aren't sure whether he is laughing with or at the alley singer.

Cassius scans the foxes and says, "This is *my* crowd. They don't dig that other mess, either."

The girls don't say anything.

"Is that your kinda music? I know it's *hers*," he says, looking at Francine, who is sitting pretty still. "She's about to fall over."

And maybe at this point somebody says, "What time is it?" And Rudy or somebody looks out the panorama window to the clock on the Paramount Building and says, "Ten minutes to ten."

Cassius had just come from the Columbia Records studio, across from the hotel at Seventh Avenue and 52nd, where he was making an album, *I Am the Greatest*, a long pastiche of poems and skits composed wholly in terms of his impending fight with Sonny Liston. The incessant rehearsing of his lines for two weeks, most of them lines he had sprung at random at press conferences and so forth over a period of a year and a half, had made Cassius aware, as probably nothing else, of the showman's role he was filling. And made him tempted by it.

After cutting up a little for Frankie Tucker and the foxes

and everybody—showing them how he could *act*, really—he went over to one side of the living room and sat in a gangster-modern swivel chair and propped his feet up on the panorama-window ledge and talked a while. Everybody else was talking away in the background. Somebody had put the cool jazz back on and some husky girl with one of those augmented-sevenths voices was singing "Moon Over Miami."

"What's that club Leslie Uggams was at?" Cassius asked.

"The Metropole."

"The Metropole, that's right. That's one of the big ones out there, ain't it?"

His designation of the Metropole Café as "a big one" is an interesting thing in itself, but the key phrase is "out there." To Cassius, New York and the hot spots and the cool life are out there beyond his and Rudy's and Tuddie's suite at the Americana and beyond his frame of reference. Cassius does not come to New York as the hip celebrity, although it would be easy enough, but as a phenomenon. He treats Broadway as though these were still the days when the choirboys at Lindy's would spot a man in a white Palm Beach-brand suit heading up from 49th Street and say, "Here comes Winchell," or "Here comes Hellinger," or even the way Carl Van Vechten's Scarlet Creeper treated 125th Street in the days of the evening promenade. Cassius likes to get out amongst them.

About 10:15 P.M. he motioned to Sophia and started leaving the suite. All five girls got up and followed. The procession was spectacular even for Seventh Avenue on a crowded night with the chocolate-drink stands open. Cassius, six feet three, two hundred pounds, was wearing a black-and-white-checked jacket, white tab-collared shirt and black tie, light gray Continental trousers, black pointed-toe Italian shoes, and walking with a very cocky walk. The girls were walking one or two steps behind, all five of them, dressed in slayingly high couture. There were high heels and garden-party hats. Down at the corner, at 52nd Street, right at the foot of the hotel, Cassius stopped, looked all around and began loosening up his shoulders, the way prizefighters do. This, I found out, is Cassius' signal, an unconscious signal, that he is now available for crowd collecting. He got none on that corner, but halfway down to 51st Street people started saying, "That's Cassius Clay, Cassius Clay, Cassius Clay, Cassius Clay," the way he had mimicked it back in the hotel. Cassius might have gotten his crowd at 51st Street—he was looking cocky and the girls were right behind him in a phalanx, looking gorgeous—but he headed on across the street, when the light changed, over to where two fellows he knew were standing a quarter of the way down the block.

"Here he comes. Whatta you say, champ?"

"Right, man. Hey," said Cassius, referring the girls to the taller and older of the two men, "I want you all to meet one of the greatest singers in New York." A pause there. "What is your name, man, I meet so many people here."

"Hi, Pinocchio," said one of the foxes, and the man smiled.

"Pinocchio," said Cassius. Then he said, "You see all these queens are with me?" He made a sweeping motion with his hand. The girls were around him on the sidewalk. "All these foxes."

"That's sump'n else, man."

Cassius could have gotten his crowd easily on the sidewalk outside the Metropole. When it's warm, there is always a mob out there looking in through the front doorway at the band strung out along the bandstand, which is really more of a shelf. If there is a rock-and-roll band, there will always be some Jersey teen-agers outside twisting their ilia to it. That night there was more of a Dixieland or jump band on, although Lionel Hampton was to come on later, and Cassius entered, by coincidence, while an old tune called "High Society" was playing. All the foxes filed in, a step or so behind. The Metropole

Café has not seen many better entrances. Cassius looked gloriously bored.

The Metropole is probably the perfect place for a folk hero to show up at in New York. It is kind of a crossroads, or ideal type, of all the hot spots and live joints in the country. I can tell you two things about it that will help you understand what the Metropole is like, if you have never been there. First, the color motif is submarine green and Prussian blue, all reflected in huge wall-to-wall mirrors. If the stand-up beer crowd gets so thick you can't see over them to the bandstand, you can always watch through the mirrors. Second, the place attracts high-livers of a sort that was there that night. I particularly remember one young guy, standing there at the bar in the submarine-green and Prussian-blue light with sunglasses on. He had on a roll-collar shirt, a silvery tie, a pale-gray suit of the Continental cut and pointed black shoes. He had a king-size cigarette pasted on his lower lip, and when the band played "The Saints," he broke into a terribly "in" and hip grin, which brought the cigarette up horizontal. He clapped his hands and hammered his right heel in time to the drums and kept his eyes on the trumpet player the whole time. The thing is, kids don't even do that at Williams College anymore, but they do it at the Metropole.

This same kid came over to ask Cassius for his autograph at one point. He thought "The Saints" was hip, but he must not have thought autograph-hunting was very hip. He wanted an autograph, however. He handed Cassius a piece of paper for his autograph and said, "It's not for me, it's for a buddy of mine, he wants it." This did not score heavily with Cassius.

"Where's your pen?" he said.

"I don't have a pen," the kid said. "It's for a friend of mine."

"You ain't got no pen, man," said Cassius.

About a minute later the kid came back with a pen, and Cassius signed the piece of paper, and the kid said, "Thank you, Cassius, you're a gentleman." He said it very seriously. "It's for a buddy of mine. You're a real gentleman."

That was the tone of things that night in the Metropole. Everything was just a little off, the way Cassius saw it.

From the moment he walked into the doorway of the Metropole, people were trying to prod him into the act.

"You *really* think you can beat Sonny Liston, man?"

"Liston must fall in eight."

"You *really* mean that?"

"If he gives me any jive, he goes in five," Cassius said, but in a terribly matter-of-fact, recitative voice, all the while walking on ahead, with the foxes moseying in behind him, also gloriously bored.

His presence spread over the Metropole immediately. As I said, it is the perfect place for folk heroes, for there is no one in there who is not willing to be impressed. The management, a lot of guys in tuxedos with the kind of Hollywood black ties that tuck under the collars and are adorned with little pearl stickpins and such devices—the management was rushing up. A guy at the bar, well-dressed, came up behind Cassius and touched him lightly at about the level of the sixth rib and went back to the bar and told his girl, "That's Cassius Clay. I just touched him, no kidding."

They sat all the foxes down in a booth at about the middle of the Metropole Café and gave Cassius a chair by himself right next to them. Lionel Hampton came up with the huge smile he has and shook Cassius' hand and made a fuss over him without any jive about when Liston must fall. Cassius liked that. But then the crowd came around for autographs, and they wanted him to go into his act. It was a hell of a noisy place.

But the crowd at the Metropole hit several wrong notes. One was hit by a white man about fifty-five, obviously a Southerner from the way he talked, who came up to Clay from behind—

people were gaggled around from all sides—and stuck the blank side of a Pennsylvania Railroad receipt, the kind you get when you buy your ticket on the train, in his face and said in a voice you could mulch the hollyhocks with:

"Here you are, boy, put your name right there."

It was more or less the same voice Mississippians use on a hot day when the colored messenger boy has come into the living room and is standing around nervously. "Go ahead, boy, sit down. Sit in that seat right there."

Cassius took the Pennsylvania Railroad receipt without looking up at the man, and held it for about ten seconds, just staring at it.

Then he said in a slightly accusing voice, "Where's your pen?"

"I don't have a pen, boy. Some of these people around here got a pen. Just put your name right there."

Cassius still didn't look up. He just said, "Man, there's one thing you gotta learn. You don't *ever* come around and ask a man for an autograph if you ain't got no pen."

The man retreated and more people pressed in.

Cassius treats the fact of color—but not race—casually. Sometimes, when he is into his act, he will look at somebody and say, "You know, man, you lucky, you seen me here in living color." One time, I remember, a CBS news crew was filming an interview with him in the Columbia Records Studio A, at 799 Seventh Avenue, when the cameraman said to the interviewer, who was moving in on Cassius with the microphone: "Hey, Jack, you're throwing too much shadow on Cassius. He's dark enough already."

All the white intellectuals in the room cringed. Cassius just laughed. In point of fact, he is not very dark at all.

But he does not go for any of the old presumptions, such as, "Put your name right there, boy."

Another wrong note was hit when a middle-aged couple

came up. They were white. The woman struck you as a kind of Arkansas Blanche Dubois. They looked like they wanted autographs at first. They did in a way. They were both loaded. She had an incredible drunk smile that spread out soft and gooey like a can of Sherwin-Williams paint covering the world. She handed Cassius a piece of paper and a pencil and wanted him to write down both his name *and* her name. He had just about done that when she put her hand out very slowly to caress his cheek.

"Can I touch you?" she said. "I just want to touch you."

Cassius pulled his head back.

"Naw," he said. "My girl friends might get jealous."

He didn't call them foxes to her. He said it in a nice way. After she left, though, he let her have it. It was the only time I ever heard him say anything contemptuously of anyone.

"Can I *touch* you, can I *touch* you," he said. He could mimic her white Southern accent in a fairly devastating way.

"Naw, you can't touch me," he said, just as if he were answering her face to face. "Nobody can touch me."

As a matter of fact, Cassius is good at mimicking a variety of white Southern accents. He doesn't do it often, but when he does it, it has an extra wallop because he has a pronounced Negro accent of his own, which he makes no attempt to polish. He only turns it on heavier from time to time for comic effect. Once I heard him mimic both himself, a Louisville Negro, and newspapermen, Louisville whites, in one act.

I had asked him if the cocky act he was putting on all over the country, and in England for that matter, surprised the people who knew him back home. What I was getting at was whether he had been a cocky kid in Louisville back in the days before anybody ever heard of him. He changed the direction slightly.

"They believe anything you tell 'em about me back in Louisville. Newspapermen used to come around and I'd give 'em predictions and they'd say, 'What is this boy doing?'

"I had a fight with Lamar Clark, I believe it was, and I said [*Clay mimicking Clay, heavy, high-flown, bombastic Negro accent*]: 'Lamar will fall in two.' I knocked him out in two, and they said [*Clay mimicking drawling Kentucky Southern accent*]: 'Suht'n'ly dee-ud.'" (Certainly did.)

"I said, 'Miteff will fall in six.'

"They said, 'Suht'n'ly dee-ud.'

"I said, 'Warren will fall in four.'

"They said, 'Suht'n'ly dee-ud.'"

Clay had a lot better look on his face when people came by to admire what he had become rather than the funny act he puts on.

One young Negro, sharp-looking, as they say, in Continental clothes with a wonderful pair of Latin-American sunglasses, the kind that are narrow like the mask the Phantom wears in the comic strip, came by and didn't ask Cassius when Liston would fall. He shot an admiring, knowing look at the foxes, and said, "Who are all these girls, man?"

"Oh, they just the foxes," said Cassius.

"Man, I like your choice of foxes, I'm telling you," the kid said.

This tickled Cassius and he leaned over and told it to Sophia.

The kid, meantime, went around to the other side of the booth. He had a glorified version of how Cassius was living. He believed Cassius as he leaned over to the girls when the waiter came around and said, "You get anything you want. I own this place. I own all of New York." (Sophia gave him a derisive laugh for that.)

The kid leaned over to one of the girls and said: "Are you all his personal property?"

"What are you talking about, boy. What do you mean, his *per*sonal *property?* "

"You know, *his,*" said the kid. He was getting embarrassed, but he still had traces of a knowing look salivating around the edges.

"Why do we have to be his personal property? "

"Well, like, I mean, you know," said the kid. His mouth had disintegrated completely into an embarrassed grin by now, but his eyes were still darting around, as if to say, "Why don't they level with me. I'm a hip guy."

Cassius also liked it when a Negro he had met a couple of nights before, an older guy, came around and didn't ask when Liston would fall.

"I saw a crowd on the sidewalk out there, and I might have *known* you'd be inside," he told Cassius. "What's going on? "

"Oh, I'm just sitting here with the foxes," said Cassius.

"You sure are," the fellow said.

A young white kid with a crew cut said, "Are you afraid of Liston?"

Cassius said mechanically, "That big ugly bear? If I was worried, I'd be out training and I'm out partying."

Cassius had a tall, pink drink. It was nothing but Hawaiian Punch, right out of the can.

"How you gonna beat him? "

"I'll beat that bear in eight rounds. I'm strong and I'm beautiful and I'll beat that bear in eight rounds."

"You promise? " said the kid. He said it very seriously and shook Cassius' hand, as though he were getting ready to go outside and drop off a couple of grand with his Weehawken bookmaker. He apparently squeezed pretty hard. This fellow being a fighter and all, a guy ought to shake hands like a man with him.

Cassius pulled his hand away suddenly and wrung it. "Don't ever squeeze a fighter's hand, man. That hand's worth about three hundred thousand dollars," he said, making a fist. "You don't have to shake hands, you doing good just to lay eyes on me."

The kid edged off with his buddy and he was saying, "He said, 'Don't ever squeeze a fighter's hand.'"

By now Cassius was looking slightly worse than gloriously bored.

"If they don't stop worrying me," he said, "I'm gonna get up and walk out of here."

Sophia leaned over and told me, "He doesn't mean that. He loves it."

Of all the girls, Sophia seemed to be closest to him. She found him amusing. She liked him.

"You know, he's really a normal boy," she told me. She threw her head to one side as if to dismiss Cassius' big front. "Oh, he's got a big mouth. But aside from that, he's a real normal boy."

The foxes were beginning to stare a little morosely into their Gin Fizzes and Brandy Alexanders and Sidecars, and even the stream of autograph seekers was slowing down. It was damned crowded and you could hardly hear yourself talk. Every now and then the drummer would go into one of those crazy sky-rocketing solos suitable for the Metropole, and the trumpet player would take the microphone and say, "That's what Cassius Clay is going to do to Sonny Liston's head!" and Cassius would holler, "Right!" but it was heavy weather. By this time Richie Pittman had dropped in, and Cassius motioned to him. They got up and went out "for some air." At the doorway there was a crowd on the sidewalk looking in at the bandstand, as always. They made a fuss over Cassius, but he just loosened his shoulders a little and made a few wisecracks. He and Richie started walking up toward the Americana.

It was after midnight, and at the foot of the hotel, where this paseo-style sidewalk pans out almost like a patio, there was a crowd gathered around. Cassius didn't miss that. They were watching three street musicians, colored boys, one with a makeshift bass—a washtub turned upside down with a cord coming up out of the bottom, forming a single string; a drum—a large tin-can bottom with spoons as sticks; and one guy dancing. They were playing "Pennies from Heaven," a pretty good number for three guys getting ready to pass the hat. Cassius just walked up to the edge of the crowd and stood there. One person noticed him, then another, and pretty soon the old "That's Cassius Clay, Cassius Clay, Cassius Clay" business started. Cassius' spirits were rising. "Pennies from Heaven" stopped, and the three colored boys looked a little nonplussed for a moment. The show was being stolen. Somebody had said something about "Sonny Liston," only this time Cassius had the 150-watt eyes turned on, and he was saying, "The only thing I'm worried about is, I don't want Sonny Liston trying to crash *my* victory party the way I crashed his. I'm gonna tell him right before the fight starts so he won't forget it, 'Sonny,' I'm gonna tell him, 'Sonny Liston, I don't want you trying to crash my victory party tonight, you hear that? I want you to hear that now, 'cause you ain't gonna be *ab*le to hear anything eight rounds from now.' And if he gives me any jive when I tell him that, if he gives me any jive, he must fall in five."

A soldier, a crank-sided kid who looked like he must have gone through the battered-child syndrome at about age four, came up to take the role of Cassius' chief debater. Cassius likes that when he faces a street crowd. He'll hold a press conference for anybody, even a soldier on leave on Seventh Avenue.

"Where you gonna go after Sonny Liston whips you?" the kid said. "I got some travel folders right here."

"Boy," said Cassius, "you talk about traveling. I want you to go to that fight, 'cause you gonna see the launching of a human satellite. Sonny Liston."

The crowd was laughing and carrying on.

"I got some travel folders," the kid said. "You better look 'em over. I can get you a mask, too."

"You gonna bet against me?" said Cassius.

"Every cent I can get my hands on," said the kid.

"Man," said Cassius, "you better save your money, 'cause there's gonna be a total eclipse of the Sonny."

Cassius was standing there looking like a million dollars, and Richie was standing by, sort of riding shotgun. By this time, the crowd was so big, it was spilling off the sidewalk into 52nd Street. All sorts of incredible people were moving up close, including sclerotic old men with big-lunch ties who edged in with jag-legged walks. A cop was out in the street going crazy, trying to prod everybody back on the sidewalk. A squad car drove up, and the cop on the street put on a real tough tone, "All right, goddamn it," he said to an old sclerotic creeper with a big-lunch tie, "get up on the sidewalk."

Cassius looked around at me as if to say, "See, man? That's only what I predicted"—which is to say, "When I walk down the street, the crowds, they have to call the police."

The autograph business had started now, and people were pushing in with paper and pens, but Cassius wheeled around toward the three colored boys, the musicians, and said, "Autographs are one dollar tonight. Everyone puts one dollar in there" (the musicians had a corduroy-ribbed box out in front of the tub) "gets the autograph of Cassius Clay, the world's strongest fighter, the world's most beautiful fighter, the onliest fighter who predicts when they will fall."

The colored boys took the cue and started up with "Pennies from Heaven" again. The kid who danced was doing the merengue by himself. The kid on the bass was flailing away like a madman. All the while Cassius was orating on the corner.

"Come on, man, don't put no fifty cents in there, get that old dollar bill outa there. Think at all you're getting free here, the music's so fine and here you got Cassius Clay right here in front of you in living color, the next heavyweight champion of the world, the man who's gon' put old man Liston in orbit."

The dollar bills started piling up in the box, and the solo merengue kid was dervishing around wilder still, and Cassius wouldn't let up.

"Yeah, they down there right now getting that Medicare ready for that old man, and if I hit him in the mouth he's gonna need Denticare. That poor ol' man, he's so ugly, his wife drives him to the gym every morning 'fore the sun comes up, so nobody'll have to look at him 'round home. Come on, man, put yo' money in that box, people pay good money to hear this—"

The bass man was pounding away, and Cassius turned to me and said, behind his hand, "Man, you know one thing? If I get whipped, they gonna run me outa the country. You know that?"

Then he threw his head back and his arms out, as if he were falling backward. "Can you see me flat out on my back like this?"

The colored kids were playing "Pennies from Heaven," and Cassius Clay had his head thrown back and his arms out, laughing, and looking straight up at the top of the Americana Hotel.

8

The Last American Hero

Ten o'clock Sunday morning in the hills of North Carolina. Cars, miles of cars, in every direction, millions of cars, pastel cars, aqua green, aqua blue, aqua beige, aqua buff, aqua dawn, aqua dusk, aqua Malacca, Malacca lacquer, Cloud lavender, Assassin pink, Rake-a-cheek raspberry, Nude Strand coral, Honest Thrill orange, and Baby Fawn Lust cream-colored cars are all going to the stock car races, and that old mothering North Carolina sun keeps exploding off the windshields.

Seventeen thousand people, me included, all of us driving out Route 421, out to the stock car races at the North Wilkesboro Speedway, 17,000 going out to a five-eighths-mile stock car track with a Coca-Cola sign out front. This is not to say there is no preaching and shouting in the South this morning. There is preaching and shouting. Any of us can turn on the old automobile transistor radio and get all we want:

"They are greedy dogs. Yeah! They ride around in big cars. Unnh-hunh! And chase women. Yeah! And drink liquor. Unnh-hunh! And smoke cigars. Oh yes! And they are greedy dogs. Yeah! Unh-hunh! Oh yes! Amen!"

There are also some commercials on the radio for Aunt Jemima grits, which cost ten cents a pound. There are also the Gospel Harmonettes, singing: "If you dig a ditch, you better dig two. . . ."

There are also three fools in a panel discussion on the New South, which they seem to conceive of as General Lee running the new Dulcidreme Labial Cream factory down at Griffin, Georgia.

And suddenly my car is stopped still on Sunday morning in the middle of the biggest traffic jam in the history of the world. It goes for ten miles in every direction from the North Wilkesboro Speedway. And right there it dawns on me that as far as this situation is concerned, anyway, all the conventional notions about the South are confined to . . . the Sunday radio. The South has preaching and shouting, the South has grits, the South has country songs, old mimosa traditions, clay dust, Old Bigots, New Liberals—and all of it, all of that old mental cholesterol, is confined to the Sunday radio. What I was in the middle of—well, it wasn't anything one hears about in panels about the South today. Miles and miles of eye-busting pastel cars on the expressway, which roar right up into the hills, going to the stock car races. Fifteen years of stock car racing, and baseball—and the state of North Carolina alone used to have forty-four professional baseball teams—baseball is all over with in the South. We were all in the middle of a wild new thing, the Southern car world, and heading down the road on my way to see a breed such as sports never saw before, Southern stock car drivers, all lined up in these two-ton mothers that go over 175 m.p.h., Fireball Roberts, Freddie Lorenzen, Ned Jarrett, Richard Petty, and—the hardest of all the hard chargers, one of the fastest automobile racing drivers in history—yes! Junior Johnson.

The legend of Junior Johnson! In this legend, here is a country boy, Junior Johnson, who learns to drive by running whiskey for his father, Johnson, Senior, one of the biggest copper-still operators of all time, up in Ingle Hollow, near North Wilkesboro, in northwestern North Carolina, and grows up to be a famous stock car racing driver, rich, grossing $100,000 in 1963, for example, respected, solid, idolized in his hometown and throughout the rural South. There is all this about how good old boys would wake up in the middle of the night in the apple shacks and hear a supercharged Oldsmobile engine roaring over Brushy Mountain and say, "Listen at him—there he goes! " although that part is doubtful, since some nights there were so many good old boys taking off down the road in supercharged automobiles out of Wilkes County, and running loads to Charlotte, Salisbury, Greensboro, Winston-Salem, High Point, or wherever, it would be pretty hard to pick out one. It was Junior Johnson specifically, however, who was famous for the "bootleg turn" or "about-face," in which, if the Alcohol Tax agents had a roadblock up for you or were too close behind, you threw the car up into second gear, cocked the wheel, stepped on the accelerator and made the car's rear end skid around in a complete 180-degree arc, a complete about-face, and tore on back up the road exactly the way you came from. God! The Alcohol Tax agents used to burn over Junior Johnson. Practically every good old boy in town in Wilkesboro, the county seat, got to know the agents by sight in a very short time. They would rag them practically to their faces on the subject of Junior Johnson, so that it got to be an obsession. Finally, one night they had Junior trapped on the road up toward the bridge around Millersville, there's no way out of there, they had the barricades up and they could hear this souped-up car roaring around the bend, and here it comes—but suddenly they can hear a siren and see a red light flashing in the grille, so they think it's another agent, and boy, they run out like ants and pull those barrels and boards and sawhorses out of the way, and then—Ggghhzzzzzzzzhhhhhhgg-ggggzzzzzzzeeeeeong!—gawdam! there he goes again, it was him, Junior Johnson! with a gawdam agent's si-reen and a red light in his grille!

I wasn't in the South five minutes before people started making oaths, having visions, telling these hulking great stories, all on the subject of Junior Johnson. At the Greensboro, North Carolina, Airport there was one good old boy who vowed he would have eaten "a bucket of it" if that would have kept Junior Johnson from switching from a Dodge racer to a Ford. Hell yes, and after that—God-almighty, remember that 1963 Chevrolet of Junior's? Whatever happened to that car? A couple of more good old boys join in. A good old boy, I ought to explain, is a generic term in the rural South referring to a man, of any age, but more often young than not, who fits in with the status system of the region. It usually means he has a good sense of humor and enjoys ironic jokes, is tolerant and easygoing enough to get along in long conversations at places like on the corner, and has a reasonable amount of physical courage. The term is usually heard in some such form as: "Lud? He's a good old boy from over at Crozet." These good old boys in the airport, by the way, were in their twenties, except for one fellow who was a cabdriver and was about forty-five, I would say. Except for the cabdriver, they all wore neo-Brummellian clothes such as Lacoste tennis shirts, Slim Jim pants, windbreakers with the collars turned up, "fast" shoes of the winkle-picker genre, and so on. I mention these details just by way of pointing out that very few grits, Iron Boy overalls, clodhoppers or hats with ventilation holes up near the crown enter into this story. Anyway, these good old boys are talking about Junior Johnson and how he has switched to Ford. This they unanimously regard as some kind of betrayal on Johnson's part. Ford, it seems, they regard as the car symbolizing the established power structure. Dodge is kind of a middle ground. Dodge is at least a challenger, not a ruler. But the Junior Johnson they like to remember is the Junior Johnson of 1963, who took on the whole field of NASCAR (National Association For Stock Car Auto Racing) Grand National racing with a Chevrolet. All the other drivers, the drivers driving Fords, Mercurys, Plymouths, Dodges, had millions, literally millions when it is all added up, millions of dollars in backing from the Ford and Chrysler Corporations. Junior Johnson took them all on in a Chevrolet without one cent of backing from Detroit. Chevrolet had pulled out of stock car racing. Yet every race it was the same. It was never a question of whether anybody was going to *outrun* Junior Johnson. It was just a question of whether he was going to win or his car was going to break down, since, for one thing, half the time he had to make his own racing parts. God! Junior Johnson was like Robin Hood or Jesse James or Little David or something. Every time that Chevrolet, No. 3, appeared on the track, wild curdled yells, "Rebel" yells, they still have those, would rise up. At Daytona, at Atlanta, at Charlotte, at Darlington, South Carolina; Bristol, Tennessee; Martinsville, Virginia—Junior Johnson!

And then the good old boys get to talking about whatever happened to that Chevrolet of Junior's, and the cabdriver says he knows. He says Junior Johnson is using that car to run liquor out of Wilkes County. What does he mean? For Junior Johnson ever to go near another load of bootleg whiskey again—he would have to be insane. He has this huge racing income. He has two other businesses, a whole automated chicken farm with 42,000 chickens, a road-grading business—but the cabdriver says he has this dream Junior is still roaring down from Wilkes County, down through the clay cuts, with the Atlas Arc Lip jars full in the back of that Chevrolet. It is in Junior's blood—and then at this point he puts his right hand up in front of him as if he is groping through fog, and his eyeballs glaze over and he looks out in the distance and he describes Junior Johnson roaring over the ridges of Wilkes County as if it is the ghost of Zapata he is describing, bounding over the Sierras on a white horse to rouse the peasants.

A stubborn notion! A crazy notion! Yet Junior Johnson has followers who need to keep him, symbolically, riding through nighttime like a demon. Madness! But Junior Johnson is one of the last of those sports stars who is not just an ace at the game itself, but a hero a whole people or class of people can identify with. Other, older examples are the way Jack Dempsey stirred up the Irish or the way Joe Louis stirred up the Negroes. Junior Johnson is a modern figure. He is only thirty-three years old and still racing. He should be compared to two other sports heroes whose cultural impact is not too well known. One is Antonino Rocca, the professional wrestler, whose triumphs mean so much to New York City's Puerto Ricans that he can fill Madison Square Garden, despite the fact that everybody, the Puerto Ricans included, knows that wrestling is nothing but a crude form of folk theatre. The other is Ingemar Johanssen, who had a tremendous meaning to the Swedish masses—they were tired of that old king who played tennis all the time and all his friends who keep on drinking Cointreau behind the screen of socialism. Junior Johnson is a modern hero, all involved with car culture and car symbolism in the South. A wild new thing—

Wild—gone wild, Fireball Roberts' Ford spins out on the first turn at the North Wilkesboro Speedway, spinning, spinning, the spin seems almost like slow motion—and then it smashes into the wooden guardrail. It lies up there with the frame bent. Roberts is all right. There is a new layer of asphalt on the track, it is like glass, the cars keep spinning off the first turn. Ned Jarrett spins, smashes through the wood. "Now, boys, this ice ain't gonna get one goddamn bit better, so you can either line up and qualify or pack up and go home—"

I had driven from the Greensboro Airport up to Wilkes County to see Junior Johnson on the occasion of one of the two yearly NASCAR Grand National stock car races at the North Wilkesboro Speedway.

It is a long, very gradual climb from Greensboro to Wilkes County. Wilkes County is all hills, ridges, woods and underbrush, full of pin oaks, sweet-gum maples, ash, birch, apple trees, rhododendron, rocks, vines, tin roofs, little clapboard places like the Mount Olive Baptist Church, signs for things like Double Cola, Sherrill's Ice Cream, Eckard's Grocery, Dr. Pepper, Diel's Apples, Google's Place, Suddith's Place and—yes!—cars. Up onto the highway, out of a side road from a hollow, here comes a 1947 Hudson. To almost anybody it would look like just some old piece of junk left over from God knows when, rolling down a country road . . . the 1947 Hudson was one of the first real "hot" cars made after the war. Some of the others were the 1946 Chrysler, which had a "kickdown" gear for sudden bursts of speed, the 1955 Pontiac and a lot of the Fords. To a great many good old boys a hot car was a symbol of heating up life itself. The war! Money even for country boys! And the money bought cars. In California they suddenly found kids of all sorts involved in vast drag racing orgies and couldn't figure out what was going on. But in the South the mania for cars was even more intense, although much less publicized. To millions of good old boys, and girls, the automobile represented not only liberation from what was still pretty much a land-bound form of social organization but also a great leap forward into twentieth-century glamor, an idea that was being dinned in on the South like everywhere else. It got so that one of the typical rural sights, in addition to the red rooster, the gray split-rail fence, the Edgeworth Tobacco sign and the rusted-out harrow, one of the typical rural sights would be . . . you would be driving along the dirt roads and there beside the house would be an automobile up on blocks or something, with a rope over the tree for hoisting up the motor or some other heavy part, and a couple of good old boys would be practically disappearing into its innards, from below and from above, draped over the side under the hood. It got so that on Sundays there wouldn't be a safe straight stretch of road in the county, because so many wild country boys would be out racing or just raising hell on the roads. A lot of other kids, who weren't basically wild, would be driving like hell every morning and every night, driving to jobs perhaps thirty or forty miles away, jobs that were available only because of automobiles. In the morning they would be driving through the dapple shadows like madmen. In the hollows, sometimes one would come upon the most incredible tarpaper hovels, down near the stream, and out front would be an incredible automobile creation, a late-model car with aerials, Continental kit overhangs in the back, mudguards studded with reflectors, fender skirts, spotlights, God knows what all, with a girl and perhaps a couple of good old boys communing over it and giving you rotten looks as you drive by. On Saturday night everybody would drive into town and park under the lights on the main street and neck. Yes! There was something about being right in there in town underneath the lights and having them reflecting off the baked enamel on the hood. Then if a good old boy insinuated his hands here and there on the front seat with a girl and began . . . necking . . . somehow it was all more *complete*. After the war there was a great deal of stout-burgher talk about people who lived in hovels and bought big-yacht cars to park out front. This was one of the symbols of a new, spendthrift age. But there was a great deal of unconscious resentment buried in the talk. It was resentment against (a) the fact that the good old boy had his money at all and (b) the fact that the car symbolized freedom, a slightly wild, careening emancipation from the old social order. Stock car racing got started about this time, right after the war, and it was immediately regarded as some kind of manifestation of the animal irresponsibility of the lower orders. It had a truly terrible reputation. It was—well, it looked *rowdy* or something. The cars were likely to be used cars, the tracks were dirt, the stands were rickety wood, the drivers were country boys, and they had regular feuds out there, putting each other "up against the wall" and "cutting tires" and everything else. Those country boys would drive into the curves full tilt, then slide maniacally, sometimes coming around the curve sideways, with red dirt showering up. Sometimes they would race at night, under those weak-eyed yellow-ochre lights they have at small tracks and baseball fields, and the clay dust would start showering up in the air, where the evening dew would catch it, and all evening long you would be sitting in the stands or standing out in the infield with a fine clay-mud drizzle coming down on you, not that anybody gave a damn— except for the Southern upper and middle classes, who never attended in those days, but spoke of the "rowdiness."

But mainly it was the fact that stock car racing was something that was welling up out of the lower orders. From somewhere these country boys and urban proles were getting the money and starting this hellish sport.

Stock car racing was beginning all over the country, at places like Allentown, Langhorne and Lancaster, Pennsylvania, and out in California and even out on Long Island, but wherever it cropped up, the Establishment tried to wish it away, largely, and stock car racing went on in a kind of underground world of tracks built on cheap stretches of land well out from the town or the city, a world of diners, drive-ins, motels, gasoline stations, and the good burghers might drive by from time to time, happen by on a Sunday or something, and see the crowd gathered from out of nowhere, the cars coming in, crowding up the highway a little, but Monday morning they would be all gone, and all would be as it was.

Stock car racing was building up a terrific following in the South during the early fifties. Here was a sport not using any abstract devices, any *bat* and *ball*, but the same automobile that was changing a man's own life, his own symbol of liberation, and it didn't require size, strength and all that, all it required was a taste for speed, and the guts. The newspapers in the South didn't seem to catch onto what was happening until late in the game. Of course, newspapers all over the country have looked backward over the tremendous rise in automobile sports, now the second-biggest type of sport in the country in terms of attendance. The sports pages generally have an inexorable lower-middle-class outlook. The sportswriter's "zest for life" usually amounts, in the end, to some sort of gruff Mom's Pie sentimentality at a hideously cozy bar somewhere. The sportswriters caught onto Grand Prix racing first because it had "tone," a touch of defrocked European nobility about it, what with a few counts racing here and there, although, in fact, it is the least popular form of racing in the United States. What finally put stock car racing onto the sports pages in the South was the intervention of the Detroit automobile firms. Detroit began putting so much money into the sport that it took on a kind of massive economic respectability and thereby, in the lower-middle-class brain, status.

What Detroit discovered was that thousands of good old boys in the South were starting to form allegiances to brands of automobiles, according to which were hottest on the stock car circuits, the way they used to have them for the hometown baseball team. The South was one of the hottest car-buying areas in the country. Cars like Hudsons, Oldsmobiles and Lincolns, not the cheapest automobiles by any means, were selling in disproportionate numbers in the South, and a lot of young good old boys were buying them. In 1955, Pontiac started easing into stock car racing, and suddenly the big surge was on. Everybody jumped into the sport to grab for themselves The Speed Image. Suddenly, where a good old boy used to have to bring his gasoline to the track in old filling-station pails and pour it into the tank through a funnel when he made a pit stop, and change his tires with a hand wrench, suddenly, now, he had these "gravity" tanks of gasoline that you just jam into the gas pipe, and air wrenches to take the wheels off, and whole crews of men in white coveralls to leap all over a car when it came rolling into the pit, just like they do at Indianapolis, as if they are mechanical apparati *merging* with the machine as it rolls in, forcing water into the radiator, jacking up the car, taking off wheels, wiping off the windshield, handing the driver a cup of orange juice, all in one synchronized operation. And now, today, the *big money* starts descending on this little place, the North Wilkesboro, North Carolina, Speedway, a little five-eights-of-a-mile stock car track with a Coca-Cola sign out by the highway where the road in starts.

The private planes start landing out at the Wilkesboro Airport. Freddie Lorenzen, the driver, the biggest money winner last year in stock car racing, comes sailing in out of the sky in a twin-engine Aero Commander, and there are a few good old boys out there in the tall grass by the runway already with their heads sticking up watching this hero of the modern age come in and taxi up and get out of that twin-engine airplane with his blonde hair swept back as if by the mother internal combustion engine of them all. And then Paul Goldsmith, the driver, comes in in a 310 Cessna, and *he* gets out, all these tall, lanky hard-boned Americans in their thirties with these great

profiles like a comic-strip hero or something, and then Glenn
(Fireball) Roberts—Fireball Roberts!—Fireball is *hard*—he
comes in a Comanche 250, like a flying yacht, and then Ray
Nichels and Ray Fox, the chief mechanics, who run big racing
crews for the Chrysler Corporation, this being Fox's last race
for Junior as his mechanic, before Junior switches over to
Ford, they come in in two-engine planes. And even old Buck
Baker—hell, Buck Baker is a middling driver for Dodge, but
even he comes rolling in down the landing strip at two hundred miles an hour with his Southern-hero face at the window
of the cockpit of a twin-engine Apache, traveling first class in
the big status boat that has replaced the yacht in America, the
private plane.

And then the Firestone and Goodyear vans pull in, huge
mothers, bringing in huge stacks of racing tires for the race,
big wide ones, 8.20's, with special treads, which are like a lot of
bumps on the tire instead of grooves. They even have special
tires for qualifying, soft tires, called "gumballs," they wouldn't
last more than ten times around the track in a race, but for
qualifying, which is generally three laps, one to pick up speed
and two to race against the clock, they are great, because they
hold tight on the corners. And on a hot day, when somebody
like Junior Johnson, one of the fastest qualifying runners in the
history of the sport, 170.777 m.p.h. in a one-hundred-mile qualifying race at Daytona in 1964, when somebody like Junior
Johnson really pushes it on a qualifying run, there will be a
ring of blue smoke up over the whole goddamned track, a ring
like an oval halo over the whole thing from the gumballs burn-
ing, and some good old boy will say, "Great smokin' blue
gumballs god almighty dog! There goes Junior Johnson!"

The thing is, each one of these tires costs fifty-five to sixty
dollars, and on a track that is fast and hard on tires, like
Atlanta, one car might go through ten complete tire changes,
easily, forty tires, or almost $2500 worth of tires just for one

race. And he may even be out of the money. And then the Ford van and the Dodge van and the Mercury van and the Plymouth van roll in with new motors, a whole new motor every few races, a 427-cubic-inch stock car racing motor, 600 horsepower, the largest and most powerful allowed on the track, that probably costs the company $1000 or more, when you consider that they are not mass produced. And still the advertising appeal. You can buy the very same car that these fabulous wild men drive every week at these fabulous wild speeds, and some of their power and charisma is yours. After every NASCAR Grand National stock car race, whichever company has the car that wins, this company will put big ads in the Southern papers, and papers all over the country if it is a very big race, like the Daytona 500, the Daytona Firecracker 400 or the Atlanta and Charlotte races. They sell a certain number of these 427-cubic-inch cars to the general public, a couple of hundred a year, perhaps, at eight or nine thousand dollars apiece, but it is no secret that these motors are specially reworked just for stock car racing. Down at Charlotte there is a company called Holman & Moody that is supposed to be the "garage" or "automotive-engineering" concern that prepares automobiles for Freddy Lorenzen and some of the other Ford drivers. But if you go by Holman & Moody out by the airport and Charlotte, suddenly you come upon a huge place that is a *factory,* for godsake, a big long thing, devoted mainly to the business of turning out stock car racers. A whole lot of other parts in stock car racers are heavier than the same parts on a street automobile, although they are made to the same scale. The shock absorbers are bigger, the wheels are wider and bulkier, the swaybars and steering mechanisms are heavier, the axles are much heavier, they have double sets of wheel bearings, and so forth and so on. The bodies of the cars are pretty much the same, except that they use lighter sheet metal, practically tinfoil. Inside, there is only the driver's seat and a heavy set of roll bars and diagonal struts that turn the inside of the car into a rigid cage, actually. That is why the drivers can walk away unhurt—most of the time—from the most spectacular crackups. The gearshift is the floor kind, although it doesn't make much difference, as there is almost no shifting gears in stock car racing. You just get into high gear and go. The dashboard has no speedometer, the main thing being the dial for engine revolutions per minute. So, anyway, it costs about $15,000 to prepare a stock car racer in the first place and another three or four thousand for each new race and this does not even count the costs of mechanics' work and transportation. All in all, Detroit will throw around a quarter of a million dollars into it every week while the season is on, and the season runs, roughly, from February to October, with a few big races after that. And all this turns up even out at the North Wilkesboro Speedway in the up-country of Wilkes County, North Carolina.

Sunday! Racing day! There is the Coca-Cola sign out where the road leads in from the highway, and hills and trees, but here are long concrete grandstands for about 17,000 and a paved five-eighths-mile oval. Practically all the drivers are out there with their cars and their crews, a lot of guys in white coveralls. The cars look huge . . . and curiously nude and blind. All the chrome is stripped off, except for the grilles. The headlights are blanked out. Most of the cars are in the pits. The so-called "pit" is a paved cutoff on the edge of the infield. It cuts off from the track itself like a service road off an expressway at the shopping center. Every now and then a car splutters, hacks, coughs, hocks a lunga, rumbles out onto the track itself for a practice run. There is a lot of esoteric conversation going on, speculation, worries, memoirs:

"What happened?"

"Mother—condensed on me. Al brought it up here with him. Water in the line."

"Better keep Al away from a stable, he'll fill you up with horse manure."

". . . they told me to give him one, a creampuff, so I give him one, a creampuff. One goddam race and the son of a bitch, he *melted* it. . . ."

". . . he's down there right now pettin' and rubbin' and huggin' that car just like those guys do a horse at the Kentucky Derby. . . ."

". . . They'll blow you right out of the tub. . . ."

". . . No, the quarter inch, and go on over and see if you can get Ned's blowtorch. . . ."

". . . Rear end's loose. . . ."

". . . I don't reckon this right here's got nothing to do with it, do you? . . ."

". . . Aw, I don't know, about yea big. . . ."

". . . Who the hell stacked them gumballs on the bottom? . . ."

". . . th'owing rocks. . . ."

". . . won't turn seven thousand. . . ."

". . . strokin' it. . . ."

". . . blistered. . . ."

". . . spun out. . . ."

". . . muvva. . . ."

Then, finally, here comes Junior Johnson. How he does come on. He comes tooling across the infield in a big white dreamboat, a brand-new white Pontiac Catalina four-door hard-top sedan. He pulls up and as he gets out he seems to get more and more huge. First his crew-cut head and then a big jaw and then a bigger neck and then a huge torso, like a wrestler's, all done up rather modish and California modern, with a red-and-white candy-striped sport shirt, white ducks and loafers.

"How you doing?" says Junior Johnson, shaking hands, and then he says, "Hot enough for ye'uns?"

Junior is in an amiable mood. Like most up-hollow people, it turns out, Junior is reserved. His face seldom shows an emo-tion. He has three basic looks: amiable, amiable and a little shy, and dead serious. To a lot of people, apparently, Junior's dead-serious look seems menacing. There are no cowards left in stock car racing, but a couple of drivers tell me that one of the things that can shake you up is to look into your rear-view mirror going around a curve and see Junior Johnson's car on your tail trying to "root you out of the groove," and then get a glimpse of Junior's dead-serious look. I think some of the sportswriters are afraid of him. One of them tells me Junior is strong, silent—and explosive. Junior will only give you three answers, "Uh-huh," "Uh-unh," and "I don' know," and so forth and so on. Actually, I found he handles questions easily. He has a great technical knowledge of automobiles and the phys-ics of speed, including things he never fools with, such as Offenhauser engines. What he never does offer, however, is small talk. This gives him a built-in poise, since it deprives him of the chance to say anything asinine. "Ye'uns," "we'uns," "H'it" for "it," "growed" for "grew" and a lot of other unusual past participles—Junior uses certain older forms of English, not ex-actly "Elizabethan," as they are sometimes called, but older forms of English preserved up-country in his territory, Ingle Hollow.

Kids keep coming up for Junior's autograph and others are just hanging around and one little old boy comes up, he is about thirteen, and Junior says: "This boy here goes coon hunting with me."

One of the sportswriters is standing around, saying: "What do you shoot a coon with?"

"Don't shoot 'em. The dogs tree 'em and then you flush 'em out and the dogs fight 'em."

"Flush 'em out?"

"Yeah. This boy right here can flush 'em out better than anybody you ever did see. You go out at night with the dogs, and soon as they get the scent, they start barking. They go on out ahead of you and when they tree a coon, you can tell it, by the way they sound. They all start baying up at that coon—h'it sounds like, I don't know, you hear it once and you not likely to forget it. Then you send a little old boy up to flush him out and he jumps down and the dogs fight him."

"How does a boy flush him out?"

"Aw, he just climbs up there to the limb he's on and starts shaking h'it and the coon'll jump."

"What happens if the coon decides he'd rather come back after the boy instead of jumping down to a bunch of dogs?"

"He won't do that. A coon's afraid of a person, but he can kill a dog. A coon can take any dog you set against him if they's just the two of them fighting. The coon jumps down on the ground and he rolls right over on his back with his feet up, and he's *got* claws about like this. All he has to do is get a dog once in the throat or in the belly, and he can kill him, cut him wide open just like you took a knife and did it. Won't any dog even fight a coon except a coon dog."

"What kind of dogs are they?"

"*Coon* dogs, I guess. Black and tans they call 'em sometimes. They's bred for it. If his mammy and pappy wasn't coon dogs, he ain't likely to be one either. After you got one, you got to train him. You trap a coon, live, and then you put him in a pen and tie him to a post with a rope on him and then you put your dog in there and he has to fight him. Sometimes you get a dog just don't have any fight in him and he ain't no good to you."

Junior is in the pit area, standing around with his brother Fred, who is part of his crew, and Ray Fox and some other good old boys, in a general atmosphere of big stock car money, a big ramp truck for his car, a white Dodge, number 3, a big crew in white coveralls, huge stacks of racing tires, a Dodge P.R. man, big portable cans of gasoline, compressed air hoses, compressed water hoses, the whole business. Herb Nab, Freddie Lorenzen's chief mechanic, comes over and sits down on his haunches and Junior sits down on his haunches and Nab says:

"So Junior Johnson's going to drive a Ford."

Junior is switching from Dodge to Ford mainly because he hasn't been winning with the Dodge. Lorenzen drives a Ford, too, and the last year, when Junior was driving the Chevrolet, their duels were the biggest excitement in stock car racing.

"Well," says Nab, "I'll tell you, Junior. My ambition is going to be to outrun your ass every goddamned time we go out."

"That was your ambition last year," says Junior.

"I know it was," says Nab, "and you took all the money, didn't you? You know what my strategy was. I was going to outrun everybody else and outlast Junior, that was my strategy."

Setting off his California modern sport shirt and white ducks Junior has on a pair of twenty-dollar rimless sunglasses and a big gold Timex watch, and Flossie, his fiancée, is out there in the infield somewhere with the white Pontiac, and the white Dodge that Dodge gave Junior is parked up near the pit area—and then a little thing happens that brings the whole thing right back there to Wilkes County, North Carolina, to Ingle Hollow and to hard muscle in the clay gulches. A couple of good old boys come down to the front of the stands with the screen and the width of the track between them and Junior, and one of the good old boys comes down and yells out in the age-old baritone raw-curdle yell of the Southern hills:

"Hey! Hog jaw!"

Everybody gets quiet. They know he's yelling at Junior, but nobody says a thing. Junior doesn't even turn around.

"Hey, hog jaw! . . ."

Junior, he does nothing.

"Hey, hog jaw, I'm gonna get me one of them fastback roosters, too, and come down there and get you!"

Fastback rooster refers to the Ford—it has a "fastback" design—Junior is switching to.

"Hey, hog jaw, I'm gonna get me one of them fastback roosters and run you right out of here, you hear me, hog jaw!"

One of the good old boys alongside Junior says, "Junior, go on up there and clear out those stands."

Then everybody stares at Junior to see what he's gonna do. Junior, he don't even look around. He just looks a bit dead serious.

"Hey, hog jaw, you got six cases of whiskey in the back of that car you want to let me have?"

"What you hauling in that car, hog jaw!"

"Tell him you're out of that business, Junior," one of the good old boys says.

"Go on up there and clean house, Junior," says another good old boy.

Then Junior looks up, without looking at the stands, and smiles a little and says, "You flush him down here out of that tree—and I'll take keer of him."

Such a howl goes up from the good old boys! It is almost a blood curdle—

"Goddam, he *will*, too!"

"Lord, he better know how to do an *about-face* hissef if he comes down here!"

"Goddam, get him, Junior!"

"Whooeeee!"

"Mother dog!"

—a kind of orgy of reminiscence of the old Junior before the Detroit money started flowing, wild *combats d'honneur* up-hollow—and, suddenly, when he heard that unearthly baying coming up from the good old boys in the pits, the good old boy retreated from the edge of the stands and never came back.

Later on Junior told me, sort of apologetically, "H'it used to be, if a fellow crowded me just a little bit, I was ready to crawl him. I reckon that was one good thing about Chillicothe.

"I don't want to pull any more time," Junior tells me, "but I wouldn't take anything in the world for the experience I had in prison. If a man needed to change, that was the place to change. H'it's not a waste of time there, h'it's good experience.

"H'it's that they's so many people in the world that feel that nobody is going to tell them what to do. I had quite a temper, I reckon. I always had the idea that I had as much sense as the other person and I didn't want them to tell me what to do. In the penitentiary there I found out that I could listen to another fellow and be told what to do and h'it wouldn't kill me."

Starting time! Linda Vaughn, with the big blonde hair and blossomy breasts, puts down her Coca-Cola and the potato chips and slips off her red stretch pants and her white blouse and walks out of the officials' booth in her Rake-a-cheek red show-girl's costume with her long honeydew legs in net stockings and climbs up on the red Firebird float. The Life Symbol of stock car racing! Yes! Linda, every luscious morsel of Linda, is a good old girl from Atlanta who was made Miss Atlanta International Raceway one year and was paraded around the track on a float and she liked it so much and all the good old boys liked it so much, Linda's flowing hair and blossomy breasts and honeydew legs, that she became the permanent glamor symbol of stock car racing, and never mind this other modeling she was doing . . . this, she liked it. Right before practically every race on the Grand National circuit Linda Vaughn puts down her Coca-Cola and potato chips. Her momma is there, she generally comes around to see Linda go around the track on the float, it's such a nice spectacle seeing Linda looking so lovely, and the applause and all. "Linda, I'm thirstin', would you bring me a Coca-Cola?" "A lot of them think I'm Freddie Lorenzen's girl friend, but I'm not any of 'em's girl friend, I'm real good friends with 'em all, even Wendell," he being Wendell Scott, the only Negro in big-league stock car racing. Linda gets up on the Firebird float. This is an extraordinary object, made of wood, about twenty feet tall, in the shape of a huge bird, an eagle or something, blazing red, and Linda, with her red showgirl's suit on, gets up on the seat, which is up between the wings, like a saddle, high enough so her long honeydew legs stretch down, and a new car pulls her—Miss Firebird!—slowly once around the track just before the race. It is more of a ceremony by now than the national anthem. Miss Firebird sails slowly in front of the stands and the good old boys let out some real curdle Rebel yells, "Yaaaa-aaaaaaaaghhhhhooooooo! Let me at that car!" "Honey, you sure do start my motor, I swear to God!" "Great God and Poona-dingdong, I mean!"

And suddenly there's a big roar from behind, down in the infield, and then I see one of the great sights in stock car racing. That infield! The cars have been piling into the infield by the hundreds, parking in there on the clay and the grass, every which way, angled down and angled up, this way and that, where the ground is uneven, these beautiful blazing brand-new cars with the sun exploding off the windshields and the baked enamel and the glassy lacquer, hundreds, thousands of cars stacked this way and that in the infield with the sun bolting down and no shade, none at all, just a couple of Coca-Cola stands out there. And already the good old boys and girls are out beside the cars, with all these beautiful little buds in short shorts already spread-eagled out on top of the car roofs, pressing down on good hard slick automobile sheet metal, their little cupcake bottoms aimed up at the sun. The good old boys are lollygagging around with their shirts off and straw hats on that have miniature beer cans on the brims and buttons that read, "Girls Wanted—No Experience Required." And everybody, good old boys and girls of all ages, are out there with

portable charcoal barbecue ovens set up, and folding tubular
steel terrace furniture, deck chairs and things, and Thermos
jugs and coolers full of beer—and suddenly it is not the up-
country South at all but a concentration of the modern sub-
urbs, all jammed into that one space, from all over America,
with blazing cars and instant goodies, all cooking under the
bare blaze—inside a strange bowl. The infield is like the bottom of a bowl. The track around it is banked so steeply at the
corners and even on the straightaways, it is like the steep sides
of a bowl. The wall around the track, and the stands and the
bleachers are like the rim of a bowl. And from the infield, in
this great incredible press of blazing new cars, there is no
horizon but the bowl, up above only that cobalt-blue North
Carolina sky. And then suddenly, on a signal, thirty stock car
engines start up where they are lined up in front of the stands.
The roar of these engines is impossible to describe. They have
a simultaneous rasp, thunder and rumble that goes right
through a body and fills the whole bowl with a noise of internal combustion. Then they start around on two build-up
runs, just to build up speed, and then they come around the
fourth turn and onto the straightaway in front of the stands
at—here, 130 miles an hour, in Atlanta, 160 miles an hour, at
Daytona, 180 miles an hour—and the flag goes down and everybody in the infield and in the stands is up on their feet going
mad, and suddenly here is a bowl that is one great orgy of
everything in the way of excitement and liberation the automobile has meant to Americans. An orgy!

The first lap of a stock car race is a horrendous, a wildly
horrendous spectacle such as no other sport approaches.
Twenty, thirty, forty automobiles, each of them weighing almost two tons, 3700 pounds, with 427-cubic-inch engines, 600
horsepower, are practically locked together, side to side and
tail to nose, on a narrow band of asphalt at 130, 160, 180 miles
an hour, hitting the curves so hard the rubber burns off the

tires in front of your eyes. To the driver, it is like being inside a car going down the West Side Highway in New York City at rush hour, only with everybody going literally three to four times as fast, at speeds a man who has gone eighty-five miles an hour down a highway cannot conceive of, and with every other driver an enemy who is willing to cut inside of you, around you or in front of you, or ricochet off your side in the battle to get into a curve first.

The speeds are faster than those in the Indianapolis 500 race, the cars are more powerful and much heavier. The prize money in Southern stock car racing is far greater than that in Indianapolis-style or European Grand Prix racing, but few Indianapolis or Grand Prix drivers have the raw nerve required to succeed at it.

Although they will deny it, it is still true that stock car drivers will put each other "up against the wall"—cut inside on the left of another car and ram it into a spin—if they get mad enough. Crashes are not the only danger, however. The cars are now literally too fast for their own parts, especially the tires. Firestone and Goodyear have poured millions into stock car racing, but neither they nor anybody so far have been able to come up with a tire for this kind of racing at the current speeds. Three well-known stock car drivers were killed last year, two of them champion drivers, Joe Weatherly and Fireball Roberts, and another, one of the best new drivers, Jimmy Pardue, from Junior Johnson's own home territory, Wilkes County, North Carolina. Roberts was the only one killed in a crash. Junior Johnson was in the crash but was not injured. Weatherly and Pardue both lost control on curves. Pardue's death came during a tire test. In a tire test, engineers from Firestone or Goodyear try out various tires on a car, and the driver, always one of the top competitors, tests them at top speed, usually on the Atlanta track. The drivers are paid three dollars a mile and may drive as much as five or six hundred miles in a single day. At 145 miles an hour average that does not take very long. Anyway, these drivers are going at speeds that, on curves, can tear tires off their casings or break axles. They practically run off from over their own wheels.

Junior Johnson was over in the garden by the house some years ago, plowing the garden barefooted, behind a mule, just wearing an old pair of overalls, when a couple of good old boys drove up and told him to come on up to the speedway and get in a stock car race. They wanted some local boys to race, as a preliminary to the main race, "as a kind of side show," as Junior remembers it.

"So I just put the reins down," Junior is telling me, "and rode on over 'ere with them. They didn't give us seat belts or nothing, they just roped us in. H'it was a dirt track then. I come in second."

Junior was a sensation in dirt-track racing right from the start. Instead of going into the curves and just sliding and holding on for dear life like the other drivers, Junior developed the technique of throwing himself into a slide about seventy-five feet before the curve by cocking the wheel to the left slightly and gunning it, using the slide, not the brake, to slow down, so that he could pick up speed again halfway through the curve and come out of it like a shot. This was known as his "power slide," and—yes! of course!—every good old boy in North Carolina started saying Junior Johnson had learned that stunt doing those goddamned *about-faces* running away from the Alcohol Tax agents. Junior put on such a show one night on a dirt track in Charlotte that he broke two axles, and he thought he was out of the race because he didn't have any more axles, when a good old boy came running up out of the infield and said, "Goddamn it, Junior Johnson, you take the axle off my car here, I got a Pontiac just like yours," and Junior took it off and put it on his and went out and broke *it* too.

Mother dog! To this day Junior Johnson loves dirt track racing like nothing else in this world, even though there is not much money in it. Every year he sets new dirt track speed records, such as at Hickory, North Carolina, one of the most popular dirt tracks, last spring. As far as Junior is concerned, dirt track racing is not so much of a mechanical test for the car as those long five- and six-hundred-mile races on asphalt are. Gasoline, tire and engine wear aren't so much of a problem. It is all the driver, his skill, his courage—his willingness to mix it up with the other cars, smash and carom off of them at a hundred miles an hour or so to get into the curves first. Junior has a lot of fond recollections of mixing it up at places like Bowman Gray Stadium in Winston-Salem, one of the minor league tracks, a very narrow track, hardly wide enough for two cars. "You could always figure Bowman Gray was gonna cost you two fenders, two doors and two quarter panels," Junior tells me with nostalgia.

Anyway, at Hickory, which was a Saturday night race, all the good old boys started pouring into the stands before sundown, so they wouldn't miss anything, the practice runs or the qualifying or anything. And pretty soon, the dew hasn't even started falling before Junior Johnson and David Pearson, one of Dodge's best drivers, are out there on practice runs, just warming up, and they happen to come up alongside each other on the second curve, and—the thing is, here are two men, each of them driving $15,000 automobiles, each of them standing to make $50,000 to $100,000 for the season if they don't get themselves killed, and they meet on a curve on a goddamned practice run on a dirt track, and neither of them can resist it. Coming out of the turn they go into a wildass race down the backstretch, both of them trying to get into the third turn first, and all the way across the infield you can hear them ricocheting off each other and bouncing at a hundred miles an hour on loose dirt, and then they go into ferocious power slides, red

dust all over the goddamned place, and then out of this goddamned red-dust cloud, out of the fourth turn, here comes
Junior Johnson first, like a shot, with Pearson right on his tail,
and the good old boys in the stands going wild, and the *qualifying* runs haven't started yet, let alone the race.

Junior worked his way up through the minor leagues, the
Sportsman and Modified classifications, as they are called,
winning championships in both, and won his first Grand National race, the big leagues, in 1955 at Hickory, on dirt. He was
becoming known as "the hardest of the hard-chargers," power
sliding, rooting them out of the groove, raising hell, and already the Junior Johnson legend was beginning.

He kept hard-charging, power sliding, going after other
drivers as though there wasn't room on the track but for one,
and became the most popular driver in stock car racing by
1959. The presence of Detroit and Detroit's big money had
begun to calm the drivers down a little. Detroit was concerned
about Image. The last great duel of the dying dog-eat-dog era
of stock car racing came in 1959, when Junior and Lee Petty,
who was then leading the league in points, had it out on the
Charlotte raceway. Junior was in the lead, and Petty was right
on his tail, but couldn't get by Junior. Junior kept coming out
of the curves faster. So every chance he got, Petty would get
up right on Junior's rear bumper and start banging it, gradually forcing the fender in to where the metal would cut Junior's
rear tire. With only a few laps to go, Junior had a blowout and
spun out up against the guardrail. That is Junior's version.
Petty claimed Junior hit a pop bottle and spun out. The fans in
Charlotte were always throwing pop bottles and other stuff
onto the track late in the race, looking for blood. In any case,
Junior eased back into the pits, had the tire changed, and
charged out after Petty. He caught him on a curve and—well,
whatever really happened, Petty was suddenly "up against the
wall" and out of the race, and Junior won.

What a howl went up. The Charlotte chief of police charged out onto the track after the race, according to Petty, and offered to have Junior arrested for "assault with a dangerous weapon," the hassling went on for weeks—

"Back then," Junior tells me, "when you got into a guy and racked him up, you might as well get ready, because he's coming back for you. H'it was dog eat dog. That straightened Lee Petty out right smart. They don't do stuff like that anymore, though, because the guys don't stand for it."

Anyway, the Junior Johnson legend kept building up and building up, and in 1960 it got hotter than ever when Junior won the biggest race of the year, the Daytona 500, by discovering a new technique called "drafting." That year stock car racing was full of big powerful Pontiacs manned by top drivers, and they would go like nothing else anybody ever saw. Junior went down to Daytona with a Chevrolet.

"My car was about ten miles an hour slower than the rest of the cars, the Pontiacs," Junior tells me. "In the preliminary races, the warmups and stuff like that, they was smoking me off the track. Then I remember once I went out for a practice run, and Fireball Roberts was out there in a Pontiac and I got in right behind him on a curve, right on his bumper. I knew I couldn't stay with him on the straightaway, but I came out of the curve fast, right in behind him, running flat out, and then I noticed a funny thing. As long as I stayed right in behind him, I noticed I picked up speed and stayed right with him and my car was going faster than it had ever gone before. I could tell on the tachometer. My car wasn't turning no more than 6000 before, but when I got into this drafting position, I was turning 6800 to 7000. H'it felt like the car was plumb off the ground, floating along."

"Drafting," it was discovered at Daytona, created a vacuum behind the lead car and both cars would go faster than they normally would. Junior "hitched rides" on the Pontiacs most of the afternoon, but was still second to Bobby Johns, the lead Pontiac. Then, late in the race, Johns got into a drafting position with a fellow Pontiac that was actually one lap behind him and the vacuum got so intense that the rear window blew out of Johns' car and he spun out and crashed and Junior won.

This made Junior the Lion Killer, the Little David of stock car racing, and his performance in the 1963 season made him even more so.

Junior raced for Chevrolet at Daytona in February, 1963, and set the all-time stock car speed record in a hundred-mile qualifying race, 164.083 miles an hour, twenty-one miles an hour faster than Parnelli Jones's winning time at Indianapolis that year. Junior topped that at Daytona in July of 1963, qualifying at 166.005 miles per hour in a five-mile run, the fastest that anyone had ever averaged that distance in a racing car of any type. Junior's Chevrolet lasted only twenty-six laps in the Daytona 500 in 1963, however. He went out with a broken push rod. Although Chevrolet announced they were pulling out of racing at this time, Junior took his car and started out on the wildest performance in the history of stock car racing. Chevrolet wouldn't give him a cent of backing. They wouldn't even speak to him on the telephone. Half the time he had to have his own parts made. Plymouth, Mercury, Dodge and Ford, meantime, were pouring more money than ever into stock car racing. Yet Junior won seven Grand National races out of the thirty-three he entered and led most others before mechanical trouble forced him out.

All the while, Junior was making record qualifying runs, year after year. In the usual type of qualifying run, a driver has the track to himself and makes two circuits, with the driver with the fastest average time getting the "pole" position for the start of the race. In a way this presents stock car danger in its purest form. Driving a stock car does not require much handling ability, at least not as compared to Grand Prix racing, because the tracks are simple banked ovals and there is almost no shifting of gears. So qualifying becomes a test of raw nerve—of how fast a man is willing to take a curve. Many of the top drivers in competition are poor at qualifying. In effect, they are willing to calculate their risks only against the risks the other drivers are taking. Junior takes the pure risk as no other driver has ever taken it.

"Pure" risk or total risk, whichever, Indianapolis and Grand Prix drivers have seldom been willing to face the challenge of Southern stock car driver. A. J. Foyt, last year's winner at Indianapolis, is one exception. He has raced against the Southerners and beaten them. Parnelli Jones has tried and fared badly. Driving "Southern style" has a quality that shakes a man up. The Southerners went on a tour of northern tracks last fall. They raced at Bridgehampton, New York, and went into the corners so hard the marshals stationed at each corner kept radioing frantically to the control booth: "They're going off the track. They're all going off the track!"

But this, Junior Johnson's last race in a Dodge, was not his day, neither for qualifying or racing. Lorenzen took the lead early and won the 250-mile race a lap ahead of the field. Junior finished third, but was never in contention for the lead.

"Come on, Junior, do my hand—"

Two or three hundred people come out of the stands and up out of the infield and onto the track to be around Junior Johnson. Junior is signing autographs in a neat left-handed script he has. It looks like it came right out of the Locker book. The girls! Levis, stretch pants, sneaky shorts, stretch jeans, they press into the crowd with lively narbs and try to get their hands up in front of Junior and say:

"Come on, Junior, do my hand!"

In order to do a hand, Junior has to hold the girl's hand in his right hand and then sign his name with a ball-point on the back of her hand.

"Junior, you got to do mine, too!"

"Put it on up here."

All the girls break into . . . smiles. Junior Johnson does a hand. Ah, sweet little cigarette-ad blonde! She says:

"Junior, why don't you ever call me up?"

"I 'spect you get plenty of calls 'thout me."

"Oh, Junior! You call me up, you hear now?"

But also a great many older people crowd in, and they say:

"Junior, you're doing a real good job out there, you're driving real good."

"Junior, when you get in that Ford, I want to see you pass that Freddie Lorenzen, you hear now?"

"Junior, you like that Ford better than that Dodge?"

And:

"Junior, here's a young man that's been waiting some time and wanting to see you—" and the man lifts up his little boy in the middle of the crowd and says: "I told you you'd see Junior Johnson. This here's Junior Johnson!"

The boy has a souvenir racing helmet on his head. He stares at Junior through a buttery face. Junior signs the program he has in his hand, and then the boy's mother says:

"Junior, I tell you right now, he's beside you all the way. He can't be moved."

And then:

"Junior, I want you to meet the meanest little girl in Wilkes County."

"She don't look mean to me."

Junior keeps signing autographs and over by the pits the other kids are all over his car, the Dodge. They start pulling off the decals, the ones saying Holly Farms Poultry and Autolite and God knows whatall. They fight over the strips, the shreds of decal, as if they were totems.

All this homage to Junior Johnson lasts about forty minutes. He must be signing about 250 autographs, but he is not a happy man. By and by the crowd is thinning out, the sun is going down, wind is blowing the Coca-Cola cups around, all one can hear, mostly, is a stock car engine starting up every now and then as somebody drives it up onto a truck or something, and Junior looks around and says:

"I'd rather lead one lap and fall out of the race than stroke it and finish in the money."

"Stroking it" is driving carefully in hopes of outlasting faster and more reckless cars. The opposite of stroking it is "hard-charging." Then Junior says:

"I hate to get whipped up here in Wilkes County, North Carolina."

Wilkes County, North Carolina! Who was it tried to pin the name on Wilkes County, "The bootleg capital of America"? This fellow Vance Packard. But just a minute. . . .

The night after the race Junior and his fiancée, Flossie Clark, and myself went into North Wilkesboro to have dinner. Junior and Flossie came by Lowes Motel and picked us up in the dreamboat white Pontiac. Flossie is a bright, attractive woman, *saftig*, well-organized. She and Junior have been going together since they were in high school. They are going to get married as soon as Junior gets his new house built. Flossie has been doing the decor. Junior Johnson, in the second-highest income bracket in the United States for the past five years, is moving out of his father's white frame house in Ingle Hollow at last. About three hundred yards down the road. Overlooking a lot of good green land and Anderson's grocery. Junior shows me through the house, it is almost finished, and when we get to the front door, I ask him, "How much of this land is yours?"

Junior looks around for a minute, and then back up the hill, up past his three automated chicken houses, and then down into the hollow over the pasture where his $3100 Santa Gertrudis bull is grazing, and then he says:

"Everything that's green is mine."

Junior Johnson's house is going to be one of the handsomest homes in Wilkes County. Yes. And—such complicated problems of class and status. Junior is not only a legendary figure as a backwoods boy with guts who made good, he is also popular personally, he is still a good old boy, rich as he is. He is also respected for the sound and sober way he has invested his money. He also has one of the best business connections in town, Holly Farms Poultry. What complicates it is that half the county, anyway, reveres him as the greatest, most fabled nightroad driver in the history of Southern bootlegging. There is hardly a living soul in the hollows who can conjure up two seconds' honest moral indignation over "the whiskey business." That is what they call it, "the whiskey business." The fact is, it has some positive political overtones, sort of like the I.R.A. in Ireland. The other half of the county—well, North Wilkesboro itself is a prosperous, good-looking town of 5,000, where a lot of hearty modern business burghers are making money the modern way, like everywhere else in the U.S.A., in things like banking, poultry processing, furniture, mirror, and carpet manufacture, apple growing, and so forth and so on. And one thing these men are tired of is Wilkes County's reputation as a center of moonshining. The U.S. Alcohol and Tobacco Tax agents sit over there in Wilkesboro, right next to North Wilkesboro, year in and year out, and they have been there since God knows when, like an Institution in the land, and every day that they are there, it is like a sign saying, Moonshine County. And even that is not so *bad*—it has nothing to do with it being immoral and only a little to do with it being illegal. The real thing is, it is—raw and hillbilly. And one thing thriving modern Industry is not is hillbilly. And one thing the burghers of

North Wilkesboro are not about to be is hillbilly. They have split-level homes that would knock your eyes out. Also swimming pools, white Buick Snatchwagons, flagstone *terrasse*-porches enclosed with louvered glass that opens wide in the summertime, and built-in brick barbecue pits and they give parties where they wear Bermuda shorts and Jax stretch pants and serve rum collins and play twist and bossa nova records on the hi-fi and tell Shaggy Dog jokes about strange people ordering martinis. Moonshining . . . just a minute—the truth is, North Wilkesboro. . . .

So we are all having dinner at one of the fine new restaurants in North Wilkesboro, a place of suburban plate-glass elegance. The manager knows Junior and gives us the best table in the place and comes over and talks to Junior a while about the race. A couple of men get up and come over and get Junior's autograph to take home to their sons and so forth. Then toward the end of the meal a couple of North Wilkesboro businessmen come over ("Junior, how are you, Junior. You think you're going to like that fast-backed Ford?") and Junior introduces them to me.

"You're not going to do like that fellow Vance Packard did, are you?"

"Vance Packard?"

"Yeah, I think it was Vance Packard wrote it. He wrote an article and called Wilkes County the bootleg capital of America. Don't pull any of that stuff. I think it was in *American* magazine. The bootleg capital of America. Don't pull any of that stuff on us."

I looked over at Junior and Flossie. Neither one of them said anything. They didn't even change their expressions.

The next morning I met Junior down in Ingle Hollow at Anderson's Store. That's about fifteen miles out of North Wilkesboro on County Road No. 2400. Junior is known in a lot of Southern newspapers as "the wild man from Ronda" or "the lead-footed chicken farmer from Ronda," but Ronda is only his post-office-box address. His telephone exchange, with the Wilkes Telephone Membership Corporation, is Clingman, North Carolina, and that isn't really where he lives either. Where he lives is just Ingle Hollow, and one of the communal centers of Ingle Hollow is Anderson's Store. Anderson's is not exactly a grocery store. Out front there are two gasoline pumps under an overhanging roof. Inside there are a lot of things like a soda-pop cooler filled with ice, Coca-Colas, Nehi drinks, Dr. Pepper, Double Cola, and a gumball machine, a lot of racks of Red Man chewing tobacco, Price's potato chips, OKay peanuts, cloth hats for working outdoors in, dried sausages, cigarettes, canned goods, a little bit of meal and flour, fly swatters, and I don't know what all. Inside and outside of Anderson's there are good old boys. The young ones tend to be inside, talking, and the old ones tend to be outside, sitting under the roof by the gasoline pumps, talking. And on both sides, cars; most of them new and pastel.

Junior drives up and gets out and looks up over the door where there is a row of twelve coon tails. Junior says:

"Two of them gone, ain't they?"

One of the good old boys says, "Yeah," and sighs.

A pause, and the other one says, "Somebody stole 'em."

Then the first one says, "Junior, that dog of yours ever come back?"

Junior says, "Not yet."

The second good old boy says, "You looking for her to come back?"

Junior says, "I reckon she'll come back."

The good old boy says, "I had a coon dog went off like that. They don't ever come back. I went out 'ere one day, back over yonder, and there he was, cut right from here to here. I swear if it don't look like a coon got him. Something. H'it must of turned him every way but loose."

Junior goes inside and gets a Coca-Cola and rings up the till himself, like everybody who goes into Anderson's does, it seems like. It is dead quiet in the hollow except for every now and then a car grinds over the dirt road and down the way. One coon dog missing. But he still has a lot of the black and tans, named Rock. . . .

. . . Rock, Whitey, Red, Buster are in the pen out back of the Johnson house, the old frame house. They have scars all over their faces from fighting coons. Gypsy has one huge gash in her back from fighting something. A red rooster crosses the lawn. That's a big rooster. Shirley, one of Junior's two younger sisters, pretty girls, is out by the fence in shorts, pulling weeds. Annie May is inside the house with Mrs. Johnson. Shirley has the radio outside on the porch aimed at her, The Four Seasons! "Dawn!—ahhhh, ahhhhh, ahhhhhh!" Then a lot of electronic wheeps and lulus and a screaming disc jockey, yessss! WTOB, the Vibrant Mothering Voice of Winston-Salem, North Carolina. It sounds like WABC in New York. Junior's mother, Mrs. Johnson, is a big, good-natured woman. She comes out and says, "Did you ever see anything like that in your life? Pullin' weeds listenin' to the radio." Junior's father, Robert Glenn Johnson, Sr.—he built this frame house about thirty-five years ago, up here where the gravel road ends and the woods starts. The road just peters out into the woods up a hill. The house has a living room, four bedrooms and a big kitchen. The living room is full of Junior's racing trophies, and so is the piano in Shirley's room. Junior was born and raised here with his older brothers, L. P., the oldest, and Fred, and his older sister, Ruth. Over yonder, up by that house, there's a man with a mule and a little plow. That's L. P. The Johnsons still keep that old mule around to plow the vegetable gardens. And all around, on all sides, like a rim are the ridges and the woods. Well, what about those woods, where Vance Packard said the agents come stealing over the ridges and good old boys go crashing through the underbrush to get away from the still and the women start "calling the cows" up and down the hollows as the signal *they were coming. . . .*

Junior motions his hand out toward the hills and says, "I'd say nearly everybody in a fifty-mile radius of here was in the whiskey business at one time or another. When we growed up here, everybody seemed to be more or less messing with whiskey, and myself and my two brothers did quite a bit of transporting. H'it was just a business, like any other business, far as we was concerned. H'it was a matter of survival. During the Depression here, people either had to do that or starve to death. H'it wasn't no gangster type of business or nothing. They's nobody that ever messed with it here that was ever out to hurt anybody. Even if they got caught, they never tried to shoot anybody or anything like that. Getting caught and pulling time, that was just part of it. H'it was just a business, like any other business. Me and my brothers, when we went out on the road at night, h'it was just like a milk run, far as we was concerned. They was certain deliveries to be made and. . . ."

A milk run—yes! Well, it was a business, all right. In fact, it was a regional industry, all up and down the Appalachian slopes. But never mind the Depression. It goes back a long way before that. The Scotch-Irish settled the mountains from Pennsylvania down to Alabama, and they have been making whiskey out there as long as anybody can remember. At first it was a simple matter of economics. The land had a low crop yield, compared to the lowlands, and even after a man struggled to grow his corn, or whatever, the cost of transporting it to the markets from down out of the hills was so great, it wasn't worth it. It was much more profitable to convert the corn into whiskey and sell that. The trouble started with the

Federal Government on that score almost the moment the Republic was founded. Alexander Hamilton put a high excise tax on whiskey in 1791, almost as soon as the Constitution was ratified. The "Whiskey Rebellion" broke out in the mountains of western Pennsylvania in 1794. The farmers were mad as hell over the tax. Fifteen thousand Federal troops marched out to the mountains and suppressed them. Almost at once, however, the trouble over the whiskey tax became a symbol of something bigger. This was a general enmity between the western and eastern sections of practically every seaboard state. Part of it was political. The eastern sections tended to control the legislatures, the economy and the law courts, and the western sections felt shortchanged. Part of it was cultural. Life in the western sections was rougher. Religions, codes and styles of life were sterner. Life in the eastern capitals seemed to give off the odor of Europe and decadence. Shay's Rebellion broke out in the Berkshire hills of western Massachusetts in 1786 in an attempt to shake off the yoke of Boston, which seemed as bad as George III's. To this day people in western Massachusetts make proposals, earnestly or with down-in-the-mouth humor, that they all ought to split off from "Boston." Whiskey—the mountain people went right on making it. Whole sections of the Appalachians were a whiskey belt, just as sections of Georgia, Alabama and Mississippi were a cotton belt. Nobody on either side ever had any moral delusions about why the Federal Government was against it. It was always the tax, pure and simple. Today the price of liquor is 60 per cent tax. Today, of course, with everybody gone wild over the subject of science and health, it has been much easier for the Federals to persuade people that they crack down on moonshine whiskey because it is dangerous, it poisons, kills and blinds people. The statistics are usually specious.

Moonshining was *illegal*, however, that was also the unvarnished truth. And that had a side effect in the whiskey belt.

The people there were already isolated, geographically, by the mountains and had strong clan ties because they were all from the same stock, Scotch-Irish. Moonshining isolated them even more. They always had to be careful who came up there. There are plenty of hollows to this day where if you drive in and ask some good old boy where so-and-so is, he'll tell you he never heard of the fellow. Then the next minute, if you identify yourself and give some idea of why you want to see him, and he believes you, he'll suddenly say, "Aw, you're talking about *so-and-so*. I thought you said—" With all this isolation, the mountain people began to take on certain characteristics normally associated, by the diffident civilizations of today, with tribes. There was a strong sense of family, clan and honor. People would cut and shoot each other up over honor. And physical courage! They were almost like Turks that way.

In the Korean War, there were seventy-eight Medal of Honor winners. Thirty-two of them were from the South, and practically all of the thirty-two were from small towns in or near the Appalachians. The New York metropolitan area, which has more people than all these towns put together, had three Medal of Honor winners, and one of them had just moved to New York from the Appalachian region of West Virginia. Three of the Medal of Honor winners came from within fifty miles of Junior Johnson's side porch.

Detroit has discovered these pockets of courage, almost like a natural resource, in the form of Junior Johnson and about twenty other drivers. There is something exquisitely ironic about it. Detroit is now engaged in the highly sophisticated business of offering the illusion of Speed for Everyman—making their cars go 175 miles an hour on racetracks—by discovering and putting behind the wheel a breed of mountain men who are living vestiges of a degree of physical courage that became extinct in most other sections of the country by 1900. Of course, very few stock car drivers have ever had anything to do with the whiskey business. A great many always lead quiet lives off the track. But it is the same strong people among whom the whiskey business developed who produced the kind of men who could drive the stock cars. There are a few exceptions, Freddie Lorenzen, from Elmhurst, Illinois, being the most notable. But, by and large, it is the rural Southern code of honor and courage that has produced these, the most daring men in sports.

Cars and bravery! The mountain-still operators had been running white liquor with hopped-up automobiles all during the thirties. But it was during the war that the business was so hot out of Wilkes County, down to Charlotte, High Point, Greensboro, Winston-Salem, Salisbury, places like that; a night's run, by one car, would bring anywhere from $500 to $1000. People had money all of a sudden. One car could carry twenty-two to twenty-five cases of white liquor. There were twelve half-gallon fruit jars full per case, so each load would have 132 gallons or more. It would sell to the distributor in the city for about ten dollars a gallon, when the market was good, of which the driver would get two dollars, as much as $300 for the night's work.

The usual arrangement in the white liquor industry was for the elders to design the distillery, supervise the formulas and the whole distilling process and take care of the business end of the operation. The young men did the heavy work, carrying the copper and other heavy goods out into the woods, building the still, hauling in fuel—and driving. Junior and his older brothers, L. P. and Fred, worked that way with their father, Robert Glenn Johnson, Sr.

Johnson, Senior, was one of the biggest individual copper-still operators in the area. The fourth time he was arrested, the agents found a small fourtune in working corn mash bubbling in the vats.

"My Daddy was always a hard worker," Junior is telling me.

"He always wanted something a little bit better. A lot of people resented that and held that against him, but what he got, he always got h'it by hard work. There ain't no harder work in the world than making whiskey. I don't know of any other business that compels you to get up at all times of night and go outdoors in the snow and everything else and work. H'it's the hardest way in the world to make a living, and I don't think anybody'd do it unless they had to."

Working mash wouldn't wait for a man. It started coming to a head when it got ready to and a man had to be there to take it off, out there in the woods, in the brush, in the brambles, in the muck, in the snow. Wouldn't it have been something if you could have just set it all up inside a good old shed with a corrugated metal roof and order those parts like you want them and not have to smuggle all that copper and all that sugar and all that everything out here in the woods and be a coppersmith and a plumber and a copper and a carpenter and a pack horse and every other goddamned thing God ever saw in this world, all at once.

And live decent hours—Junior and his brothers, about two o'clock in the morning they'd head out to the stash, the place where the liquor was hidden after it was made. Sometimes it would be somebody's house or an old shed or some place just out in the woods, and they'd make their arrangements out there, what the route was and who was getting how much liquor. There wasn't anything ever written down. Everything was cash on the spot. Different drivers liked to make the run at different times, but Junior and his brother always liked to start out from 3 to 4 A.M. But it got so no matter when you started out you didn't have those roads to yourself.

"Some guys liked one time and some guys liked another time," Junior is saying, "but starting about midnight they'd be coming out of the woods from every direction. Some nights the whole road was full of bootleggers. It got so some nights they'd be somebody following you going just as fast as you were and you didn't know who h'it was, the law or somebody else hauling whiskey."

And it was just a business, like any other business, just like a milk route—but this funny thing was happening. In those wild-ass times, with the money flush and good old boys from all over the country running that white liquor down the road ninety miles an hour and more than that if you try to crowd them a little bit—well, the funny thing was, it got to be competitive in an almost aesthetic, a pure sporting way. The way the good old boys got to hopping up their automobiles—it got to be a science practically. Everybody was looking to build a car faster than anybody ever had before. They practically got into industrial espionage over it. They'd come up behind one another on those wild-ass nights on the highway, roaring through the black gulches between the clay cuts and the trees, pretending like they were officers, just to challenge them, test them out, race . . . *pour le sport,* you mothers, careening through the darkness, old Carolina moon. All these cars were registered in phony names. If a man had to abandon one, they would find license plates that traced back to . . . nobody at all. It wasn't anything, particularly, to go down to the Motor Vehicle Bureau and get some license plates, as long as you paid your money. Of course, it's rougher now, with compulsory insurance. You have to have your insurance before you can get your license plates, and that leads to a lot of complications. Junior doesn't know what they do about that now. Anyway, all these cars with the magnificent engines were plain on the outside, so they wouldn't attract attention, but they couldn't disguise them altogether. They were jacked up a little in the back and had 8.00 or 8.20 tires, for the heavy loads, and the sound—

"They wasn't no way you could make it sound like an ordinary car," says Junior.

God-almighty, that sound in the middle of the night, groaning, roaring, humming down into the hollows, through the clay gulches—yes! And all over the rural South, hell, all over the South, the legends of wild-driving whiskey running got started. And it wasn't just the plain excitement of it. It was something deeper, the symbolism. It brought into a modern focus the whole business, one and a half centuries old, of the country people's rebellion against the Federals, against the seaboard establishment, their independence, their defiance of the outside world. And it was like a mythology for that and for something else that was happening, the whole wild thing of the car as the symbol of liberation in the postwar South.

"They was out about every night, patroling, the agents and the State Police was," Junior is saying, "but they seldom caught anybody. H'it was like the dogs chasing the fox. The dogs can't catch a fox, he'll just take 'em around in a circle all night long. I was never caught for transporting. We never lost but one car and the axle broke on h'it."

The fox and the dogs! Whiskey running certainly had a crazy gamelike quality about it, considering that a boy might be sent up for two years or more if he were caught transporting. But these boys were just wild enough for that. There got to be a code about the chase. In Wilkes County nobody, neither the good old boys or the agents, ever did anything that was going to hurt the other side physically. There was supposed to be some parts of the South where the boys used smoke screens and tack buckets. They had attachments in the rear of the cars, and if the agents got too close they would let loose a smoke screen to blind them or a slew of tacks to make them blow a tire. But nobody in Wilkes County ever did that because that was a good way for somebody to get killed. Part of it was that whenever an agent did get killed in the South, whole hordes of agents would come in from Washington and pretty soon they would be tramping along the ridges practically inch by inch, smoking out the stills. But mainly it was—well, the code. If you got caught, you went along peaceably, and the agents never used their guns. There were some tense times. Once was when the agents started using tack belts in Iredell County. This was a long strip of leather studded with nails that the agents would lay across the road in the dark. A man couldn't see it until it was too late and he stood a good chance of getting killed if it got his tires and spun him out. The other was the time the State Police put a roadblock down there at that damned bridge at Millersville to catch a couple of escaped convicts. Well, a couple of good old boys rode up with a load, and there was the roadblock and they were already on the bridge, so they jumped out and dove into the water. The police saw two men jump out of their car and dive in the water, so they opened fire and they shot one good old boy in the backside. As they pulled him out, he kept saying.

"What did you have to shoot at me for? What did you have to shoot at me for?"

It wasn't pain, it wasn't anguish, it wasn't anger. It was consternation. The bastards had broken the code.

Then the Federals started getting radio cars.

"The radios didn't do them any good," Junior says, "As soon as the officers got radios, then *they* got radios. They'd go out and get the same radio. H'it was an awful hard thing for them to radio them down. They'd just listen in on the radio and see where they're setting up the roadblocks and go a different way."

And such different ways. The good old boys knew back roads, dirt roads, up people's backlanes and every which way, and an agent would have to live in the North Carolina hills a lifetime to get to know them. There wasn't hardly a stretch of road on any of the routes where a good old boy couldn't duck off the road and into the backcountry if he had to. They had wild detours around practically every town and every intersection in the region. And for tight spots—the legendary devices, the "bootleg slide," the siren and the red light. . . .

It was just a matter of keeping up with the competition. You always have to have the latest equipment. It was a business thing, like any other business, you have to stay on top—"They was some guys who was more dependable, they done a better job"—and it may have been business to Junior, but it wasn't business to a generation of good old boys growing up all over the South. The Wilkes County bootleg cars started picking up popular names in a kind of folk hero worship—"The Black Ghost," "The Grey Ghost," which were two of Junior's, "Old Mother Goose," "The Midnight Traveler," "Old Faithful."

And then one day in 1955 some agents snuck over the ridges and caught Junior Johnson at his daddy's still. Junior Johnson, the man couldn't *any*body catch!

The arrest caught Junior just as he was ready to really take off in his career as a stock car driver. Junior says he hadn't been in the whiskey business in any shape or form, hadn't run a load of whiskey for two or three years, when he was arrested. He says he didn't need to fool around with running whiskey after he got into stock car racing, he was making enough money at that. He was just out there at the still helping his daddy with some of the heavy labor, there wasn't a good old boy in Ingle Hollow who wouldn't help his daddy lug those big old cords of ash wood, it doesn't give off much smoke, out in the woods. Junior was sentenced to two years in the Federal reformatory in Chillicothe, Ohio.

"If the law felt I should have gone to jail, that's fine and dandy," Junior tells me. "But I don't think the true facts of the case justified the sentence I got. I never had been arrested in my life. I think they was punishing me for the past. People get a kick out of it because the officers can't catch somebody, and this angers them. Soon as I started getting publicity for racing, they started making it real hot for my family. I was out of the whiskey business, and they knew that, but they was just waiting to catch me on something. I got out after serving ten months and three days of the sentence, but h'it was two or three years I was set back, about half of fifty-six and every bit of fifty-seven. H'it takes a year to really get back into h'it after something like that. I think I lost the prime of my racing career. I feel that if I had been given the chance I feel I was due, rather than the sentence I got, my life would have got a real boost."

But, if anything, the arrest only made the Junior Johnson legend hotter.

And all the while Detroit kept edging the speeds up, from 150 m.p.h. in 1960 to 155 to 165 to 175 to 180 flat out on the longest straightaway, and the good old boys of Southern stock car racing stuck right with it. Any speed Detroit would give them they would take right with them into the curve, hard-charging even though they began to feel strange things such as the rubber starting to pull right off the tire casing. And God! Good old boys from all over the South roared together after the Stanchion—Speed! Guts!—pouring into Birmingham, Daytona Beach, Randleman, North Carolina; Spartanburg, South Carolina; Weaverville, Hillsboro, North Carolina; Atlanta, Hickory, Bristol, Tennessee; Augusta, Georgia; Richmond, Virginia; Asheville, North Carolina; Charlotte, Myrtle Beach—tens of thousands of them. And still upper- and middle-class America, even in the South, keeps its eyes averted. Who cares! They kept on heading out where we all live, after all, out amongst the Drive-ins, white-enameled filling stations, concrete aprons, shopping-plaza apothecaries, show-window steak houses, Burger-Ramas, Bar-B-Cubicles and Miami aqua-swimming-pool motor inns, on out the highway . . . even outside a town like Darlington, a town of 10,000 souls, God, here they come, down route 52, up 401, on 340, 151 and 34, on through the South Carolina lespedeza fields. By Friday night already the good old boys are pulling the infield of the Darlington raceway with those blazing pastel dreamboats stacked this way and that on the clay flat and the tubular terrace furniture and the sleeping bags and the Thermos jugs and the brown whiskey bottles coming on out. By Sunday—the race!—there are 65,000 piled into the racetrack at Darlington. The sheriff, as always, sets up the jail right there in the infield. No use trying to haul them out of there. And now—the *sound* rises up inside the raceway, and a good old boy named Ralph goes mad and starts selling chances on his Dodge. Twenty-five cents and you can take the sledge he has and smash his car anywhere you want. How they roar when the windshield breaks! The police could interfere, you know, but they are busy chasing a good old girl who is playing Lady Godiva on a hogbacked motorcycle, naked as sin, hauling around and in and out of the clay ruts.

Eyes averted, happy burghers. On Monday the ads start appearing—for Ford, for Plymouth, for Dodge—announcing that we gave it to you, speed such as you never saw. There it was! At Darlington, Daytona, Atlanta—and not merely in the Southern papers but in the albino pages of the suburban women's magazines, such as *The New Yorker*, in color—the Ford winners, such as Fireball Roberts, grinning with a cigar in his mouth in *The New Yorker* magazine. And somewhere, some Monday morning, Jim Pascal of High Point, Ned Jarrett of Boykin, Cale Yarborough of Timmonsville and Curtis Crider from Charlotte, Bobby Isaac of Catawba, E. J. Trivette of Deep Gap, Richard Petty of Randleman, Tiny Lund of Cross, South Carolina; Stick Elliott of Shelby—and from out of Ingle Hollow—

And all the while, standing by in full Shy, in alumicron suits—there is Detroit, hardly able to believe itself what it has discovered, a breed of good old boys from the fastnesses of the Appalachian hills and flats—a handful from this rare breed—who have given Detroit . . . speed . . . and the industry can present it to a whole generation as . . . yours. And the

Detroit P.R. men themselves come to the tracks like folk wor-
shipers and the millions go giddy with the thrill of speed. Only
Junior Johnson goes about it as if it were . . . the usual. Junior goes on down to Atlanta for the Dixie 400 and drops by the
Federal penitentiary to see his Daddy. His Daddy is in on his
fifth illegal distillery conviction; in the whiskey business that's
just part of it; an able craftsman, an able businessman, and the
law kept hounding him, that was all. So Junior drops by and
then goes on out to the track and gets in his new Ford and sets
the qualifying speed record for Atlanta Dixie 400, 146.301
m.p.h.; later on he tools on back up the road to Ingle Hollow
to tend to the automatic chicken houses and the road-grading
operation. Yes.

Yet how can you tell that to . . . anybody . . . out on the
bottom of that bowl as the motor thunder begins to lift up
through him like a sigh and his eyeballs glaze over and his
hands reach up and there, riding the rim of the bowl, soaring
over the ridges, is Junior's yellow Ford . . . which is his white
Chevrolet . . . which is a White Ghost, forever rousing the
good old boys . . . hard-charging! . . . up with the automobile into their America, and the hell with arteriosclerotic old
boys trying to hold onto the whole pot with arms of cotton
seersucker. Junior!

9

Loverboy of the Bourgeoisie

On their way into the Edwardian Room of the Plaza Hotel all they had was that sort of dutiful, forward-tilted gait that East Side dowagers get after twenty years of walking small dogs up and down Park Avenue. But on their way out the two of them discover that all this time, in the same room, there has been their dreamboat, Cary Grant, sitting in the corner. Actually, Grant had the logistics of the Edwardian Room figured out pretty well. In the first place, the people who come to the Plaza for lunch are not generally the kind who are going to rise up and run, skipping and screaming, over to some movie star's table. And in the second place, he is sitting up against the wall nearest the doorway. He is eating lunch, consisting of a single bowl of Vichyssoise, facing out the window towards three old boys in silk toppers moseying around their horses and hansoms on 59th Street on the edge of Central Park.

Well, so much for logistics. The two old girls work up all the courage they need in about one-fourth of a second.

"Cary Grant!" says the first one, coming right up and putting one hand on his shoulder. "Look at you! I just had to come over here and touch you!"

Cary Grant plays a wonderful Cary Grant. He cocks his head and gives her the Cary Grant mock-quizzical look—just like he does in the movies—the look that says, "I don't know what's happening, but we're not going to take it very seriously, are we? Or are we?"

"I have a son who's the spitting image of you," she is saying.

Cary Grant is staring at her hand on his shoulder and giving her the Cary Grant fey-bemused look and saying, "Are you trying to hold me down?"

"My son is forty-nine," she's saying. "How old are you?"

"I'm fifty-nine," says Cary Grant.

"*Fifty-nine!* Well, he's forty-nine and he's the spitting image of you, except that he looks *older* than you!"

By this time the other old girl is firmly planted, and she says: "I don't care if you hate me, I'm going to stand here and *look* at you."

"Why on earth should I hate you?" says Cary Grant.

"You can say things about me after I'm gone. I don't care, I'm going to stand here and look at you!"

"You poor dear!"

Which she does, all right. She takes it all in; the cleft chin; this great sun tan that looks like it was done on a rotisserie; this great head of steel-gray hair, of which his barber says: "It's real; I swear, I yanked it once"; and the Cary Grant clothes, all worsteds, broadcloths and silks, all rich and underplayed, like a viola ensemble.

"Poor baby," says Cary Grant, returning to the Vichyssoise.

"She meets some one for the first time and already she's saying, 'I don't care if you hate me.' Can you imagine? Can you imagine what must have gone into making someone feel that way?"

Well, whatever it was, poor old baby knows that Cary Grant is one leading man who, at least, might give it a second thought. Somehow Cary Grant, they figure, is the one dreamboat that a lady can walk right up to and touch, pour soul over and commune with.

And by the time Grant's picture, "Charade," with Audrey Hepburn, had its première at the Radio City Music Hall, thousands turned out in lines along 50th Street and Sixth Avenue, many of them in the chill of 6 A.M., in order to get an early seat. This was Grant's 61st motion picture and his 26th to open at Radio City. He is, indeed, fifty-nine years old, but his drawing power as a leading man, perhaps the last of the genuine "matinee idols," keeps mounting toward some incredible, golden-aged crest. Radio City is like a Nielsen rating for motion pictures. It has a huge seating capacity and is attended by at least as many tourists, from all over the country, as New Yorkers. Grant's first 25 premiers there played a total of 99 weeks. Each one seems to break the records all over again. Before "Charade," "That Touch of Mink," with Doris Day, played there for 10 weeks and grossed $1,886,427.

And the secret of it all is somehow tied up with the way he lit up two aging dolls in the Edwardian Room at the Plaza Hotel. In an era of Brandoism and the Mitchumism in movie heroes, Hollywood has left Cary Grant, by default, in sole possession of what has turned out to be a curiously potent device. Which is to say, to women he is Hollywood's lone example of the Sexy Gentleman. And to men and women, he is Hollywood's lone example of a figure America, like most of the West, has needed all along: a Romantic Bourgeois Hero.

One has only to think of what the rest of Hollywood and the international film industry, for that matter, have been up to since World War II. The key image in film heroes has certainly been that of Marlon Brando. One has only to list the male stars of the past 20 years—Brando, Rock Hudson, Kirk Douglas, John Wayne, Burt Lancaster, Robert Mitchum, Victor Mature, William Holden, Frank Sinatra—and already the mind is overpowered by an awesome montage of swung fists, bent teeth, curled lips, popping neck veins, and gurglings. As often as not the Brandoesque hero's love partner is some thyroid hoyden, as portrayed by Brigitte Bardot, Marilyn Monroe, Jayne Mansfield, Gina Lollobrigida or, more recently, Sue Lyons and Tuesday Weld. The upshot has been the era of Rake-a-Cheek Romance on the screen. Man meets woman. She rakes his cheek with her fingernails. He belts her in the chops. They fall in a wallow of passion.

The spirit of these romances, as in so many of the early Brando, James Dean and Rock Hudson pictures, has been borrowed from what Hollywood imagines to be the beer-and-guts verve of the guys-and-dolls lower classes. Undoubtedly, the rawness, the lubricity, the implicit sadism of it has excited moviegoers of all classes. Yet it should be clear even to Hollywood how many Americans, at rock bottom, can find no lasting identification with it. The number of American men who can really picture themselves coping with a little bleached hellion who is about to rake a cheek and draw blood with the first kiss is probably embarrassingly small. And there are probably not many more women who really wish to see Mister Right advancing toward them in a torn strap-style undershirt with his latissimae dorsae flexed.

After all, this is a nation that, except for a hard core of winos at the bottom and a hard crust of aristocrats at the top, has been going gloriously middle class for two decades, as far as the breezeways stretch. There is no telling how many millions of American women of the new era know exactly what Ingrid Bergman meant when she said she loved playing opposite

Cary Grant in "Notorious" (1946): "I didn't have to take my shoes off in the love scenes."

Yet "Notorious," one will recall, was regarded as a highly sexy motion picture. The Grant plot formula—which he has repeated at intervals for 25 years—has established him as the consummate bourgeois lover: consummately romantic and yet consummately genteel. Grant's conduct during a screen romance is unfailingly of the sort that would inspire trust and delight, but first of all trust, in a middle-class woman of any age. Not only does Grant spare his heroines any frontal assault on their foundation garments, he seldom chases them at all at the outset. In fact, the Grant plot formula calls for a reverse chase. First the girl—Audrey Hepburn in "Charade," Grace Kelly in "To Catch a Thief," Betsy Drake in "Every Girl Should Be Married"—falls for Grant. He retreats, but always slowly and coyly, enough to make the outcome clear. Grant, the screen lover, and Grant, the man, were perfectly combined under the escutcheon of the middle-class American woman— "Every Girl Should Be Married"—when Grant married Betsy Drake in real life.

During the chase Grant inevitably scores still more heavily with the middle-class female psyche by treating the heroine not merely as an attractive woman but as a witty and intelligent woman. And, indeed, whether he is with Katharine Hepburn or Audrey Hepburn or Irene Dunne or Doris Day, both parties are batting incredibly bright lines back and forth, and halfway through the film they are already too maniacally witty not to click one way or another.

Because of the savoir faire, genial cynicism and Carlyle Hotel lounge accent with which he brings it all off, Grant is often thought of as an aristocratic motion picture figure. In fact, however, the typical Grant role is that of an exciting bourgeois. In "Charade" he is a foreign service officer in Paris; in "Bringing Up Baby" he was a research professor; in "Mr.

Blandings Builds His Dream House" he was an enthusiastic suburbanite; and in countless pictures—among them "Crisis," "People Will Talk," "Kiss and Make Up"—he was in the most revered middle-class role of them all, exploited so successfully by television over the past three years: the doctor. Seldom is Grant portrayed as a lower-class figure—he did not make a good beatnik Cockney in "None But the Lonely Heart"—and rarely is he anything so formidable as the trucking tycoon he played in "Born To Be Bad" in 1934. The perfect Grant role is one in which he has a job that gives him enough free time so that he does not have to languish away at the office during the course of the movie; but he has the job and a visible means of support and highly visible bourgeois respectability all the same.

Grant, of course, has had no Hollywood monopoly on either savoir faire or gentility on the screen. Many suave, humorous gentlemen come to mind: Jimmy Stewart, David Niven, Fred Astaire, Ronald Colman, Franchot Tone. None of them, however, could approach Grant in that other part of being the world's best bourgeois romantic: viz., sex appeal. It was Cary Grant that Mae West was talking about when she launched the phrase "tall, dark and handsome" in "She Done Him Wrong" (1933), and it was Cary Grant who was invited up to see her sometime. Even at age fifty-nine, the man still has the flawless squared-off face of a comic strip hero, a large muscular neck and an athletic physique which he still exhibits in at least one scene in each picture. Every good American girl wants to marry a doctor. But a Dr. Dreamboat? Is it too much to hope for? Well, that is what Cary Grant is there for.

So Cary Grant keeps pouring it on, acting out what in the Age of Brando seems like the most unlikely role in the world: the loverboy of the bourgeoisie. The upshot has been intriguing. In 1948, at the age of forty-four he came in fourth in the box-office poll of male star popularity, behind Clark Gable, Gary Cooper and Bing Crosby. By 1958, when he was fifty-four, he had risen to No. 1. This fall—when he was fifty-nine—the motion picture Theater Owners Association named him as the No. 1 box-office attraction, male or female.

Well, the two old dolls had left, and the next crisis in the Edwardian Room was that an Italian starlet had walked in, a kind of tabescent bijou blonde. Old Cary Grant knows he has met her somewhere, but he will be damned if he can remember who she was. His only hope is that she won't see him, so he has his head tucked down to one side in his Cary Grant caught-out-on-a-limb look.

He can't keep that up forever, so he keeps his head turned by talking to the fellow next to him, who has on a wild solarocloth suit with a step-collared vest.

"Acting styles go in fads," Cary Grant is saying. "It's like girls at a dance. One night a fellow walks in wearing a motorcycle jacket and blue jeans and he takes the first girl he sees and embraces her and crushes her rib cage. 'What a man!' all the girls say, and pretty soon all the boys are coming to the dances in motorcycle jackets and blue jeans and taking direct action. That goes on for a while, and then one night in comes a fellow in a blue suit who can wear a necktie without strangling, carrying a bouquet of flowers. Do they still have bouquets of flowers? I'm sure they do. Well, anyway, now the girls say, 'What a charmer!' and they're off on another cycle. Or something like that.

"Well, as for me, I just keep going along the same old way," says Cary Grant with his Cary Grant let's-not-get-all-wrapped-up-in-it look.

But now that the secret is out, the prospects are almost forbidding. Think of all those Actors Studio people trussed up in worsted, strangling on Foulard silk, speaking through the mouth instead of the nose, talking nice to love-stricken old ladies in the Edwardian Room of the Plaza Hotel. The mind boggles, baby.

10

Purveyor of the Public Life

Up there in the office at Broadway and 52nd Street during the last days of *Confidential,* the old *Confidential* (1952–58), the most scandalous scandal magazine in the history of the world, everybody seemed to be richocheting around amid the dolly lights and cracking up. Everybody, save one, namely, Robert Harrison himself, the publisher. Jay Breen's liver had gone into its last necrotic, cirrhotic foliation. Jay Breen used to write half the magazine, but it had gotten to the point where Breen couldn't stand to listen to the Reader anymore. Breen and his wife would come in and sit in the next room while the Reader read the stories for the next issue out loud. The Reader, whatever his name was, had a truly great voice, like Sir Ralph

Richardson reading Lear soliloquies at a Bauhaus Modern lec‑
tern under a spotlight. Great diction, great resonance, etc.
Harrison hired him just to read out loud. Harrison had a the‑
ory that if you read the stories out loud, every weak spot in a
story would stand out. So there would be the Reader with a
voice like Sir Ralph Richardson enunciating such works as
"Errol Flynn and His Two-Way Mirror," "White Women
Broke Up My Marriage" [to a Negro entertainer], and "How
Mike Todd Made a Chump of a Movie Mogul." One of the
writers would be in there muttering away because he claimed
that the Reader had it in for him and was blundering over his
best-turned phrases on purpose, thereby causing Harrison to
throw whole stories out. But Jay Breen was long, long past all
that, and presently he died, of cirrhosis of the liver. Mean‑
while, Howard Rushmore, the editor, was beginning to look
awful. He used to be such a big robust guy, and now he looked
like a couple of eye sockets mounted on a piece of modern
solder sculpture. Rushmore was an ex-Communist and a com‑
plex person. He had a talent for gossip stories, but somehow it
was all wrapped up with the anti-Communist crusade he was
carrying on. There came a day when Rushmore and his wife
were riding in a cab on the upper East Side and he took out a
revolver and shot her to death and then shot himself to death.
Harrison was the publisher of *Confidential* and he remem‑
bered that day very well. He had just come into Idlewild
Airport from someplace and gotten into a cab. The first he
heard about Rushmore was when the cabdriver said, "Hey, did
you hear that? The publisher of *Confidential* just shot himself!"

"The publisher of *Confidential*," says Harrison, the publisher
of *Confidential*. "Where did the publisher of *Confidential* shoot
himself?"

"In the head, in a cab," says the cabdriver. "He shot himself
through the head, right in the back of a cab!"

Harrison remembers that, well, here he was, right in the

back of a cab, and he didn't have the slightest inclination to pull a gun on anybody inside or outside a cab. It had been wild for a while, forty million dollars' worth of libel suits, the whole movie industry had been after him, jukebox gangsters or somebody like that had hung him upside down by his heels out his office window, Congressmen and half the newspapers in the country were crucifying him, some guy from Chicago was going to fly in and break every bone in his body, starting with his fingers and toes—but that was all pressure from outside. Inside, he wasn't drowning in his own turbulent juices like Breen or Rushmore. He was serene, and *Confidential* was beautiful. This may be a hard idea to put across—the way Harrison found *Confidential* beautiful. But the fact is, the man is an aesthete, the original *aesthete du schlock.*

At the outset all I knew about Harrison was that he was living under an assumed name in a place called the Hotel Madison. To imagine the kind of picture that brought to mind, all you have to think of was the libel suits, the outrage, all the big people who were after him in 1957 when he sold *Confidential* and dropped from view. They must have crushed him like a Phrygian sacrifice. So the picture I had of Robert Harrison, the ex-publisher of *Confidential,* in someplace called the Hotel Madison was of a skulking fifty-nine-year-old man holed up in a hotel room where the view was a close-up of the air-conditioning duct of the short-order restaurant out back, hung with heavy-duty New York lint in clots like Spanish moss. That was until I saw the Madison, Reggie, Lately Miss BMC of Canada, and Harrison's cravat.

The Madison, on East 58th Street, between Fifth and Madison, turned out to be a fairly posh and conservative old place full of big cooperative apartments and a lobby with plum and umber walls and servitors in white dickies. Harrison's sister, Helen, a polite, quiet woman with grey-blonde hair who has been his personal secretary all these years, opened the door, and there was what I later learned was the very same apartment he had lived in during the heyday of *Confidential*. It has a thirty-foot living room all buttressed with yards of faceted mirrors, a bar with hilarious novelties on it, a pygmy tropical tree with a wooden ape hanging in the branches, ochre-colored neo-Moloch art objects, black and tan furniture, the total effect being the decorator style known as Malay Peninsula Modern. Pretty soon, out of one of the two side rooms, came Harrison, trampling through the wall-to-wall and tying the cravat.

"Have you had breakfast yet?" he says. It was one in the afternoon. "I've been on this goddamned diet. Let's go to Lindy's, I can't stand it anymore. I lost two pounds. I got to have something to eat, some of that fish or something; you know, lox."

Judging from his 1957 pictures, Harrison, now fifty-nine and grey-haired, may have a little more heft in the bags above and below the eyes, and a little more erosion in the jowls, but he is wearing his hair combed back long and on the rakish side, like Jon Hall in *The Hurricane*, and he has this silk cravat debouching like mad from the throat of his sports shirt. Furthermore, he still has a Broadway promoter's accent, the kind that seems to be created by hidden pistons, and one of those voices that comes from back in the throat as if it has been mellow-cured like a Dr. Grabow pipe.

And then, from exactly where I forget, materializes Reggie, a blonde. Reggie is one of these girls who strikes you as more of an ensemble, a chorus, a tableau, an opulent colonial animal, than as one person. She has great blonde bouffant hair, a coat of white fur whose locks fluff out wider than she is tall, and a dog, a toy greyhound named Tessie. Reggie and Helen get into a discussion about the dog's recent alimentary history to see if it will be safe to leave it in the apartment with Helen while Reggie, Harrison and I go off to Lindy's. The dog looks just like a racing greyhound except that it is two feet long and wears a town coat.

While they're talking, Harrison shows me a copy of his latest enterprise, a newspaper he started last year called *Inside News*.

"What do you think of it?" he says.

Obviously, from the tone he is not asking if I felt all informed by its inside news or was even entertained by it. It is an aesthetic question, as if he were showing me a Hiroshige print he just bought. The front-page headline in the newspaper is set in a great burst of red and says: "Castro's Sex Invasion of Washington." The story postulates—that seems to be the word for it—that Castro is planning to smuggle a lot of Christine Keelers into Washington to ruin the careers of prominent officials—and features a picture of a girl in a checkerboard bikini and these odd shoes: "The Castro cutie who could change Capitol Hill into Fanny Hill. Pics smuggled from Cuba by writer," one "Marc Thorez." The picture reveals mainly that Castro has stockpiled a pair of six-inch spiked-heel shoes of the sort that turned up in the girlie magazines Harrison used to publish in the Forties.

"This is going to be bigger than *Confidential*," says Harrison. "The keyhole stuff is dead. The big thing now is getting behind the news. This is going to be big. What's his name, the big Hollywood producer, he drives up here to the newsstand every week in a limousine just to get *Inside News*. I see him every week. He comes up in a limousine and he doesn't reach out for it. He gets out of the car and goes over and picks it up himself. Now, I think that's a goddamned compliment!"

From Harrison's face you can see that here is a man who is still trying to free his features from the sebaceous stickum of having just woke up, but he is already on the move. The old *aesthetique du schlock* is already stirred up and he is already thinking about his own story, the story about him and *Confidential*.

"I think I've got a story angle for you," he says. "The angle I like is, 'Now It Can Be Told.' You know? Of course, you guys probably have your own ideas about it, but that's the way I see it—'Now It Can Be Told.' "

And as the day wore on, you could see the first splash of red with a montage of photographs, tabloid headlines and feverish brush script over it, saying something like "Now It Can Be Told—'Inside' *Confidential!*" Harrison always liked to begin a story like that, with a layout with a big stretch of red and a lot of pictures and lettering and type faces exploding on top of it. Actually, he would probably see it not as an article but a whole one-shot. A one-shot is a magazine, or a book in magazine form, that is published just once, to capitalize on some celebrity or current event. James Dean, the movie actor, dies and a lot of one-shots come out, with titles like *The James Dean Story, The Real James Dean, James Dean Lives!* or just *James Dean.* One-shots have been among Harrison's enterprises since he sold *Confidential* in 1958. He has put out one-shots like *Menace of the Sex Deviates, New York Confidential, That Man Paar,* as well as *Naked New York.* You can almost see Harrison putting together the stories for "Now It Can Be Told." The lead piece would no doubt be called: "How *Confidential* Got Those 'Prying' Stories—from the Stars Themselves!" And there would be another big one entitled, "Why I've Started *Inside News*—To Prove I Can Do It Again!" by Bob Harrison.

And along about then Helen comes into the living room from the room they use as an office. She has a worried look on her face.

"What's wrong?" Harrison says.

"Oh, I don't know," Helen says. "Why are you bringing up all that?"

"It's all the truth, isn't it?"

"Yes, but it's all over. That's the past. It's finished. *Confi-*

dential is over. I don't know, I just don't like to bring it all up again."

"Why not?" said Harrison. "I'm not ashamed of anything I ever did!"

Helen says in a weary voice, as if to say, That's not even the point, "But what about _____?"

"He was a nice guy," Harrison says. "I liked him."

"What do you mean, *was*," Helen says. "What is he going to say if he reads about this. You had an agreement."

"That was a long time ago," Harrison says. "Anyway, he admits it. He's writing a book and he admits I gave him his real start in his career, the publicity he got in *Confidential*. He admits it."

"What about Mike Todd, and Cohn, that was part of the agreement."

"They're both dead," says Harrison. "Besides, that was a very amusing story. Nobody got hurt."

"Still . . . " says Helen, and then she just sighs.

Then he says, "Let's go to Lindy's. You go to Lindy's much?" I had never been in there. "How long have you been in New York? You ought to start getting around to places like that. That's where everybody is."

A couple of minutes later we all—Harrison, Reggie and the dog, and myself—get into a cab, and Harrison sinks back and says, "Lindy's."

The cabbie gets that bemused, Jell-O-faced look that New York cabdrivers get when they are stumped and they have to admit it.

"Let's see," he says, "where is that, again?"

"Where is Lindy's!" Harrison says in his Dr. Grabow voice. "What the hell is happening in this goddamned town!"

At Lindy's there is trouble right away about the dog. Harrison and Reggie were counting on it being Sunday and things are slow. But the maître d' at Lindy's says it is true that this is Sunday and things are slow and he still can't let any dogs in; there is a law. One trouble, I think, is that the dog has this fey grin on his face. Harrison weighs the whole thing on the scales of life and does not protest. Reggie leaves in her remarkable profusion of hair, fur and toy greyhound to take the dog back to the apartment, but she will be back. Well, that is just a setback, that is all. Harrison gets a table where he wants it, over to one side where everything is orange curves decorated with stylized emblems of such things as martinis, trombones, and pretty girls, all set at a swingy angle that reminds you of the Busy City music from the opening montage of a Fred Astaire-Ginger Rogers movie. Harrison takes a seat where he can see the door. One of the waiters comes up and says, "Mr. Harrison! How are you? You look like a million dollars!"

"I must be living right," says Harrison. "I've been on this goddamned diet. I can't stand it anymore. That's why I came over here. Has Walter been in?"

Walter hasn't been in.

"Do you know Winchell?" Harrison asks me. "No? You ought to meet him. He's a terrific guy. He's the one who really put *Confidential* over."

The waiter is saying, "Now all you need is a couple of good-looking broads and it will be just like old times."

Harrison says, "Well, you just keep your eyes open in a minute."

The great pink-orange slabs of lox, the bagels, the butter and the cups of coffee start coming, and Harrison pitches in, and to hell with the diet. Lindy's is not crowded, but people are starting to crane around to look at Harrison. A lot of people remember *Confidential*, if not Harrison himself, and in any case the word is going around the restaurant that the publisher of *Confidential* in its most notorious days is there, and everyone has a look on the face that says, in indignation or stupefaction, How did that guy get out from under the deluge and come in here to feast on all that orange-blossomy lox?

"You want to know what happened to the libel suits?" Harrison says. "Nothing happened, that's what happened." [Harrison has a tendency toward oversimplification. Some suits against *Confidential* resulted in substantial settlements.] "Forty million dollars and nothing happened. It was all a show. They loved it. I was the one who took all the responsibility. I was the one who got crucified. I was terribly condemned. And all the time some big shots were giving me the stories themselves!"

"The movie stars were giving you scandal stories about themselves?"

"That's what I'm trying to explain," Harrison says. "That's how we used to get them! From the big shots! And I was the one who always took the rap. I couldn't tell the world then, because it would jeopardize someone's standing. I'll tell you, _____ sat right there in my living room and gave me two stories about himself. We had already run one about him and an actress, I forget where we got that one. But he was up in my living room. The deal was, he would give me the stories, but 'I'll deny the whole thing,' he says.

"And Mike Todd. I knew Mike. I'll tell you a funny story about him. Mike Todd called me up from California to give me a story about Harry Cohn. Cohn was a big producer at Columbia Pictures. Mike Todd says, 'I'll meet you at the Stork Club, I'll meet you tonight, I've got a great story for you.' So he flew all the way to New York and he gave me this story about Harry Cohn.

"There was this girl who wanted to break into the pictures, and Mike Todd wanted to help her out, but he really didn't have any use for her, so what he did was, he started raving to Cohn about this girl he'd discovered and told him he was getting ready to sign her up, but for $500 a week he'd lend her to him. So Cohn decided to outsmart Mike Todd and without saying anything he puts her under contract himself and she has her job.

"Well, you should have heard Mike Todd telling me that story. He howled! He almost died! And you know, he was so interested in that story, he came over and he worked on it with us. We almost had the story done, but we were having trouble getting a last line, and Mike Todd had to go back to Hollywood. Well, that night, in the middle of the night, he called me up from Hollywood and he said, 'I've got it! I've got that last line for you!' Here was a guy who was one of the busiest guys in Hollywood, he was doing a million things, but he called me up in the middle of the night just to get that story right. My respect for him went up a million per cent!"

There it was again! The *aesthetique du schlock!* There is only one Mike Todd in Harrison's book. More bagels, more lox, more coffee; Harrison is going strong now—names, names, names. The names *Confidential* was built on keep bubbling up. He used to meet these people in the damnedest places, he says. He was too hot to be seen with. He used to meet Lee Mortimer, a writer, in some damned telephone booth. Both of them would get right in there in the same booth and talk, and Mortimer would give him stories, for Christ's sake. "Then we'd glare at each other at some nightclub that night." Other people Harrison remembers because they were supposed to be mad as hell at him but all of a sudden were acting very friendly when they met him. Harrison tended to overestimate the world's store of goodwill for him, but the fact was that even when *Confidential* was at its most notorious peak, people would meet Harrison for the first time, brace themselves for the worst, talk to him for a while and come away telling about his "curious charm." Well, practically everybody seemed to like him in varying degrees, as Harrison recalls it, but there was only one Mike Todd. Mike Todd was not only friendly, he not only provided stories about himself, but he saw the beauty of *Confidential* as usually only Harrison could see it, he participated in it, he understood the *aesthetique du schlock!*

"I get along fine with all those people," Harrison is saying. "The only one who never liked me was _____. Did you ever read that story we did about _____, about how he ate Wheaties? That was a fabulous story. That was the best story Breen ever did. Here is this girl, and she told me the story herself. She just told it to me when we were sitting in some place, I forget the name of it, it might have been Harwyn's, that was a big place then. Anyway, in this story, here is this girl, and every time she hears the 'crunch crunch crunch' of the Wheaties, she knows _____ is coming back in the room. He thinks Wheaties are good for, you know, virility, and every time he goes out in the kitchen for the Wheaties and this girl can hear the 'crunch crunch crunch'—it was a fabulous story. You've got to read it. And that's the funny thing, he is the only one who never liked me. I ran into him one night in the Copacabana and he just looked right past me—and that was the best story we ever did!"

Yes! The *aesthetique du schlock! Schlock*, which is Yiddish for a kind of "ersatz," is the New York publishing-trade term for the sort of periodical, known academically as subliterature, in which there is a story about, say, bars where young women from Utica and Akron are lured, seduced, hooked and shanghaied as call girls, and the title is "Sin Traps for Secretaries!" and there is an illustration made up of half photograph, of models with black censor bars across their eyes and a lot of thigh and garter strap, and half superimposed drawing, of a leering devil in a silk topper, all on a layout that the editor has returned to the art department with a crayon notation that says, "Make devil red." Harrison would fret and enthuse over a *schlock* tale like the Wheaties one with the same flaming passion for art as Cardinal Newman or somebody dubbing a few oxymorons and serpentinae carminae into his third draft. Well, even *schlock* has its classics. All during the mid-fifties, the outrage was building up about *Confidential,* the sales were going up to more than four million at the newsstands per issue, the record for newsstand sales, and everybody was wondering, outraged, how such a phenomenon could crop up in the middle of the twentieth century after the lessons of the war, hate and all, and what kind of creature could be producing *Confidential.* That was because no one really knew about Harrison, the "air business," and the Cézanne, the Darwin, the Aristotle of *schlock*—the old New York *Graphic.*

Harrison's father, he was saying, had wanted him to have a trade. Like plumbing, he says, that being the worst trade Harrison can imagine on short notice. The thing was, Harrison's father had been an immigrant, from Mitau. Harrison doesn't know where that is. His father and he were as different as black and white, he was saying. His father had the Old World idea of having a trade so inculcated in him that he was suspicious about any job that wasn't a trade. Harrison says he was about fifteen or sixteen when he got a job in an advertising agency, and he was getting seventy-five bucks a week. His old man went right down to the office of the place to see what kind of funny stuff his son had gotten mixed up in. Even after he found out it was legit, he wrote it off as "air business." "This *air business,*" he kept saying.

But the air business to end all air business was the New York *Daily Graphic.* Harrison went to work for the *Graphic* as an office boy, or copy boy, when the paper was the hottest thing in New York. It was one of those Xanadus of inspired buncombe in the twenties. The *Graphic* blew up scandal and crime stories like pork bladders. When the *Graphic* wanted to do a sensational story, they had writers, photographers and composograph artists who could not only get in there and milk every gland in the human body—but do it with verve, with patent satisfaction, and, by god, celebrate it and pronounce it good with a few bawling red-eyed rounds after work. The *Graphic*'s ghost writers developed the knack of putting a story, first-person and sopping with confession, into a famous person's mouth until it seemed like the guy was lying right out there on the page like a flat-out Gulliver. And those composograph artists. The composograph was a way of developing photographs of a scene at which, unfortunately, no photographers were present. If a gal were nude when the action took place but was uncooperatively fully clothed when the *Graphic* photographers zeroed in, the composographers had a way of recollecting the heated moment in tranquillity with scissors, paste and the retouch brush. These were wild times all around. These were the days of Texas Guinan and all that kind of stuff, Harrison was saying. Harrison was only sixteen or seventeen when he went to work on the *Graphic*, and he was only an office boy, or copy boy, but this piece of air business fixed his mind like an aspic mold. Okay, it was bogus. It was ballyhoo. It was outrageous. Everybody was outraged and called the *Daily Graphic* "gutter journalism"—that's how that one got started—and the Daily Pornographic. But by god the whole thing had style. Winchell was there, developing a column called "Broadway Hearsay" that set the style for all the hot, tachycardiac gossip columns that were to follow. Even in the realm of the bogus, the *Graphic* went after bogosity with a kind of Left Bank sense of rebellious discovery. Those composographs, boy! Those confession yarns!

By 1957 people were starting to rustle through all the cerebral fretwork of Freud, Schopenhauer and Karl Menninger for an explanation of the *Confidential* phenomenon, when all the time they could have found it in some simpler, brighter stuff— that old forgotten bijou, the *aesthetique du Daily Graphic*. That was a long-faced year, 1957. Hate? Venom? Smut peddling? Scandal mongering? All those long faces floated past

Harrison like a bunch of emphysematous investment counselors who had missed the train.

After his days on the *Graphic*, Harrison worked for a long time for Martin Quigley, publisher of the *Motion Picture Daily* and the *Motion Picture Herald*. Then, as he puts it, a funny thing happened. He got canned. He got canned for publishing the first of his girlie magazines, *Beauty Parade*, in Quigley's office after hours. "Quigley fired me and it was on Christmas Eve, I want you to know," says Harrison. "Yeah! Christmas Eve!" But *Beauty Parade* clicked, and by the late forties Harrison was publishing six girlie magazines, among them being *Titter*, *Wink* and *Flirt*. Harrison's first great contribution to the art, sort of like Braque coming up with the collage at a crucial point in the history of painting, was the editorial sequence. Which is to say, instead of just having a lot of unrelated girlie shots stuck into a magazine of, say, *Breezy Stories*, the way it used to be done, Harrison arranged the girlie shots in editorial sequences. A whole set of bust-and-leg pictures would be shot around the theme, "Models Discover the Sauna Baths!" Class. Harrison's second great contribution was really the brainchild of one of his editors, an educated gal who was well-versed on Krafft-Ebing. It was she who sold Harrison on the idea of fetishism, such as the six-inch spiked-heel shoes, and the eroticism of backsides or of girls all chained up and helpless, or girls whipping the hides off men and all the rest of the esoterica of the Viennese psychologists that so thoroughly pervades the girlie magazines today. She once put a volume of Krafft-Ebing on Harrison's desk, but he never read it. Apparently, life in the Harrison offices was memorable. There are commercial artists in New York today who will tell you how they would be quietly working away on some layout when a door would open and in would tramp some margarine-faced babe in a brassiere, panties and spike heels, with a six-foot length of chain over her shoulder, dragging it over the floor. Harrison, who half the time slept in the office and worked around the clock, would be just waking up and out he would charge, fighting off the sebaceous sleepers from his eyes and already setting up the day's shots, with his piston-driven Dr. Grabow voice, as if the sound of the dragging chain had been the gong of dawn.

"And then a funny thing happened," Harrison is saying, "one day my accountant calls up and asks me to meet him down at Longchamps. So I am talking to him in Longchamps and he informs me that I am broke. Broke! After making all that money! I couldn't believe what he was telling me! I think the thing was, we had six magazines, and if six magazines start losing money for a few months, you can lose hundreds of thousands of dollars and not even know what happened.

"Now, listen to this, I think this is a hell of a story. He told me I was busted, so I was looking for an idea. And that same week, I thought up *Confidential*. That same week. I think this is a hell of a story, because I'm not a rich man's son. I'm not one of these guys like Huntington Hartford who can start one thing, and if that flops, so what, start something else.

"Anyway, we put together the first issue of *Confidential*. It must have taken about six months to do it.

"But that first issue of *Confidential* was lousy. I must have ripped that thing apart three times before I published it, and it still wasn't right. The first one went for 250,000 copies. That was in December, 1952. Those first issues were terrible. If you saw them and then you saw what we did later, you wouldn't even think it was the same magazine."

In point of fact, to the unpracticed eye they look precisely alike; but, then, the unpracticed eye does not comprehend the *aesthetique du schlock*.

"But in that second issue we had a story about Winchell, and he really liked that story. That was what really—"

And here comes Reggie. She's back, as bouffant blonde and furred out as ever, bereft only of the dog, and in Lindy's all these necks are sloshing around in the shirt fronts watching her progress to the table. Harrison is blasé about the whole thing. Reggie settles in. The dog is all right. Reggie wants some lox, too. Harrison goes on about Winchell.

"I took the magazine over to Winchell and showed it to him. We had this story called, 'Winchell Was Right About Josephine Baker.' Josephine Baker had made a scene in some club, I forget which one, she said she was being discriminated against because she was a Negro or something like that, and Winchell said she was exploiting the race thing, and there was a lot of criticism of Winchell over what he wrote. So we ran this story, 'Winchell Was Right About Josephine Baker,' and he loved it."

Just then there is a page call for Harrison to go to the telephone, so he gets up and I get to talking with Reggie. For such a visual phenomenon, she has a small voice and a quiet manner. She is telling me how she met Harrison. Her family had fled Eastern Europe after the war and had settled in Canada. Reggie had done a lot of modeling and been Miss this and that, such as Miss BMC, but she really wants to act. Anyway, a couple of years ago somebody had gotten her a job doing some modeling for something Harrison was working on.

"But as soon as I met him," Reggie says, "I wasn't interested in the job. I was interested in him. He's a very, you know, a very exciting guy."

Well, Reggie was having some problems with the immigration people over her status in the U.S.A., and one day there is a knock on the door of the apartment where she is staying with this girl friend, and it is the immigration people. They ask her all these questions about what she's doing, and then one of them tells her that she has been seen quite a bit in the company of this elderly man.

"That was Bob they were talking about!" Reggie says. She

certainly does laugh at that. "I told Bob that he was The Elderly Man. He didn't like that too much, I don't think."

But everything had been straightened out and it was an exciting life. Just the other day Bob had called up Winchell's office to ask about something, and his secretary said she would take the message.

"And do you know," Reggie says, "in a little while Winchell called back himself. Bob was happy about that. They were good friends, you know. Bob comes over here to Lindy's quite a bit. He'd like to, you know, he kind of hopes he'll run into Winchell and sort of see if they're still friends. You know."

Harrison comes back to the table and says. "That was Helen."

Reggie says, "Is Tessie behaving?"

Harrison says, "Yeah." He seems a little distracted.

"I was telling him," Reggie says, "about how you were The Elderly Man."

Reggie laughs. Harrison finesses the whole subject and looks up toward the door.

"Winchell hasn't been in," Reggie says.

Harrison looks back. The cloud passes.

"Anyway," Harrison resumes, "Winchell liked that story so much, he plugged it on the air. Winchell had this program on, I forget what network, it was the hottest thing on television then. One night he held up a copy of *Confidential*, right on television. And I'm telling you, from then on, this thing flew. That was what really made *Confidential*, the publicity.

"Well, we started running a Winchell piece every issue. We'd try to figure out who Winchell didn't like and run a piece about them. One of them was 'Broadway's Biggest Double Cross.' It was about all the ingrates who Winchell had helped to start their careers who turned their backs on him and double-crossed him or something. We had one in every issue. And he kept on plugging *Confidential*. It got to the point

where some days we would sit down and rack our brains trying to think of somebody else Winchell didn't like. We were
running out of people, for Christ's sake!

"Pretty soon everybody believes we have a deal going with
Winchell or that he owns a piece of *Confidential*. I think they
called him in over at the *Mirror* and asked him about it. They
thought he was investing in the magazine. But there was never
anything like that. We never offered Winchell anything, and it
wouldn't have been any use anyway. A lot of people tried to
buy their way into his column, and they never got to first base.
You can't buy Winchell. With *Confidential*, he was just crazy
about the stuff we were printing, and he kept plugging it on
television. Well, we had advance word once that he was going
to plug one issue on television, and I happened to tell the
distributor about it. And this guy sends out a notice to the
dealers all over the goddamned country to stock up on a lot of
this issue because Winchell is going to plug it on television.
That was a stupid thing for this guy to do, because it makes it
look like we have a deal with Winchell. Well, somehow, Winchell heard about this, and he really blew his stack. Luckily,
none of this ever got in the papers, but by now even Winchell
himself is wondering what's going on. One day he meets me in
here, in Lindy's, and he sits down and says, 'Bob, you've got to
tell me one thing. How the hell did I ever get involved with
Confidential, I can't figure it out.' I had to laugh over that."

Well, the money was pouring in, Harrison is saying. *Confidential* opened a big office, about 4,000 square feet, at 1697
Broadway, but they never had more than about fifteen people
on the staff.

"After we got going, people would come to us with stories
about themselves, or their families, like I was telling you.

"Breen wrote half the stories himself. That guy was a fabulous writer! But you know what ruined Breen? He was making
too much money, and that started him drinking. He must have

been making forty or fifty thousand a year, and he never had money like that before, and he was living high and he started drinking. The trouble was, I guess, he had it too good! After a while he was drunk all the time. I remember we put out one whole issue up in Memorial Hospital, I think that was the name of it. He was in one room, for treatment, and I took the room next to it, and we put out the whole goddamned issue up there.

"Anyway we were selling five million. There's never been anything like it. And the real thing behind it was, we had a definite style. Nothing was just thrown together. Sometimes we would work on a layout for days. And those stories were beautifully written. They were s*uperb!* We were asked by many schools of journalism to come and lecture. Yeah! They wanted to know how we did it."

Pretty soon, though, for the *aesthetes du schlock,* life began to get too goddamned much with them.

"There was all this indignation," Harrison is saying, "and it got so the insurance companies canceled everybody's life insurance who worked for *Confidential.* We were supposed to be 'poor risks.' One of the columnists ran a story saying I had been taken for a ride by some gangsters. It was a completely phony story, but when Winchell read about it, he was mad as hell and he called up and said, 'What's the idea of not giving me that story first?' I told him there was nothing to it, it never happened, but he didn't believe it.

"Some guys did start to take me for a ride one night, though, right out here on Broadway, some gangsters, we had run some story about the jukeboxes or the garment industry, I forget which one. They pushed me in this car, and they said, 'This is it, Harrison, this is where you get yours,' or something like that, I don't remember. So I said, 'Let's get it over with. You'll be doing me a favor.' 'A favor?' this guy says. 'Yeah,' I said, 'I have cancer, it's incurable, I'm in pain all the time, I'm living on morphine, but I haven't got the guts to shoot myself. You'll be doing me a favor. I haven't got the guts.' So they throw me back out of the car on the sidewalk and this guy says, 'Let the bastard suffer!' I always had to use psychology with those guys.

"That's one thing everybody forgets about *Confidential.* We ran a lot of stories exposing the rackets, the jukebox rackets, the garment rackets, gambling, this deal where they had a regular casino going in an airplane. We drove that operation out of New York. I covered that one myself and took pictures in the airplane with a concealed camera. When those guys want to get you, that's a compliment. We ran stories exposing how children were dying from eating candy-flavored aspirin, and how boric acid was poison, and a lot of things like that. But we had to have the other stuff, the gossip, to sell the magazine, or we could have never run these stories at all. Nobody remembers that part of it, but that magazine was a goddamned public service."

Another time, Harrison was saying, somebody's goons, the jukebox mob he believes it was, came in his office and hung him out the window by his heels, head down. They wanted a retraction. He didn't remember what psychology he used then, but anyhow they pulled him back up. Another time he ran into a big mobster, he forgets what his name was, happened to be sitting at the table next to him in one of the nightclubs with his lawyer, and he tells Harrison, "One night, buddy, you're liable to find yourself in the East River with a concrete suit on, you know that, don't you?" They really talk like that, Harrison is saying. So he just tells the guy, "You know what the circulation of *Confidential* is?" The guy says, What. Six million, says Harrison. He ups it a million or so for good measure. He's right, the lawyer says. Better lay off. It would create too big a noise. Psychology.

"But the wildest thing was Izzy the Eel. One day I walk in

here, in Lindy's, and here is this girl I know. She's sitting with this guy, a very well-dressed guy, and I think I know him from someplace. He looks like a garment manufacturer I knew on Seventh Avenue. 'Don't I know you?' I says to him. 'Yeah, and don't I know you?' he says. And the girl introduces us.

"So we're talking, and this guy is very friendly, he asks me where I live. So I tell him, it's the same place I live in now, the Madison. 'Oh, yeah,' the guy says, 'the Madison, a nice place, I've been in apartments in there, it's nice, where is yours in there?' So I tell him, in fact, I practically give him a blueprint of the place, how the rooms are laid out, everything. So we talk a little more, and then I leave and I don't think anymore of it.

"Well, the next day I get a call from this girl, and her voice is shaking. She's really upset. 'Bob,' she says, 'I got to see you. It's urgent. You're in trouble.' So I meet her someplace and she says, 'You know who that guy was you were talking to with me yesterday?' And I say, 'Yeah.' And she says, 'That was Izzy the Eel!!' 'Izzy the Eel?' I says. And she says, 'Yeah, and he's planning to kidnap you, for ransom. He thinks you and him were in Dannemora together, and now that you're making a lot of money from *Confidential,* he's going to get some of it.' 'He's out of his mind,' I said, 'I've never been in a prison in my life.'

"Well, this was one of those times I was lucky again. About a week after that I pick up the papers and Izzy the Eel has been picked up in a shooting case. Eventually they put him away for fifteen years.

"All this time I was getting all these phone calls. They'd say something like 'You're gonna get it tonight,' and hang up. Sure, I was scared, but I couldn't stay locked up in the apartment all day. So I used some psychology. I bought the biggest white Cadillac convertible they make, it was like a goddamned

Caribbean yacht, and I drove all over New York, telling the world I didn't give a damn and I wasn't scared of anybody."

Well, there was that time when Harrison got shot in the Dominican Republic. But that was different. He says he was down there doing a story on a drug the Dominicans developed, called Pego-Palo, that was supposed to do great things for virility. He was out in the wilds when he got shot under "mysterious circumstances." There were headlines all over the United States saying "*Confidential* Publisher Shot."

"Anyway, that thing brought us tremendous publicity. Not long after that I was on the Mike Wallace show on television. Wallace was known as the great prosecutor then or something like that." Inquisitor? "Yeah, one of those things. There was nothing prearranged on that show. All I knew was that he would really try to let me have it. So he starts after me right away. He's very sarcastic. 'Why don't you admit it, Harrison, that so-called shooting in the Dominican Republic was a fake, a publicity stunt, wasn't it? You weren't shot at all, were you?' So I said to him, 'Would you know a bullet wound if you saw one?' He says, 'Yeah.' So I start taking off my shirt right there in front of the camera. Those guys didn't know what to do, die or play organ music. I can see the cameramen and everybody is running around the studio like crazy. Well, I have this big mole on my back, a birthmark, and the cameramen are all so excited, they think that's the bullet hole and they put the camera right on that. Well, that mole's the size of a nickel, so on television it looked like I'd been shot clean through with a cannon! That was funny. They never heard the end of it, about that show!"

All these things kept happening, Harrison said. His life was always full of this drama, it was like living in the middle of a hurricane. It finally wore him out, he is saying. "It wasn't the libel suits.

"Some of these people we wrote about would be very indignant at first, but I knew goddamned well it was a beautiful act. What they really wanted was *another* story in *Confidential*. It was great publicity for them. You couldn't put out a magazine like *Confidential* again. You know why? Because all the movie stars have started writing books about *themselves!* Look at the stuff Flynn wrote, and Zsa Zsa Gabor, and all of them. They tell all! No magazine can compete with that. That's what really finished the *Confidential* type of thing."

So Harrison retired with his soap-bubble lawsuits and his pile of money to the sedentary life of stock-market investor.

"I got into the stock market quite by accident," Harrison is saying. "This guy told me of a good stock to invest in, Fairchild Camera, so I bought a thousand shares. I made a quarter of a million dollars the first month! I said to myself, 'Where the hell has *this* business been all my life!'"

Harrison's sensational good fortune on the stock market lasted just about that long, one month.

"So I started putting out the one-shots, but there was no *continuity* in them. So then I got the idea of *Inside News.*"

Suddenly Harrison's eyes are fixed on the door. There, by god, in the door is Walter Winchell. Winchell has on his snap-brim police reporter's hat, circa 1924, and an overcoat with the collar turned up. He's scanning the room, like Wild Bill Hickock entering the Crazy Legs Saloon. Harrison gives him a big smile and a huge wave. "There's Walter!" he says.

Winchell gives an abrupt wave with his left hand, keeps his lips set like bowstrings and walks off to the opposite side of Lindy's.

After a while, a waiter comes around, and Harrison says, "Who is Walter with?"

"He's with his granddaughter."

By and by Harrison, Reggie and I got up to leave, and at the door Harrison says to the maître d':

"Where's Walter?"

"He left a little while ago," the maître d' says.

"He was with his granddaughter," Harrison says.

"Oh, was that who that was," the maître d' says.

"Yeah," says Harrison. "It was his granddaughter. I didn't want to disturb them."

In the cab on the way back to the Madison Hotel Harrison says, "You know, we've got a hell of a cute story in *Inside News* about this girl who's divorcing her husband because all he does at night is watch the Johnny Carson show and then he just falls into bed and goes to sleep and won't even give her a tumble. It's a very cute story, very inoffensive.

"Well, I have an idea. I'm going to take this story and show it to Johnny Carson. I think he'll go for it. Maybe we can work out something. You know, he goes through the audience on the show, and so one night Reggie can be in the audience and she can have this copy of *Inside News* with her. When he comes by, she can get up and say, 'Mr. Carson, I see by this newspaper here, *Inside News*, that your show is breaking up happy marriages,' or something like that. And then she can hold up *Inside News* and show him the story and he can make a gag out of it. I think he'll go for it. What do you think? I think it'll be a hell of a cute stunt."

Nobody says anything for a minute, then Harrison says, sort of moodily,

"I'm not putting out *Inside News* for the money. I just want to prove—there are a lot of people say I was just a flash in the pan. I just want to prove I can do it again."

11

The Girl of the Year

Bangs manes bouffants beehives Beatle caps butter faces brush-on lashes decal eyes puffy sweaters French thrust bras flailing leather blue jeans stretch pants stretch jeans honeydew bottoms eclair shanks elf boots ballerinas Knight slippers, hundreds of them, these flaming little buds, bobbing and screaming, rocketing around inside the Academy of Music Theater underneath that vast old mouldering cherub dome up there—aren't they super-marvelous!

"Aren't they super-marvelous!" says Baby Jane, and then: "Hi, Isabel! Isabel! You want to sit backstage—with the Stones!"

The show hasn't even started yet, the Rolling Stones aren't

even on the stage, the place is full of a great shabby mouldering dimness, and these flaming little buds.

Girls are reeling this way and that way in the aisle and through their huge black decal eyes, sagging with Tiger Tongue Lick Me brush-on eyelashes and black appliqués, sagging like display window Christmas trees, they keep staring at—her—Baby Jane—on the aisle. What the hell is this? She is gorgeous in the most outrageous way. Her hair rises up from her head in a huge hairy corona, a huge tan mane around a narrow face and two eyes opened—swock!—like umbrellas, with all that hair flowing down over a coat made of . . . zebra! Those motherless stripes! Oh, damn! Here she is with her friends, looking like some kind of queen bee for all flaming little buds everywhere. She twists around to shout to one of her friends and that incredible mane swings around on her shoulders, over the zebra coat.

"Isabel!" says Baby Jane, "Isabel, hi! I just saw the Stones! They look super-divine!"

That girl on the aisle, Baby Jane, is a fabulous girl. She comprehends what the Rolling Stones *mean*. Any columnist in New York could tell them who she is . . . a celebrity of New York's new era of Wog Hip . . . Baby Jane Holzer. Jane Holzer in *Vogue,* Jane Holzer in *Life,* Jane Holzer in Andy Warhol's underground movies, Jane Holzer in the world of High Camp, Jane Holzer at the rock and roll, Jane Holzer is—well, how can one put it into words? Jane Holzer is This Year's Girl, at least, the New Celebrity, none of your old idea of sexpots, prima donnas, romantic tragediennes, she is the girl who knows . . . The Stones, East End vitality . . .

"Isabel!" says Jane Holzer in the small, high, excited voice of hers, her Baby Jane voice, "Hi, Isabel! Hi!"

Down the row, Isabel, Isabel Eberstadt, the beautiful socialite who is Ogden Nash's daughter, has just come in. She doesn't seem to hear Jane. But she is down the row a ways.

Next to Jane is some fellow in a chocolate-colored Borsalino hat, and next there is Andy Warhol, the famous pop artist.

"Isabel!" says Jane.

"What?" says Isabel.

"Hi, Isabel!" says Jane.

"Hello, Jane," says Isabel.

"You want to go backstage?" says Jane, who has to speak across everybody.

"Backstage?" says Isabel.

"With the Stones!" says Jane. "I was backstage with the Stones. They look di*vine!* You know what Mick said to me? He said, 'Koom on, love, give us a kiss!' "

But Isabel has turned away to say something to somebody.

"Isabel!" says Jane.

And all around, the little buds are batting around in the rococo gloom of the Academy of Arts Theater, trying to crash into good seats or just sit in the aisle near the stage, shrieking. And in the rear the Voice of Fifteen-year-old America cries out in a post-pubertal contralto, apropos of nothing, into the mouldering void: "Yaaaagh! Yuh dirty fag!"

Well, so what; Jane laughs. Then she leans over and says to the fellow in the Borsalino hat:

"Wait'll you see the Stones! They're so sexy! They're pure sex. They're di*vine!* The Beatles, well, you know, Paul Mc-Cartney—*sweet* Paul McCartney. You know what I mean. He's such a *sweet person.* I mean, the Stones are *bitter*—" the words seem to spring from her lungs like some kind of wonderful lavender-yellow Charles Kingsley bubbles "—they're all from the working class, you know? the East End. Mick Jagger—well, it's all Mick. You know what they say about his lips? They say his lips are *diabolical.* That was in one of the magazines.

"When Mick comes into the Ad Lib in London—I mean, there's nothing like the Ad Lib in New York. You can go into the Ad Lib and everybody is there. They're all young, and they're taking over, it's like a whole revolution. I mean, it's *exciting*, they're all from the lower classes, East End-sort-of-thing. There's nobody exciting from the upper classes anymore, except for Nicole and Alec Londonderry, Alec is a British marquis, the Marquis of Londonderry, and, O.K., Nicole has to put in an appearance at this country fair or something, well, O.K., she does it, but that doesn't mean—you know what I mean? Alec is so—you should see the way he walks, I could just watch him walk—*Undoes-one-ship!* They're *young*. They're all young, it's a whole new thing. It's not the Beatles. Bailey says the Beatles are *passé*, because now everybody's mum pats the Beatles on the head. The Beatles are getting fat. The Beatles—well, John Lennon's still thin, but Paul McCartney is getting a big bottom. That's all right, but I don't particularly care for that. The Stones are thin. I mean, that's why they're beautiful, they're so thin. Mick Jagger—wait'll you see Mick."

Then the show begins. An electronic blast begins, electric guitars, electric bass, enormous speakers up there on a vast yellow-gray stage. Murray the K, the D. J. and M. C., O.K.?, comes out from the wings, doing a kind of twist soft shoe, wiggling around, a stocky chap, thirty-eight years old, wearing Italian pants and a Sun Valley snow lodge sweater and a Stingy Brim straw hat. Murray the K! Girls throw balls of paper at him, and as they arc onto the stage, the stage lights explode off them and they look like falling balls of flame.

And, finally, the Stones, now—how can one express it? the Stones come on stage—

"Oh, God, Andy, aren't they *divine!*"

—and spread out over the stage, the five Rolling Stones, from England, who are modeled after the Beatles, only more lower-class-deformed. One, Brian Jones, has an enormous blonde Beatle bouffant.

"Oh, Andy, look at Mick! Isn't he *beautiful*! Mick! Mick!"

In the center of the stage a short thin boy with a sweat shirt on, the neck of the sweat shirt almost falling over his shoulders, they are so narrow, all surmounted by this . . . enormous head . . . with the hair puffing down over the forehead and ears, this boy has exceptional lips. He has two peculiarly gross and extraordinary red lips. They hang off his face like giblets. Slowly his eyes pour over the flaming bud horde soft as Karo syrup and then close and then the lips start spreading into the most lanquid, most confidential, the wettest, most labial, most concupiscent grin imaginable. Nirvana! The buds start shrieking, pawing toward the stage.

The girls have Their Experience. They stand up on their seats. They begin to ululate, even between songs. The looks on their faces! Rapturous agony! There, right up there, under the sulphur lights, that is *them.* God, they're right there! Mick Jagger takes the microphone with his tabescent hands and puts his huge head against it, opens his giblet lips and begins to sing . . . with the voice of a bull Negro. Bo Diddley. You movung boo meb bee-uhtul, bah-bee, oh vona breemb you' honey snurks oh crim pulzy yo' mim down, and, camping again, then turning toward the shrieking girls with his wet giblet lips dissolving . . .

And, occasionally, breaking through the ululation:

"Get off the stage, you finks!"

"Maybe we ought to scream," says Jane. Then she says to the fellow in the hat: "Tell me when it's five o'clock, will you, pussycat? I have to get dressed and go see Sam Spiegel." And then Baby Jane goes: "Eeeeeeeeeeeeeeeeeeeeee

eeeeeeeeeeeeeeeeyes!" says Diana Vreeland, the editor of *Vogue.* "Jane Holzer is the most contemporary girl I know."

Jane Holzer at the rock and roll—

Jane Holzer in the underground movies—in Andy's studio,

Andy Warhol, the famous Pop artist, experiencing the rare world of Jonas and Adolph Mekas, truth and culture in a new holy medium, underground movie-making on the lower East Side. And Jane is wearing a Jax shirt, strung like a Christmas tree with Diamonds, and they are making *Dracula,* or *Thirteen Beautiful Women* or *Soap Opera* or *Kiss*—in which Jane's lips . . . but how can one describe an underground movie? It is . . . avant-garde. "Andy calls everything super," says Jane. "I'm a super star, he's a super-director, we make super epics— and I mean, it's a completely new and natural way of acting. You can't imagine what really beautiful things can happen!"

Jane Holzer—with The New Artists, photographers like Jerry Schatzberg, David Bailey and Brian Duffy, and Nicky Haslam, the art director of *Show.* Bailey, Duffy and Haslam are English. Schatzberg says the photographers are the modern-day equivalents of the Impressionists in Paris around 1910, the men with a sense of New Art, the excitement of the salon, the excitement of the artistic style of life, while all the painters, the old artists, have moved uptown to West End Avenue and live in apartment buildings with Kwik-Fiks parquet floors and run around the corner to get a new cover for the ironing board before the stores close.

Jane in the world of High Camp—a world of thin young men in an environment, a decor, an atmosphere so—how can one say it?—so indefinably Yellow Book. Jane in the world of Teen Savage—Jane modeling here and there—wearing Jean Harlow dresses for *Life* and Italian fashions for *Vogue* and doing the most fabulous cover for Nicky at *Show,* David took the photograph, showing Jane barebacked wearing a little yacht cap and a pair of "World's Fair" sunglasses and holding an American flag in her teeth, so—so Beyond Pop Art, if you comprehend.

Jane Holzer at the LBJ Discotheque—where they were handing out aprons with a target design on them, and Jane

Holzer put it on backward so that the target was behind and
then did The Swim, a new dance.

Jane Holzer—well, there is no easy term available, Baby
Jane has appeared constantly this year in just about every
society and show business column in New York. The magazines have used her as a kind of combination of model, celebrity and socialite. And yet none of them have been able to do
much more than, in effect, set down her name, Baby Jane
Holzer, and surround it with a few asterisks and exploding
stars, as if to say, well, here we have . . . What's Happening.

She is a socialite in the sense that she lives in a twelve-room
apartment on Park Avenue with a wealthy husband, Leonard
Holzer, heir to a real estate fortune, amid a lot of old Dutch
and Flemish paintings, and she goes to a great many exciting
parties. And yet she is not in Society the way the Good Book,
the *Social Register*, thinks of Society, and the list of hostesses
who have not thought of inviting Jane Holzer would be im-
pressive. Furthermore, her stance is that she doesn't care, and
she would rather be known as a friend of the Stones, anyway—
and here she is at the April in Paris Ball, $150 per ticket, amid
the heaving white and gold swag of the Astor Hotel ballroom,
yelling to somebody: "If you aren't nice to me, I'll tell everybody you were here!"

Jane Holzer—the sum of it is glamor, of a sort very specific to
New York. With her enormous corona of hair and her long
straight nose, Jane Holzer can be quite beautiful, but she never
comes on as A Beauty. "Some people look at my pictures and
say I look very mature and sophisticated," Jane says. "Some
people say I look like a child, you know, Baby Jane. And, I
mean, I don't know what I look like, I guess it's just 1964
Jewish." She does not attempt to come on sexy. Her excitement
is something else. It is almost pure excitement. It is the excitement of the New Style, the New Chic. The press watches Jane
Holzer as if she were an exquisite piece of . . . radar. It is as

if that entire ciliate corona of hers were spread out as an antenna for new waves of style. To the magazine editors, the newspaper columnists, the photographers and art directors, suddenly here is a single flamboyant girl who sums up everything new and chic in the way of fashion in the Girl of the Year.

How can one explain the Girl of the Year? The Girl of the Year is a symbolic figure the press has looked for annually in New York since World War I because of the breakdown of conventional High Society. The old establishment still holds forth, it still has its clubs, cotillions and coming-out balls, it is still basically Protestant and it still rules two enormously powerful areas of New York, finance and corporate law. But alongside it, all the while, there has existed a large and ever more dazzling society, Cafe Society it was called in the twenties and thirties, made up of people whose status rests not on property and ancestry but on various brilliant ephemera, show business, advertising, public relations, the arts, journalism or simply new money of various sorts, people with a great deal of ambition who have congregated in New York to satisfy it and who look for styles to symbolize it.

The establishment's own styles—well, for one thing they were too dull. And those understated clothes, dark woods, high ceilings, silver-smithery, respectable nannies, and so forth and so on. For centuries their kind of power created styles—Palladian buildings, starched cravats—but with the thickening democratic façade of American life, it has degenerated to various esoteric understatements, often cryptic—Topsiders instead of tennis sneakers, calling cards with "Mr." preceding the name, the right fork.

The magazines and newspapers began looking for heroines to symbolize the Other Society, Café Society, or whatever it should be called. At first, in the twenties, they chose the more flamboyant debutantes, girls with social credentials who also moved in Cafe Society. But the Other Society's styles began to shift and change at a madder and madder rate, and the Flaming Deb idea no longer worked. The last of the Flaming Debs, the kind of Deb who made The Cover of *Life*, was Brenda Frazier, and Brenda Frazier and Brenda Frazierism went out with the thirties. More recently the Girl of the Year has had to be more and more exotic. . . . and extraordinary. Christina Paolozzi! Her exploits! Christina Paolozzi threw a twenty-first birthday party for herself at a Puerto Rican pachanga palace, the Palladium, and after that the spinning got faster and faster until with one last grand centripetal gesture she appeared in the nude, face on, in *Harper's Bazaar*. Some became Girls of the Year because their fame suddenly shed a light on their style of life, and their style of life could be easily exhibited, such as Jackie Kennedy and Barbra Streisand.

But Baby Jane Holzer is a purer manifestation. Her style of life has created her fame—rock and roll, underground movies, decaying lofts, models, photographers, Living Pop Art, the twist, the frug, the mashed potatoes, stretch pants, pre-Raphaelite hair, Le Style Camp. All of it has a common denominator. Once it was power that created high style. But now high styles come from low places, from people who have no power, who slink away from it, in fact, who are marginal, who carve out worlds for themselves in the nether depths, in tainted "undergrounds." The Rolling Stones, like rock and roll itself and the twist—they come out of the netherworld of modern teenage life, out of what was for years the marginal outcast corner of the world of art, photography, populated by poor boys, pretenders. "Underground" movies—a mixture of camp and Artistic Alienation, with Jonas Mekas crying out like some foggy echo from Harold Stearn's last boat for Le Havre in 1921: "You filthy bourgeois pseudo-culturati! You say you love art—then why don't you give us money to buy the films to make our masterpieces and stop blubbering about the naked asses we show?—you mucky pseuds." Teen-agers, bohos, camp culturati, photographers—they have won by default, because, after all, they *do* create styles. And now the Other Society goes to them for styles, like the decadenti of another age going down to the wharves in Rio to find those raw-vital devils, damn their potent hides, those proles, doing the tango. Yes! Oh my God, those raw-vital proles!

The ice floe is breaking, and can't one see, as Jane Holzer sees, that all these people—well, they *feel*, they are alive, and what does it mean simply to be sitting up in her Park Avenue apartment in the room with the two Rubenses on the wall, worth half a million dollars, if they are firmly authenticated? It means almost nothing. One doesn't feel it.

Jane has on a "Poor" sweater, clinging to the ribs, a new fashion, with short sleeves. Her hair is up in rollers. She is wearing tight slacks. Her hips are very small. She has a boyish body. She has thin arms and long, long fingers. She sits twisted about on a couch, up in her apartment on Park Avenue, talking on the telephone.

"Oh, I know what you mean," she says, "but, I mean, couldn't you wait just two weeks? I'm expecting something to jell, it's a movie, and then you'd have a real story. You know what I mean? I mean you would have something to write about and not just Baby Jane sitting up in her Park Avenue apartment with her gotrocks. You know what I mean? . . . well, all right, but I think you'll have more of a story— . . . well, all right . . . bye, pussycat."

Then she hangs up and swings around and says, "That makes me mad. That was——. He wants to do a story about me and do you know what he told me? 'We want to do a story about you,' he told me, 'because you're very big this year.' Do you know what that made me feel like? That made me feel like, All right, Baby Jane, we'll let you play this year, so get out there and dance, but next year, well, it's all over for you next year, Baby Jane. I mean,—! You know? I mean, I felt like telling him, 'Well, pussycat, you're the Editor of the Minute, and you know what? Your minute's up.'"

The thought leaves Jane looking excited but worried. Usually she looks excited about things but open, happy, her eyes wide open and taking it all in. Now she looks worried, as if the world could be such a simple and exhilarating place if there weren't so many old and arteriosclerotic people around to muck it up. There are two dogs on the floor at her feet, a toy poodle and a Yorkshire terrier, who rise up from time to time in some kind of secret needle-toothed fury, barking coloratura.

"Oh, ——," says Jane, and then, "You know, if you have anything at all, there are so many bitchy people just *waiting* to carve you up. I mean, I went to the opening of the Met and I wore a white mink coat, and do you know what a woman did? A woman called up a columnist and said, 'Ha, ha, Baby Jane rented that coat she went to the Met in. Baby Jane rents her clothes.' That's how bitchy they are. Well, that coat happens to be a coat my mother gave me two years ago when I was married. I mean, I don't care if somebody thinks I rent clothes. O.K. ——! Who cares?"

Inez, the maid, brings in lunch on a tray, one rare hamburger, one cheeseburger and a glass of tomato juice. Jane tastes the tomato juice.

"Oh, ——!" she says. "It's diet."

The Girl of the Year. It is as though nobody wants to give anyone credit for anything. They're only a *phenomenon*. Well, Jane Holzer did a great deal of modeling before she got married and still models, for that matter, and now some very wonderful things may be about to happen in the movies. Some of it, well, she cannot go into it exactly, because it is at that precarious stage—you know? But she has one of the best managers, a woman who manages the McGuire Sisters. And there has been talk about Baby Jane for *Who's Afraid of Virginia Woolf*, the movie, and *Candy*—

"Well, I haven't heard anything about it—but I'd *love* to play Candy."

And this afternoon, later on, she is going over to see Sam Spiegel, the producer.

"He's wonderful. He's, you know, sort of advising me on things at this point."

And somewhere out there in the apartment the dogs are loose in a midget coloratura rage amid patina-green walls and paintings by old Lowland masters. There is a great atmosphere in the apartment, an atmosphere of patina-green, faded plush and the ashy light of Park Avenue reflecting on the great black and umber slicks of the paintings. All that stretches on for twelve rooms. The apartment belongs to the Holzers, who have built a lot of New York's new apartment houses. Jane's husband, Leonard, is a slim, good-looking young man. He went to Princeton. He and Jane were married two years ago. Jane came from Florida, where her father, Carl Brookenfeld, also made a lot of money in real estate. But in a way they were from New York, too, because they were always coming to New York and her father had a place here. There was something so stimulating, so flamboyant, about New York, you know? Fine men with anointed blue jowls combed their hair straight back and had their shirts made at Sulka's or Nica-Rattner's, and their wives had copper-gold hair, real chignons and things, and heavy apricot voices that said the funniest things—"Honey, I've got news for you, you're crazy!"—things like that, and they went to El Morocco. Jane went to Cherry Lawn School in Darien, Connecticut. It was a progressive school.

And then she went to Finch Junior College:

"Oh, that was just ghastly. I wanted to flunk out and go to work. If you miss too many classes, they campus you, if you have a messy room, they campus you, they were always campusing me, and I always sneaked out. The last spring term I didn't spend one night there. I was supposed to be campused and I'd be out dancing at El Morocco. I didn't take my exams because I wanted to flunk out, but do you know what they did? They just said I was out, period. I didn't care about that, because I wanted to flunk out and go to work anyway—but the way they did it. I have a lot of good paintings to give away, and it's too bad, they're not getting any. They were not *educators*. They could have at least kept the door open. They could have said, 'You're not ready to be a serious student, but when you decide to settle down and be a serious student, the door will be open.' I mean, I had already paid for the whole term, they *had* the money. I always wanted to go there and tell them, well, ha ha, too bad, you're not getting any of the paintings. So henceforth, Princeton, which was super-marvelous, will get all the paintings."

Jane's spirits pick up over that. Princeton! Well, Jane left Finch and then she did quite a bit of modeling. Then she married Lennie, and she still did some modeling, but the real break—well, the whole *thing* started in summer in London, the summer of 1963.

"Bailey is fantastic," says Jane. "Bailey created four girls that summer. He created Jean Shrimpton, he created me, he created Angela Howard and Susan Murray. There's no photographer like that in America. Avedon hasn't done that for a girl, Penn hasn't, and Bailey created four girls in one summer. He did some pictures of me for the English *Vogue*, and that was all it took."

But how does one really explain about the Stones, about Bailey, Shrimp and Mick—well, it's not so much what they *do*, that's such an old idea, what people *do*—it's what they *are*, it's a revolution, and it's the kids from the East End, Cockneys, if you want, who are making it.

"I mean today Drexel Duke sits next to Weinstein, and why

216

shouldn't he? They both made their money the same way, you know? The furniture king sits next to the catsup king, and why shouldn't he-sort-of-thing. I mean, that's the way it was at the opening of the Met. A friend of mine was going to write an article about it.

"I mean, we don't lie to ourselves. Our mothers taught us to be pure and you'll fall in love and get married and stay in love with one man all your life. O.K. But we know it doesn't happen that way and we don't lie to ourselves about it. Maybe you won't ever find anybody you love. Or maybe you find somebody you love four minutes, maybe ten minutes. But I mean, why lie to yourself? We know we're not going to love one man all our lives. Maybe it's the Bomb—we know it could all be over tomorrow, so why try to fool yourself today. Shrimp was talking about that last night. She's here now, she'll be at the party tonight—"

The two dogs, the toy poodle and the Yorkshire terrier, are yapping, in the patina-green. Inez is looking for something besides diet. The two Rubenses hang up on the walls. A couple of horns come up through the ashy light of Park Avenue. The high wind of East End London is in the air—whhhooooooooo

ooooooooooooosh! Baby Jane blows out all the candles. It is her twenty-fourth birthday. She and everybody, Shrimp, Nicky, Jerry, everybody but Bailey, who is off in Egypt or something, they are all up in Jerry Schatzberg's . . . *pad* . . . his lavish apartment at 333 Park Avenue South, up above his studio. There is a skylight. The cook brings out the cake and Jane blows out the candles. Twenty-four! Jerry and Nicky are giving a huge party, a dance, in honor of the Stones, and already the people are coming into the studio downstairs. But it is also Jane's birthday. She is wearing a black velvet jump suit by Luis Estevez, the designer. It has huge bell-bottom pants. She puts her legs together . . . it looks like an evening dress. But she can also spread them apart, like so, and strike very Jane-like poses. This is like the Upper Room or something. Downstairs, they're all coming in for the party, all those people one sees at parties, everybody who goes to the parties in New York, but up here it is like a tableau, like a tableau of . . . Us. Shrimp is sitting there with her glorious pout and her textured white stockings, Barbara Steele, who was so terrific in 8½, with thin black lips and wrought-iron eyelashes. Nicky Haslam is there with his Byron shirt on and his tiger skin vest and blue jeans and boots. Jerry is there with his hair flowing back in curls. Lennie, Jane's husband, is there in a British suit and a dark blue shirt he bought on 42nd Street for this party, because this is a party for the Rolling Stones. The Stones are not here yet, but here in the upper room are Goldie and the Gingerbreads, four girls in gold lamé tights who will play the rock and roll for the party. Nicky discovered them at the Wagon Wheel. Gold lamé, can you imagine? Goldie, the leader, is a young girl with a husky voice and nice kind of slightly thick—you know—glorious sort of *East End* features, only she is from New York—ah, the delicacy of minor grossness, unabashed. The Stones' music is playing over the hi-fi.

Finally the Stones come in, in blue jeans, sweat shirts, the usual, and people get up and Mick Jagger comes in with his mouth open and his eyes down, faintly weary with success, and everybody goes downstairs to the studio, where people are now piling in, hundreds of them. Goldie and the Gingerbreads are on a stand at one end of the studio, all electric, electric guitars, electric bass, drums, loudspeakers, and a couple of spotlights exploding off the gold lamé. *Baby baby baby where did our love go.* The music suddenly fills up the room like a giant egg slicer. Sally Kirkland, Jr., a young actress, is out on the studio floor in a leopard print dress with her vast mane flying, doing the frug with Jerry Schatzberg. And then the other Girl of the Year, Caterine Milinaire, is out there in a black dress, and then Baby Jane is out there with her incredible mane and her Luis Estevez jump suit, frugging, and then everybody is out there. Suddenly it is very odd. Suddenly everybody is out there in the gloaming, bobbing up and down with the music plugged into *Baby baby baby*. The whole floor of the studio begins to bounce up and down, like a trampoline, the whole floor, some people are afraid and edge off to the side, but most keep bobbing in the gloaming, and—pow!—glasses begin to hit the floor, but every one keeps bouncing up and down, crushing the glass underfoot, while the brown whiskey slicks around. So many heads bobbing, so many bodies jiggling, so many giblets jiggling, so much anointed flesh shaking and jiggling this way and that, so many faces one wanted so desperately to see, and here they are, red the color of dried peppers in the gloaming, bouncing up and down with just a few fights, wrenching in the gloaming, until 5 A.M.—gleeeang—Goldie pulls all the electric cords out and the studio is suddenly just a dim ochre studio with broken glass all over the floor, crushed underfoot, and the sweet high smell of brown whiskey rising from the floor.

Monday's papers will record it as the Mods and Rockers Ball, as the Party of the Year, but that is Monday, a long way off. So they all decide they should go to the Brasserie. It is the only place in town where anybody would still be around. So they all get into cabs and go up to the Brasserie, up on 53rd Street between Park and Lexington. The Brasserie is the right place, all right. The Brasserie has a great entrance, elevated over the tables like a fashion show almost. There are, what?, 35 people in the Brasserie. They all look up, and as the first salmon light of dawn comes through the front window, here come . . . four teen-age girls in gold lamé tights, and a chap in a tiger skin vest and blue jeans and a gentleman in an English suit who seems to be wearing a 42nd Street hood shirt and a fellow in a sweater who has flowing curly hair . . . and then, a girl with an incredible mane, a vast tawny corona, wearing a black velvet jump suit. One never knows who is in the Brasserie at this hour—but are there any so dead in here that they do not get the point? Girl of the Year? Listen, they will *never* forget.

3

A METROPOLITAN SKETCHBOOK

OLD FACES, NEW FASHIONS

The Modern Churchman at the
hootenanny, *reaching* the Urban Young People.

The New Dandies:
cart-pullers in the Garment District,
also known as "Seventh Avenue aviators," wearing
Continental clothes exclusively.

The Suburban Bohemians,
showing the world that despite baby, hubby, and mortgage
and the breezeway, they are still . . . *hip.*

TEENAGE MALE HAIRDOS

The basic ducktail: rear view

The flat top

The basic ducktail: side view

The "Chicago Boxcar," a combination of the flat top
and the ducktail

The Presley haircut

The ducktail tease

THE SUN-WORSHIPPERS

Lunch-break Acapulco:
aluminum-foil reflector under the chin in Verdi Square.

Shop-owner's Boca Chica:
basking on *his* sidewalk in Chelsea.

The Working Girl's weekend resort:
rooftop on 19th Street.

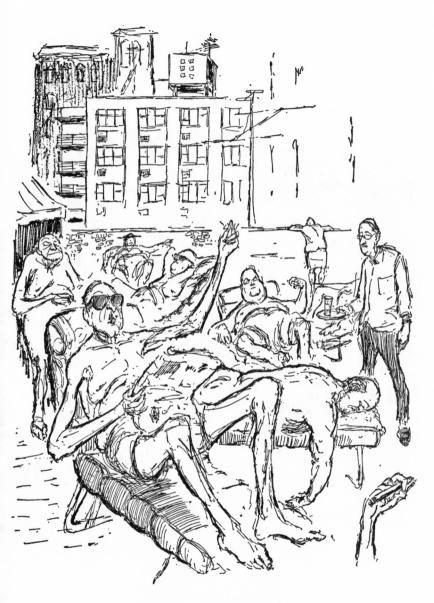

The Biggies' weekday resort:
rooftop at a midtown men's club.

THE ZOO IN CENTRAL PARK

THE VIEW IN CENTRAL PARK

NEW YORK'S BEAUTIFUL PEOPLE

The maître de

The tour guide

The cab driver

The parking lot attendant

The parking ticket patrol

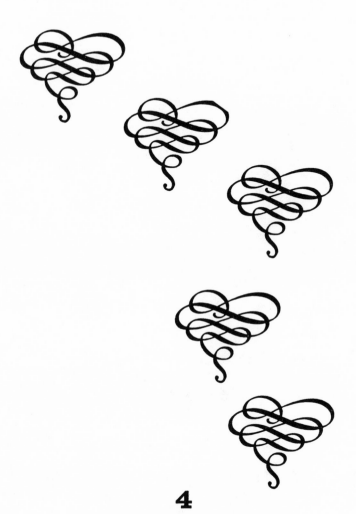

4

STATUS STRIFE AND
THE HIGH LIFE

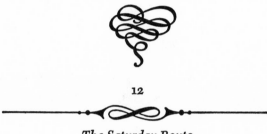

12

The Saturday Route

Is that Joan Morse, the fabulous dressmaker, over there on the curb? With that fabulous Claude-yellow heath coat, those knee-high Rolls-Royce-maroon boots and the biggest sunglasses since Audrey Hepburn sunbathed on a cantilevered terrace in the Swiss Alps? Well, it *has* to be Joan Morse.

"Joan!"

And there at Madison Avenue and 74th Street Joan Morse, owner of A La Carte, which ranks in fabulosity with Mainbocher, swings around and yells:

"Freddie! I saw you in Paris, but what happened to you in London?"

One is not to find out immediately, because the light has just changed. Joan is doing the Saturday Route *down* Madison Avenue. Freddie is doing the Saturday Route *up* Madison Avenue. But they keep on walking because they know they will meet sooner or later at Parke-Bernet and catch up on London. Or if not there, at the Wildenstein Gallery, the Emmerich or Duveen's or Castelli's or one of those places.

And so will Greta Garbo and her old friend, George Schlee —nothing retiring about Greta Garbo on the Saturday Route, no Garbo glasses, no peekaboo Ulster collar. And so will lovely Mimi Russell and her sister Serena and Nick Villiers—Mimi is not giving up the Saturday Route just because the newspapers run headlines such as "Indicted Deb Denies All."

And so will Herbert Lehman, Kirk Douglas, Norman Norell, August Heckscher, Emmett Hughes, Jan Mitchell, Pierre Scapula, Kenneth J. Lane, Alfred Barr, Dorothy Miller, Ted Peckham and, well, you know, everybody.

The thing is, any old boy from the loblolly flatlands of Georgia knows how Saturday is supposed to work out in the United States. All the old people drive down to the railroad station and park alongside the tracks and rare back and socialize on the car fenders until the main event, which is the Seaboard sleeper barreling through to New York City. And the young people drive in from all over and park along the street near the Rexall and neck under the Bright Lights stimulation of the street lamps.

But what about New York City? Just because one lives in New York and is Greta Garbo, there is no need to give the whole business up. Never mind the charisma of the Seaboard sleeper. In New York there is the new religion, Art. And none of your parking alongside the tracks. In New York there is a route from 57th Street to 86th Street through the art galleries that line Madison Avenue and the streets just off it. And, naturally, no necking under the arc lights. In New York, on the

Saturday Route, they give each other New York's newest grace, the Social Kiss.

As the sound of the wet smack begins ricocheting between the charming little buildings of upper Madison Avenue, about noon, everyone knows the Saturday Route is on. Babs Simpson of *Vogue* Magazine lives up on East 83rd Street, so she starts out near the 86th Street end, walks down as far as 78th Street to Schrafft's, for brunch, and then moves on down Madison Avenue. She meets "hundreds" of people she knows. So does Jan Mitchell, the owner of Luchow's, and his wife, the gorgeous, demure-looking blonde, who start out from 57th Street. So does everybody, because everybody is starting out from one end or the other.

"Martha!" "Tony!" "Edmond!" "Jennifer!" "Sarah!" "Bryce!" And Tony and Martha embrace and he pastes a Social Kiss on her cheek, and she pastes one on his cheek, and Edmond pastes one on Jennifer, and Jennifer pastes one on Edmond, and then Tony and Martha trade them and Bryce and Jennifer and Sarah and Martha and Martha and Jennifer.

Irresistibly, this promenade of socialites, stars, literati and culturati begins to attract a train of vergers, beadles and hierophants of fashion. One whole set is called "Seventh Avenue"— as in, "Her? That's Marilyn. She's Seventh Avenue"—designers, manufacturers' agents, who want to know what They are wearing on the Saturday Route. Also a vast crowd of interior decorators, both young and foppish and old and earnest. And jewelry makers, young museum curators and curates, antique dealers, furniture designers, fashion journalists, art journalists, press agents, social climbers, culture climbers, moochers, oglers, duns and young men who have had pairs of leather slacks made or young women in black stretch nylon pants and alligator coat outfits who have been looking all week for somewhere to wear them. So by 2:30 P.M. the promenade is roaring up and down Madison Avenue like a comet with the little stars trailing out like dust at the end.

At the Wildenstein Gallery on East 64th Street, Greta Garbo, a turban hat on her head and a vicuna coat over her shoulders, is standing in a corner before the Wildenstein's inevitable velvet-draped walls, between two drawings, a Tchelitchew and a Prendergast. She is with a smashingly well turned-out woman, who is no decoy, however. All around people are starting the business with the elbows, nudging, saying, "That's Greta Garbo, Greta Garbo, Garbo, Garbo, Garbo, Garbo." Everyone sort of falls back, except Marilyn, who is trying to peek around to the front to see what is under the vicuna.

"What's that?" Marilyn says to Lila, who is also Seventh Avenue, as they say. "It looks like one of those Pucci knit things."

"Oh, for crying out loud, relax," says Lila. "She can't be in the corner forever."

Downstairs, by the door, where the ironwork rises up, inspired, in filigrees, is Pierre Scapula, the interior decorator. He is wearing a leather overcoat with a sash belt and talking in French to one of Mr. Wildenstein's people and in English to a friend: "It's the most marvelous place. Seven French sofas, and the minute you. . . ."

Four blocks away, at 68th Street, Mimi Russell is walking down Madison Avenue in the direction of T. Anthony's, the leather goods shop. Mimi, of 1 Sutton Place, granddaughter of the Duke of Marlborough, daughter of the publisher of *Vogue*, is the one girl among 14 young persons of good blood, good bone, indicted by the Suffolk County Grand Jury, accused of taking part in the big smashup at the Ladd house after Fernanda Wetherill's coming-out ball. Right now, though, on Mimi that story, like good memoir material, is wearing as well as a checked coat, which she has on. Right now, on the Saturday Route, she looks like a million dollars, flanked by good-looking kids, her sister Serena, for one, and Nick Villiers.

On the other side of the street, the fellow with the trench coat and the two little girls in tow is Mindy Wager, the actor.

But up at 77th Street, on the corner near Parke-Bernet, the big fellow with the gray plaid shirt and the striped gray tie and the plaid sport jacket is an artist, Mark Rothko. How did he get out here? Well, he is heading for the Rauschenberg show at the Castelli gallery, 4 East 77th Street, where, later, Marilyn will say, "Well, some of the small ones would be nice," and Lila says, "Oh, for God's sake, Marilyn, you're not buying lingerie."

Rothko is standing out in the midst of the incredible comet and saying he usually doesn't go near the Saturday Route with a ten-foot pole. "Yes, I go to openings," he says, "the openings of my friends. I am an old man and I have a lot of friends. This time I just happened to be in the neighborhood."

To the beautiful people on the Saturday Route, however, it does not matter in the least that artists, and serious collectors, look down on the promenade as a social and, therefore, not very hip spectacle. The fact is, the Route through the art galleries bears approximately the same relation to Art as church-going, currently, bears to the Church. Formerly, Saturday was the big day for the collectors. Now they come around knowingly Tuesday through Friday, avoiding "the mob"—although at this moment at Wildenstein's the Charles Wrightsmans are in that room of port-colored velvet and, as always, a single painting is up on an easel by the north light, and two others, never more, are propped up against the wall nearby.

"I love it," says J————, a customer and admirer. "It's like a game of yellow dog. Two down and one up."

But never mind Art in the abstract. It is almost 3 P.M. and the whole comet seems to be veering toward Parke-Bernet. August Heckscher has just finished up at the Kootz (Raymond

Parker's hard-edge abstracts) and the Staempfli (those wild things by Jorge Piqueras) and is heading for Parke-Bernet. The fellow in the black Chesterfield, across from Parke-Bernet, near Stark's, is John Loeb of the Loeb & Loeb Loebs, grandson of Arthur Lehman. All the Lehmans seem to be out on the Saturday Route. Robert Lehman has just left Wildenstein's. Herbert Lehman, the Governor, the Senator, the 88-year-old patriarch, is already up in the great meeting place, the third floor at Parke-Bernet. The two big gallery rooms are, as always, a profusion of antiques that will be auctioned off next week, all numbered and set out for inspection: beechwood Louis XVI chairs of mustard yellow plush, Zonsei armchairs of vermilion lacquer inlaid with the playing card faces of Chinese aristocrats, draped bronze maidens holding fluted cornucopiae out of which sprout light fixtures, a Kulah prayer rug, a curved cigarette holder of Cloissoné enamel, malachite Easter eggs, a pair of gilded palm trees about 8½ feet high, bibelots, silver creamers, snuff boxes, low tables, chandeliers, napkin rings and all the assorted tabourets, bibelots and marquetry inlays of bygone Czars, noblemen, Mayfair jousters and isolated West of England gentry.

On the walls—more velvet—is a crashingly forthright assortment of 19th century paintings, all condemned forty years ago by the avant-gardeists of Paris as "literary," "academic" and "soppy," but now rather fiercely, if sometimes perversely, "in"—Messonier, von Bremen, Vibert, Millet, Ridgway Knight.

Off to the left is the auction hall where porters in green uniforms are lugging Adam settees, pedestal desks, dwarf cabinets and other formidable objects out onto the stage while John Marion of Parke-Bernet chants in his pulpit. But everybody is waiting for the two *pièces de résistance,* two serpentine-front Chippendale commodes with splayed feet.

G——, the young man who is selling commodes, looks a little anxious, but his wife, a blonde, is looking beautiful mainly, and his friends are not going to let this be too serious an occasion.

"G———, where are you going? You look so cross."

"I'm going to see Marion," he says. That would be Louis J. Marion, the president of Parke-Bernet.

"Well, I'm glad you're not hunting for me, looking so cross."

Meantime, the comet is going full force, around and around the gallery rooms and in and out of the auction hall. Governor Lehman is looking at the Rousseau—that is Pierre Etienne Theodore Rousseau—the picture of the cows moseying around the marsh puddle. Jan Mitchell and his wife are looking at a sketch Gainsborough did for some gal's portrait. Norman Norell, the dress designer, is walking into the auction hall. August Heckscher is sitting in the back row. Mrs. Edmund Lynch, whose husband is Lynch, as in Merrill Lynch, is walking out. Emmett Hughes is looking in through the back door.

"It seems to me that in the last year this place has become *very* social," says Emmett Hughes. "It's a little like those little cafés on the Via Veneto used to be."

Society, the bright young people, the celebrities, Seventh Avenue, the vergers, the beadles, the hierophants are bubbling up on all sides.

"Darling, don't keep telling me you're not going to *buy* anything. Go buy a malachite *egg* or something."

"Of course, I know what to do with two eight-foot-high palm trees. You put gas jets in the top and . . ."

". . . What do I *do?* One doesn't *do* anything, but you're a darling to ask. . ."

". . . Oh, go to Hell. I think you read that some place. . ."

". . . the thing is, I was in his studio. But *too* blinding. . ."

". . . *Smart* set? Everybody is from Kew Gardens. . ."

". . . Good Lord, the *galleries.* . ."

". . . This place is getting to be the coffee break. . ."

"Tony!"

"Martha!"

"Edmond!"

Wet smack!

Then—pow—the second of the two commodes is sold, for
$10,000, just like the first. And everybody feels it, even those
who paid no attention at all. When the last of the heavy business is over at Parke-Bernet, it is like the warning bell at the
Metropolitan, and everybody starts to wind up the Saturday
Route. It is as if someone let the magic out.

August Heckscher is out by the elevators.

"Do you have change for a quarter?" he says.

Then he heads off to the telephone booth.

Of course, it is not all over yet. Ted Peckham and about 19
others have headed down to the Parke-Bernet garage for the
auctioning of the last item on the list, No. 403, a Mercedes-
Benz limousine, built three years ago for $16,000, with Nauga-
hyde inside and on the roof, and a roll-up glass partition and
portholes. The garage is rather *basic*-looking, you know, for
Parke-Bernet. The door is up and it is already dark outside.

Ted Peckham smiles arcanely all through the chanting and
picks up the Mercedes for $3,800.

Somehow it seems like an awesome acquisition.

"Ted, boy, can I be your chauffeur?"

"Sure," says Ted. "In fact, you can buy it. It's for sale if you
want to buy it."

Outside, on Madison Avenue, G——— and his wife—she
has on a plain suede coat lined like mad with sable—are smoking and breathing easier. They now have a small entourage in
their magnetic field.

Across 77th Street, Kenneth J. Lane, the jewelry designer, is
walking up Madison Avenue with his hands in his pockets and
his tweed coattails flying out like wings.

Up at Staempfli's, Phillip Bruno is winding up the Piqueras
show. He says goodbye to Paula Johnson of the Osborne Gal

lery—she hadn't been able to get up to see the Piqueras until now—with the proper social kiss. It is really getting black outside now, and colder, but he still has some kid in his office who is looking at about a dozen pieces of jade-green sculpture resting on a pile carpet.

"Looks sort of like the ruins of Karnak," says the kid, who has the biggest black Borsalino hat on Madison Avenue.

Mr. Bruno suppresses a few immediate responses.

"Well, they won't look like that on Tuesday."

Tuesday—another opening! And four days from then, Saturday, like filaments skidding toward the mother lode, all the old people and all the young people will stride down to the Avenue and rare back alongside the pedestals and socialize until the main event, which will probably be another prodigious serpentine-front commode with splayed feet at Parke-Bernet, and get the wet smacks echoing between the limestone fronts, while Joan Morse finds out, to be sure, just what *did* happen to everybody else during the warm season in London.

13

The Luther of Columbus Circle

One look at that Kipling stuff Huntington Hartford had carved on the wall down by the elevator in his new museum—well, you can imagine how they sniggered about that. *Kip*ling! It was practically the first thing they saw. Ah, the culturati. Hartford's museum, the Gallery of Modern Art, the tallest art museum in the world, ten stories of white marble out on an island in Columbus Circle, opened with a series of special nights, one of them being for the leaders of the art world. Everybody came rolling into Columbus Circle and debouched from cabs and Carey Cadillacs and went gaggling past the golden subway stairs Hartford built out there and into the arcade at the bottom of the building and over to the elevators where—pow! —there was this stanza from Rudyard Kipling, cut in marble. You can almost see the scene, the sniggering, the nudging and so forth. Hartford himself was up on the fifth floor receiving guests. One minute he was in his mood of Paradise Island charm. He has terrific teeth and a great smile. The next he was in his distracted mood, in which he looks as if he were off walking in a mimosa grove somewhere. It didn't matter. Either way the culturati missed the point, which was that Huntington Hartford, the megamillionaire, had come amongst them in the role of a Martin Luther for modern Culture.

Hartford's Luther role has been suffering because for thirteen years now the New York intelligentsia has been taking him and his works lightly. Nobody ever knew what else to make of him. All of a sudden, in the fall of 1951, into the world of the arts came Huntington Hartford, G. Huntington Hartford II. He had been known chiefly as a playboy who squired around Marta Toren, Lana Turner and other Hollywood glamorosi and then married a cigarette girl in Ciro's restaurant, Marjorie Steele. He was one of the couple of hundred or so richest men in the world, grandson of George Huntington Hartford, founder of the A&P, the Great Atlantic & Pacific Tea Company, the fifth largest corporation in America, General Motors, Jersey Standard, AT&T and Ford being one through four. Hartford was then forty years old. He had all his hair. He was good-looking, boyish, shy, and well-preserved from playing a lot of squash and tennis and getting sun at great watering places in both hemispheres. And now he turned up with seventy-odd million dollars, an eye for Culture and the most flagrantly unfashionable taste anybody in New York had ever heard of.

Hartford always swung from the heels. From the first his transgressions against artistic fashion were so severe that nobody ever noticed the theme that ran through them, over and over. To begin with, in 1951 he wrote, paid the printer, and published a pamphlet entitled, "Has God Been Insulted Here?" which rebuked James Jones, Tennesssee Williams, William Faulkner, Pablo Picasso and modern art and letters generally as unspeakably vulgar and profane. Was this guy serious? Several months later he publicly rejected a couple of artists who were applying to the Huntington Hartford Foundation art colony, calling them "too abstract." This brought to light the art colony, which Hartford had set up on 154 acres in Pacific Palisades, Calif. On the face of it, it looked like the answer to everything American bohemians had been demanding of society in their manifestoes since 1908. Every budding talent got a cottage studio tucked amid sylvan verdure for peace, solitude, inspiration and unharried work; plus all the food he could eat and spending money. For bonhommie and fruitful discussion with one's fellow artists there was a community house. The bohos, of course, turned out to be great flaming ingrates. One thing that got them was the way a little man came around at midday and left a basket of warm food on the cottage doorstep so they would not have to break off in mid-surge of genius to go get lunch. That, and the way a chauffeur showed up with eight cylinders cooing anytime somebody wanted to go into town. Besides, after the "too abstract" rhubarb, the place was unfashionable, even though Ernst Toch's ninth symphony and some other important work had come out of there. By and by there were fewer than three hundred applicants a year for utopia.

In 1955 he bought a full page ad in six New York newspapers and printed another Hartford creed. This one was entitled, "The Public Be Damned?" It said, in sum, that abstract and abstract-expressionist art were a piece of barbaric humbug being put over on the public by a cabal of museum directors, gallery owners and critics in sacrilege of the great tradition of representational art in the West. He singled out Picasso, William De Kooning and Georges Rouault as three of the sorriest of the lot. He himself began collecting some marvelously blatant back numbers such as Sir John Everett Millais, John Singer Sargent, Sir John Constable and Sir Edward Coley Burne-Jones.

In 1958, at the peak of the pop-eyed gasper school of drama—in which the hero was always a kind of emaciated Jack London writhing at center stage with a leather belt strapped above his elbow squirting eau du heroin into his brachial artery with a Vicks nose dropper—Huntington Hartford wrote a thoroughly Victorian stage version of Jane Eyre and produced it on Broadway. You had to see it to believe it. It would have closed the first night, but Hartford kept it going six weeks with sheer money.

All the while, from Hollywood to the Bahamas, he was setting up what looked like such a mixed bag of projects, some of them staggeringly expensive, that magazines spoke repeatedly of his "eccentric whims": A million-dollar legitimate theater for Hollywood (1953). A handwriting analysis (graphology) institute (1955). A $25 million-dollar conversion of Hog Island, off Nassau, into "Paradise Island," a resort for refined people (1959). A gift of $862,500 to New York City for a Central Park café and pavilion (1960—still bogged down in law suits). *Show*, a slick magazine (1961). By 1958 he had paid between $900,000 and one million dollars for an old office building with a Mansard slope, a Chevrolet sign and a clock on top of it on an island in Columbus Circle, where Broadway, Eighth Avenue and Central Park South converge. He tore the building down, hired Edward D. Stone, the famous architect, and started building his Gallery of Modern Art.

Just before the museum opened, Hartford came back from Nassau, his winter home, to give a final inspection. At fifty-three, he had lost none of the Hartford air. He was as boyish,

shy, athletically graceful and distracted as ever. He was also—
once more—as single-minded as a Ganges mystic. As he looked
over the museum's Aeolian-Skinner organ, built into an alcove
between the second and third floors, Hartford turned to a
visitor and said: "I thought a museum ought to have organ
music. You know, it's really like a church." The moment someone mentioned his first book, Hartford underscored his own
message: "I had a hard time deciding on a title. Before I
settled on *Art or Anarchy?* I had wanted to call it 'Armageddon of Art.' Armageddon means 'the final and conclusive battle
between the forces of good and evil.'" And in the lobby, on
the way out, he turned to the four lines from Kipling on the
wall near the elevators:

> But each for the joy of the working,
> And each, in his separate star,
> Shall draw the thing as he sees it
> For the God of things as they are.

"It says exactly what I want to say," said Hartford. "Do you
know what I mean?"

Kipling! Hartford could scarcely have chosen a more unfashionable writer, of course. British intellectuals began denouncing Kipling in the 1920's as a kind of P. R. man for
colonialism, and ever since he has come to be known as the
great Anti-Culture, even among culturati who have never read
a line of him. For Hartford, however, there is the voice of the
Lord and the voice of Victorian England—and what more is
there to be said?

It is impossible to pay any attention to what Hartford has
actually been saying about culture over the past thirteen years
without noticing how often he speaks of good and evil, god-
liness, the moral order, sacred values—in short, religion. I
mention paying attention, because his trouble is that nobody
really has. The intelligentsia just thrill to the gaucheness of his
gestures. Yet Hartford has been consistent all the way. First of

all there was the odd title of the pamphlet he published in 1951, "Has God Been Insulted Here?"—a quote from Balzac. All through his essays on art, then and since, he has used expressions such as "the spiritual life of our times," "right and wrong," "that Deity," "the Most High," "a Man Who was once called the Prince of Peace," "Jesus Christ Himself." He speaks of his museum as "a church." He carves a Kipling quotation about "the God of things as they are" on the wall. Yet the subject of all this gospel diction is art. Some of his phrases have a curious 19th century antique quality about them. "A Man Who was once called the Prince of Peace"—I doubt that there is a minister in all of the Union Theological Seminary who would dare use such a phrase today.

That, however, would not faze Hartford. Much of his thinking is a deliberate return to the mental atmosphere of Victorian England, a *Zeitgeist* into which he was thoroughly initiated by his mother, Henrietta Guerard Hartford, a Southern gentlewoman.

There is a wonderful photograph of Hartford and his mother that says a great deal. In this picture he is sixteen years old and standing up straight in a double-breasted blazer and ice cream pants with his hair fluffing down over his forehead in golden Gainsborough curves. His mother is standing just behind him looking out from under a great loopy garden party hat with a smile that says, "My Boy." The atmosphere is that of verandahs in Newport, R. I., singing-rounds in the parlor, croquet on the far lawn, straw hats, piqué fans, iced tea, mint leaves, at-homes on Thursday, Tiffany candlesticks, batik parasols, tennis shirts, Morocco leather, verbena beds, blue flies and green-and-yellow afternoons in the shade; which is to say, the genteel life of about 1880. The picture was taken in 1927, two years before the Depression began.

Hartford was brought up in Newport, which in 1927 was already a period piece, left over from *fin de siècle*. Hartford had the sort of isolated upper class childhood that most Americans get a glimpse of only in Marquand novels. His father, Edward Hartford, was one of three sons of George Huntington Hartford, who founded the A&P. The other two, George L. and John, went into the business and ran it after the death of "The Old Gentleman," as he was called. Edward, who was more the sensitive introvert, branched out by himself, invented a shock absorber and made a small fortune of his own. He died when Hartford was eleven. Hartford remembers him chiefly as a quiet figure who was always in his study with his back to the door and his face to the desk. So Hartford grew up with millions of dollars but without the slightest knowledge of or taste for the atmosphere of strong men using their fortunes as instruments of power. His uncles, George L. and John, lived and breathed the A&P and had little to do with him. The person who fashioned Hartford's entire style of life was his mother.

The boarding school she sent him off to was not likely to insinuate much of the din of the outside world into his life. It was St. Paul's, which, like all the best Eastern boarding schools, was a kind of country rector's Emersonian version of an English public school. The place was calcimined and bleached with the good odor of 19th century sententiae and precepts concerning God, gentility, noblesse oblige and the virtues of active sport. In an astounding confessional piece he wrote for his Harvard class of 1934 in 1959, Hartford told how St. Paul's molded him into a miserable, self-effacing "mouse."

At Harvard, Hartford had the money to cut any figure he wanted. But his classmates seem to remember him chiefly as this boy who was said to be fabulously rich and who stayed in his rooms reading Thackeray, Dickens and Sir Walter Scott. This was in 1930, at a time when—the literary histories assure us—all Harvard boys were reading Hemingway, Dos Passos and F. Scott Fitzgerald. Santa Barranza!—Sir Walter Scott!

Writers like Thackeray, Dickens and Scott were American

Victorian *fin de siècle* ideals in Culture. They were British, which gave them the right cultural cachet. They had established their reputations a good fifty years before. They were diverting, but with a tendency toward the profound. They were morally sound; which is to say, they exposed the evil of man without trifling with the social order. The same set of names—British writers and painters favored as cultural idols by the American genteel classes from about 1880 to World War II—turn up again and again in Hartford's life. He named his yachts *Joseph Conrad.* In his living room at 1 Beekman Place he has a bust of Conrad and leatherbound sets of Scott, Thackeray, Charles Lamb and Robert Louis Stevenson. The play he wrote and produced was an adaptation of Miss Charlotte Brontë's *Jane Eyre.* Many of the eighty paintings he has collected, at a cost of about $2.5 million for the lot, are by 19th century British painters long out of fashion, such as Burne-Jones, Constable, Millais, Sir Edwin Henry, and Paul Gustave Doré—whose drawings illustrate those lush editions of the classics wealthy matrons gave their children fifty years ago.

In his second year at Harvard, Hartford married a girl named Mary Lee Epling, who is now Mrs. Douglas Fairbanks Jr. The marriage may have been some sort of rebellion against the hold his mother had on his life—she had moved to Cambridge to be near him while he was in college—but he never lost his devotion to her style of life and intellectual ideals. For example, after Harvard, he went to work for the A&P but quit after a year, partly because his mother found the idea of his going into "commerce" repulsive.

The idea that no gentleman should be a businessman was left over from the British feudal aristocracy of the Middle Ages, but has governed the thinking of many American millionaires, especially on the Eastern seaboard, once the money has been made. In the old aristocratic scheme the eldest son took over the property and assumed the dynastic power. For a younger son three acceptable careers were open: warrior, diplomat or clergyman above the rank of vicar. Many American millionaires' sons have become diplomats, of course, and some, W. Averell Harriman for one, have wielded great influence. As for the role of warrior, the American armed forces are so highly bureaucratized and so lacking in style—the shabbiest South American colonel has a better-looking uniform than an American general—that the military is out. This category has hazed over into the general area of government service. An elected position is acceptable, so long as it is governor or better; Congressman is too lowly. A Cabinet or "Little Cabinet" appointment in any branch of government will do, or even assistant secretarial rank in the older branches, State Department (diplomat) or Defense (warrior).

But no matter how far the lines hazed, there was nothing in it for Hartford. First of all, he never had the slightest interest in politics or the exercise of temporal power. Second, even if he had, there would have been nobody to appoint him; his loyalties, when he felt them, were conservative Republican, and from his twenty-second to his forty-second birthday, there were nothing but Democrats doing the appointing in Washington. Besides, by his forty-second birthday, Hartford had already given up his dilettante-ish meanderings and entered the only sphere left open to him: religion.

Anyone who takes the trouble to read Hartford's first manifesto, "Has God Been Insulted Here?", will realize immediately that while the subject is arts and letters, the pamphlet is a religious tract. His thesis is that the artist, as "the spokesman for mankind," has great power. But the modern artist, particularly in literature and paintings, has become the tool of barbaric forces that would destroy civilization through fear, despair, vulgarity and rebellion. He sees the modern artist as a man "engrossed with evil and the destruction of life," wandering off "to some streamlined inferno in which he has burned in effigy the normal people of the earth. Nor have the people always objected, for it is often interesting to watch the devil at work, and a good bonfire is fun to see, even if it happens to be your own spirit that is going up in flames." He exhorts America's artists to reform. "A tremendous task it is!—the regeneration of the spiritual life of our times. Among all classes and all walks of people, the burden of this responsibility falls most weightily upon the shoulder of the artist."

The tone of this manifesto is excruciatingly naïve, even allowing for the old-fashioned Ruskinian rhetoric, and yet its argument is not unsophisticated. Plato makes much the same case in *The Republic*, arguing that poets who stress man's despair and play up to his weaker passions, his faintings, his fallings, his swoonings, should be banished from the state.

Even the religious rubric of Hartford's writing, for all its archaic flavor, is curiously appropriate. For by the time the pamphlet appeared, 1951, Culture was already becoming the new religion of America's intelligentsia, not figuratively but quite literally. For example, it was no happenstance that the 1961 Presidential Inaugural ceremonies included a succession of Roman Catholic, Protestant, Jewish and Greek Orthodox clergymen reading prayers, followed closely by Robert Frost reading a poem. For untold thousands of intellectuals today Culture, not church, is the favored form of religious rejection of the world. Young men and women may be seen riding to work on the subway every morning in New York with volumes by Rilke, Rimbaud, Herman Hesse and LeRoi Jones or somebody like that in their laps as if to say, This filthy train, this filthy office, this rotten Gotham and this roaring rat race are not my real life. My real life is Culture. Prints and paintings are on every wall today like ikons. Renoirs are virtually unobtainable; they are clutched like Columbus' bones. Bach, Mozart, Monteverdi and Schoenberg issue forth from the hi-fi with liturgical solemnity.

Hartford, then, is a curious combination of the shockingly old and the startlingly new. He arrives as a Martin Luther to reform modern Culture even before its religious nature has been generally recognized. Like Luther, he comes from out of nowhere with a manifesto decrying the evil and corruption of the established religion, i.e., modern art. Like Luther, he calls for a reformation, a return to a simpler and more blessed age. He has an age in mind: Victorian England—which the cultural religicos regard as the most reactionary phase of cultural history. *They* would, says Hartford. To go back "to the much-despised Victorian era might do less harm than the artists of our day believe," he wrote in "Has God Been Insulted Here?"

That pamphlet, like Luther's opening blast, the "95 Theses," was addressed to the high priests of the religion; in Hartford's case, artists and curators of Culture. Getting nowhere with the hierarchy, Hartford, like Luther, appealed directly to the people. He published his second big manifesto, "The Public Be Damned?", in daily newspapers.

He exhorts the multitudes: "Ladies and gentlemen, form your own opinions concerning art. Don't be afraid to dis-agree—loudly, if necessary—with the critics. Stand up and be heard. And when the high priests of criticism and the museum directors and the teachers of mumbo jumbo begin to realize that you mean business you will be astonished, in my humble opinion, how fast they will change their tune."

Hartford's attempt to take his Reformation to the people had actually begun in Los Angeles. He had hit upon the idea of holding a huge art exhibition—requiring the cooperation of Los Angeles' leading museums and galleries—in which the critics would select the paintings they liked best and the public would vote for the paintings they liked best. Hartford felt sure the discrepancy in taste would be crushing to the critics. In any case, he says, the project was blocked at every turn by the museum directors and he began to sense the extraordinary power of the museums in the art world. In New York, he says, the situation was even more dictatorial. One museum—the Museum of Modern Art—was determining the whole course of American painting, and much of European painting, through an extraordinary control over reputations and publicity. The strategy of his Gallery of Modern Art was to provide a counterforce to the Museum of Modern Art, even to the point of insisting on the same phrase—Modern Art—in the name.

Meantime, many of the other Hartford projects, his "eccentric whims," have actually been integral parts of the same religious crusade. His art colony was an attempt to create a benevolent environment in which a non-bitter, non-despairing, non-destructive generation of Thackerays, Constables and Sir Walter Scotts might develop. A legitimate theater he bankrolled in Hollywood was an attempt to plant wholesome Culture in the heart of the evil movie industry. Paradise Island, the resort, has been Hartford's idea of reintroducing the *fin de siècle*, Victorian gentility of Newport, R.I., into the lives of influential Americans who might want to loll in the Bahamas. His Central Park pavilion scheme has much the same idea behind it. He founded *Show* magazine with the idea of recreating *Vanity Fair,* an elegant cultural magazine of the 1920's. Hartford could appreciate the photographs he saw in bound copies of *Vanity Fair,* often of polished-looking men in wing collars, wide foulard cravats and double-breasted waistcoats exuding an air of leisurely British drawing room grace.

Throughout, Hartford has been far from the mild millionaire with "whims" that he is often depicted as. He has been a plunger. He has taken risks that would make an oil millionaire flinch. By his own estimate, he has gone through certainly a fourth and perhaps as much as a half of his $70 million fortune, although the figure could go back up if certain investments, such as Paradise Island, pay off. He has devoted himself to his chosen field—the religion of Culture—with a zealous and enduring disdain of the cultural Establishment. And if the culturati still do not fathom his Luther role, even with this white marble tower on Columbus Circle to illustrate it, Hartford will not be downhearted. He is taking the long view. For as it says in the rest of the Kipling poem, "When Earth's Last Picture is Painted," whose last stanza is on the wall down there by the elevators, someday even the youngest critic will be out of the picture:

When Earth's last picture is painted and the tubes are twisted and dried,
When the oldest colours have faded, and the youngest critic has died,
We shall rest, and, faith, we shall need it—lie down for an aeon or two,
Till the Master of All Good Workmen shall put us to work anew.

And those that were good shall be happy: they shall sit in a golden chair;
They shall splash at a ten-league canvas with brushes of comets' hair.
They shall find real saints to draw from—Magdalene, Peter, and Paul;
They shall work for an age at a sitting and never be tired at all.

14

The New Art Gallery Society

Picasso's Goat! Little Alexander, with a glass of Scotch whiskey in one hand, lolls on the base of Picasso's immortal bronze goat. His other hand is hooked like a coat hanger over the nose of the goat as if he intends to hang forever from this baggy-dugged milestone of Culture in the lobby of the Museum of Modern Art. It is sacrilege, God knows. This is Picasso's goat. The occasion is the reopening of the Museum of Modern Art. The Museum was closed for certain renovations, and the building of a new wing. All it took was six months. But, my god, the reopening of this place turns out to be a stupendous occasion.

Everybody who was invited came—except Salvador Dali—and only big donors, big socialites, big politicians, big artists and a few satellites were invited. Thousands, literally thousands, about six thousand, are caroming around the place, careening, ricocheting amid a lot of 1930-Modern rectangles and a yellow haze like the Ninth Avenue end of the Port Authority bus terminal. They are all wearing dinner clothes and high-waisted gowns and glaring at Little Alexander, who dangles from Picasso's goat and stares back. How insolent! How epicene!

Oddly enough, Little Alexander is proof of just how stupendous the reopening of the Museum of Modern Art is. He is one of those thin young men who live in one-and-a-half-room apartments, as they are known in New York, but at perfectly fine addresses, such as East 55th Street, and come out, when summoned, to escort rich, splendid, dazzling but aging women. It has to be a pretty fine occasion or they aren't going to the trouble of getting someone like Little Alexander. As for himself, he has only to worry that someone like his current charge, Mrs. Annette———, will drink too much and conclude, in the dawn, that it is she, at last, who will be able to coax passion out of this beautiful boy.

Already Annette, in a gown like an Arthur Rackham soul bird, is abroad in the museum garden. She is circling like a sea pigeon around this and that splendid group. Out in the garden, near the new black pools, which, for a fact, look like rectangles in the architect's drawing, stands Saul Steinberg, the artist, with the face of a Bronx cleaning and pressing shopowner, talking to Zaidee Parkinson—a daughter of the Parkinsons who helped found the museum thirty-five years ago—a beautiful girl, and the others, charming people, about mnemonics:

". . . and then 2 and 1 and 4 and 8 . . ."

"Well, I never in my life, if you know what I mean!"

Up on the terrace, Stewart Udall, the Secretary of the Interior of the United States, is sort of aw-shucksing around, wearing a white dinner jacket and a crew cut, still looking as though he is standing on the free throw line in the school gymnasium in June wondering if he is going to ask anybody to dance. Stewart Udall is talking to Nicole Alphand, the wife of the French Ambassador. Madame Alphand is still a symbol of all that is, at this late date, still glamorous about the diplomatic life. On the other side of the terrace, across the bobbing heads, Mrs. Jacob Javits, Marion Javits, the wife of the Senator from New York, is standing just beyond the welded legs of a huge black widow spider by Alexander Calder. Mrs. Javits would probably be the symbol of what little remains glamorous about the life of congressmen, but most of the time she won't go near Washington. Both of them, Nicole Alphand and Marion Javits are caught in the strange spot, on the one hand, of not quite being celebrities themselves but being, on the other hand, more than just wives of the illuminati. All sorts of people are paying court to Helena Rubinstein, looking serene as a Taoist mask; she is currently a local heroine because when robbers broke into her apartment, she said "Go ahead and kill me; I'm an old woman and I'm not going to give my jewels to two ferrets like you," and they fled without them. Jacques Lipchitz, the sculptor, walks by, and Kathy Marcus walks by. Ah, good for Kathy Marcus. She is East Texas turning right into the boutique-land of East 64th Street. Beautifully! And in the middle of the caroming mob, in the doorway from the new wing to the garden, while the Burns guards gaze, Huntington Hartford, the millionaire who opened his own museum in New York last March, is saying: "I haven't seen so many people since J. Paul Getty's party and I lost everybody for three hours there."

The Burns guards have white ribbons up in the garden between the pools and the terrace. On the pool side are five thousand people, haunch to paunch, who merely gave a hundred dollars or a couple of thousand or something of the sort to the building fund for the museum's new wing. They just have unimpeachable, not staggering, credentials. The spotlights in the garden beam down on their skulls with a pale ochre haze, as at a night baseball game in Denison, Texas. On the terrace, on the other side of the ribbons, stand the true illuminati, for example, Adlai Stevenson and Lady Bird Johnson, the President's wife. In a few minutes she will address them all, in a drawl that sounds like it came in by mail order from Pine Bluff, concerning God, Immortality and Inspiration through Art for the free peoples.

Mark Rothko, the painter, is talking to Thomas Hess, the executive editor of *Art News*, and Frank O'Hara, the museum employee who writes poems and blue plays, about the funny time Hedy Lamarr—it was Hedy Lamarr's birthday—about the funny time it was Hedy Lamarr's birthday and they were all in Franz Kline's studio.

Hedy Lamarr and everybody and Mark Rothko in Franz Kline's studio in New York. And Adlai and Lady Bird and Huntington and Nicole and Marion and Stewart and Zaidee and Kathy and everybody standing around on the terrace of the Museum of Modern Art. It doesn't even seem unusual. There may have been a time, sixty years ago, or whenever it was, when Renoir was walking down a road and ran into Cézanne, who was stumbling down the road dragging a big painting of some bathers, with one end of it bumping up and down in the dust. Well, he told Renoir, he was taking this over to a friend who liked it who was very sick. Fat chance of any of that bohemian homefolks stuff going on today. Today Robert Rauschenberg does some comic paintings, now known as Pop Art, for a couple of years and here he is in dinner clothes and a seat of honor at the Museum of Modern Art, being lionized by Adlai and Lady Bird and Nicole and the rest. Today the world of art in New York, the world of celebrities, the world of society, press agents, gossip columnists, fashion designers, interior decorators and other hierophants have all converged on Art, now in a special, exalted place. Art—and the Museum of Modern Art in particular—has become the center of social rectitude, comparable to the Episcopal Church in Short Hills. The people involved look to the opening of new art gallery shows the way they used to look to theatre openings. Today they consider a theatre opening pretty bland stuff, unless it is at least Richard Burton in *Hamlet*. But the galleries! Sometimes two or three or more galleries will get together and assemble the work of a major painter, such as they did in the spring of 1962 with Picasso, or last spring with Braque. They divide up a man's lifework among them, and the grand opening is like a cattle call, with all these people roaring in clusters from one gallery to another on and right off Madison Avenue, plastering each other with social kisses and blazing away with 150-watt eyeballs.

The thing is, then, that the reopening of the Museum of Modern Art is the biggest gallery opening possible. It was only closed six months, but never mind. When it reopens, it is a state occasion. The wife of the President of the United States delivers the re-inaugural address. The Cabinet is there, the diplomats are there, Adlai Stevenson, Ambassador to the United Nations, is there. The clergy is there; some noted Chicago preacher is reading the text of an address by Paul Tillich, the theologian, who prepared a sacred discourse for the occasion. The new realm of man's holy spirit!

Years ago a nice woman with a million dollars' worth of real estate she wanted to dispose of in some devout way would have left it to the church. But Mrs. E. Parmalee Prentice left both her town houses on West 53rd Street to the museum. It seemed only natural and proper. Then the new wing goes up. No church building fund, except for some Mormon churches, ever piled up so fast. They stormed the place with tens, hundreds of thousands, millions at a time. In the banquet hall,

David Rockefeller extends his big right hand like a frond toward the chairman of the fund drive, Gardner (Mike) Cowles, the publisher, who stands with a large red flower in his buttonhole and his teeth ablaze.

And then David Rockefeller is telling how he remembers when he was a little boy just watching and listening on those afternoons back in 1928 when Mr. and Mrs. John D. Rockefeller, Jr., and Lizzie Bliss and A. Conger Goodyear and the Parkinsons and the others were sitting down in the Rockefellers' living room to found a museum of modern art, which they did, the next year. Modern Art had no uphill battle in America, not with Rockefeller, Goodyear, Bliss, all that irresistible, golden cachet. They had discovered Modern Art in Europe, where it was fashionable in the 1920's. It became fashionable in the United States from the moment the group founded the Museum of Modern Art in 1929. In fact, they had to go into the provinces and beat the bushes to find enough opposition to Modern Art to give the project a sense of spiritual mission, wicked outrage and zest. And today—they rally behind modern art in *Kaffeklatches* at the supermarkets in Bethesda.

Only six hundred people could be invited to the dinner at the reopening, and there were a few heartaches over that. Outside, the six thousand other culturati, who will stand behind the white ribbons in the garden, are still piling up in front of the new main entrance. Marvelous! The poor—the poor artists—are picketing the place. In front of the museum, men and women debouch from back seats in a billow of couturier colors and ribbed silk and on the other side the police have backed up the poor artists and the bystanders behind the barricades in front of America House and other places across the street. The artists are marching with placards bearing huge question marks. The artists are from the Artists-Tenants Association and the question they are asking is, What do you fat, posh, splendid, starched consumers of culture really care about art? What are you doing to see to it that the City of New York allows us—the progenitors of the art and of the openings of the future, the carriers of the sacred standard—to keep our lofts? The leader, Jean-Pierre Merle, short, slight, wearing a marvelously elaborate mustache, runs back and forth across the street, delivering manifestos and appeals to the museum, passing out buttons bearing the symbol, the question mark.

Inside, William Burden, former Ambassador to Belgium, is talking surrounded by yellow felt. Felt lines the walls of the room and bears the signatures, blown up huge, of the entire pantheon—Picasso, Matisse, Cézanne, Braque, Jackson Pollack, Robert Rauschenberg, him, too, all of them. At Huntington Hartford's table sits Edward Steichen, the immortal photographer, eighty-five years old, who can look up from the table and see his own signature a foot high on the yellow felt. Across the table, his wife, Joanna, who is thirty-one years old, sits there with the smile of the queen who tells no secrets. Steichen's beard is full, long and squared off at the bottom. He wears clear plastic spectacles and sits up straight. One has only to look and almost see a magenta ribbon of silk stretching across his shirt front with little taffeta pools of shadow on it and maybe a sunburst here and there on his dinner jacket. But of course. What is the Museum of Modern Art but the American academy? The Royal Academy in London—the National Academy in Paris—a hundred, a thousand dinners with thin crystal, long-tined lobster forks, aging aesthetes, art, honor and national glory. Somebody comes up and hands Steichen a plum-colored velvet pouch. He peers down through spectacles and eases the drawstrings open in what is known as a stately manner. It is a gift from Shirley Burden, the Ambassador's brother, celebrating the opening of the museum's new photography gallery, named after Steichen. Steichen reaches in the pouch and pulls out a miniature silver candlestick. Huntington Hartford looks over, Mrs. Edward Hopper looks over. He sets it up on the table and the poor artists are hollering for lofts in front of America House.

Six hundred leading artists were invited to the reopening of the Museum of Modern Art. Except for twelve who were asked. to dinner, they are all waiting out on the sculpture terrace. About 9:30 everybody leaves the banquet hall and already there are six thousand minor culturati packed behind the ribbons in the garden. There are no lights on the terrace, and the six hundred artists are waiting up there like sacred monsters in a pen. The six hundred dinner guests follow Mrs. Johnson, and the television crews and the reporters and the photographers following Mrs. Johnson, and the hustling, elbowing procession is like a flying wedge, plowing into the artists and driving them back into their own corner.

Six hundred sacred egos are getting batted around. It is dark up there, and nobody recognizes these damned artists anyway, especially in dinner jackets. Somehow Jean-Pierre Merle materializes up there with his question mark buttons, and some of the artists, the guests of honor, start saying, Here, give me one of those damned buttons, man, like we're tired of being batted around up here. J———, the abstract expressionist, has had enough of this———. He jostles and elbows his way down the steps from the terrace, glares at the Burns guards, glares at Babe Paley, even though she looks like a million dollars, and then he comes upon Little Alexander, hanging from Picasso's goat. He just stops. "What the hell—," he says.

"Screw you," says Little Alexander, in his most forthright way.

J——— doesn't know what to do, so he just turns around slowly, and in so doing he has an awful moment, one of those awful moments when you find out that the despised enemy is, after all, right. Through the plate glass, he can see quite clearly in the garden another of those pieces of immortality, the outstretched arms of "Mother and Child" by Jacques Lipchitz.

There are empty champagne glasses stacked all around it. One glass is on top of another and up, up, up they rise like crystal stalks. J—— sinks, drowns, decays in the smell of old grape and the morning after.

The Museum of Modern Art has reopened. And Little Alexander hangs there from Picasso's goat.

15

The Secret Vice

Real buttonholes. That's it! A man can take his thumb and forefinger and unbutton his sleeve at the wrist because this kind of suit has real buttonholes there. Tom, boy, it's terrible. Once you know about it, you start seeing it. All the time! There are just two classes of men in the world, men with suits whose buttons are just sewn onto the sleeve, just some kind of cheapie decoration, or—yes!—men who can unbutton the sleeve at the wrist because they have real buttonholes and the sleeve really buttons up. Fascinating! My friend Ross, a Good Guy, thirty-two years old, a lawyer Downtown with a good head of Scotch-Irish hair, the kind that grows right, unlike lower-class hair, is sitting in his corner on East 81st St., in his Thonet chair, with the Flemish brocade cushion on it, amid his books, sets of Thackeray, Hazlitt, Lamb, Walter Savage Landor, Cardinal Newman, and other studs of the rhetoric game, amid his prints, which are mostly Gavarni, since all the other young lawyers have Daumiers or these cute muvvas by "Spy," or whatever it is, which everybody keeps laying on thatchy-haired young lawyers at Christmas—Ross is sitting among all these good tawny, smoke-cured props drinking the latest thing somebody put him onto, port, and beginning to talk about coats with real buttonholes at the sleeves. What a taboo smirk on his face!

It is the kind of look two eleven-year-old kids get when they are riding the Ferris wheel at the state fair, and every time they reach the top and start down they are staring right into an old midway banner in front of a sideshow, saying, "THE MYSTERIES OF SEX REVEALED! SIXTEEN NUDE GIRLS! THE BARE TRUTH! EXCITING! EDUCATIONAL!" In the sideshow they get to see 16 female foetuses in jars of alcohol, studiously arranged by age, but—that initial taboo smirk!

Ross, thirty-two years old, in New York City—the same taboo smirk.

"I want to tell you a funny thing," he says. "The first time I had any idea about this whole business of the buttonholes was a couple of Christmases ago, one Saturday, when I ran into Sturges at Dunhill's." Dunhill the tobacco shop. Sturges is a young partner in Ross's firm on Wall Street. Ross idealizes Sturges. Ross stopped carrying an attaché case, for example, because Sturges kept referring to attaché cases as leather lunch pails. Sturges is always saying something like, "You know who I saw yesterday? Stolz. There he was, walking along Exchange Place with his leather lunch pail, the poor bastard." Anyway,

Ross says he ran into Sturges in Dunhill's. "He was trying to get some girl a briar pipe for Christmas or some damn thing." That Sturges! "Anyway, I had just bought a cheviot tweed suit, kind of Lovat-colored—you know, off the rack—actually it was a pretty good-looking suit. So Sturges comes over and he says, 'Well, old Ross has some new togs,' or something like that. Then he says, 'Let me see something,' and he takes the sleeve and starts monkeying around with the buttons. Then he says, 'Nice suit,' but he says it in a very half-hearted way. Then he goes off to talk to one of those scientific slenderellas he always has hanging around. So I went over to him and said, 'What was all that business with the buttons?' And he said, 'Well, I thought maybe you had it custom made.' He said it in a way like it was now pretty goddamned clear it wasn't custom made. Then he showed me his suit—it was a window-pane check, have you ever seen one of those?—he showed me his suit, the sleeve, and *his* suit had buttonholes on the sleeve. It was custom made. He showed me how he could unbutton it. Just like this. The girl wondered what the hell was going on. She stood there with one hip cocked, watching him undo a button on his sleeve. Then I looked at mine and the buttons were just sewn on. You know?" And you want to know something? That really got to old Ross. He practically couldn't *wear* that suit anymore. All right, it's ridiculous. He probably shouldn't even be confessing all this. It's embarrassing. And—the taboo smirk!

Yes! The lid was off, and poor old Ross was already hooked on the secret vice of the Big men in New York: custom tailoring and the mania for the marginal differences that go into it. Practically all the most powerful men in New York, especially on Wall Street, the people in investment houses, banks and law firms, the politicians, especially Brooklyn Democrats, for some reason, outstanding dandies, those fellows, the blue-chip culturati, the major museum directors and publishers, the kind who sit in offices with antique textile shades—practically all of these men are fanatical about the marginal differences that go into custom tailoring. They are almost like a secret club insignia for them. And yet it is a taboo subject. They won't talk about it. They don't want it known that they even care about it. But all the time they have this fanatical eye, more fanatical than a woman's, about the whole thing and even grade men by it. The worst jerks, as far as they are concerned—and people can lose out on jobs, promotions, the whole can of worms, because of this—are men who have dumped a lot of money, time and care into buying ready-made clothes from some Englishy dry goods shop on Madison Avenue with the belief that they are really "building fine wardrobes." Such men are considered to be bush leaguers, turkeys and wet smacks, the kind of men who tote the leather lunch pail home at night and look forward to having a drink and playing with the baby.

God, it's painful to hear old Ross talk about all this. It's taboo! Sex, well, all right, talk your head off. But this, these men's clothes—a man must have to have beady eyes to even see these things. But these are Big men! But—all right!

It's the secret vice! In Europe, all over England, in France, the mass ready-made suit industry is a new thing. All men, great and small, have had tailors make their suits for years, and they tend to talk a little more with each other about what they're getting. But in America it's the secret vice. At Yale and Harvard, boys think nothing of going over and picking up a copy of *Leer, Poke, Feel, Prod, Tickle, Hot Whips, Modern Mammaries,* and other such magazines, and reading them right out in the open. Sex is not taboo. But when the catalogue comes from Brooks Brothers or J. Press, that's something they whip out only in *private.* And they can hardly wait. They're in the old room there poring over all that tweedy, thatchy language about "Our Exclusive Shirtings," the "Finest Lairdsmoor Heather Hopsacking," "Clearspun Rocking Druid Worsteds," and searching like detectives for the marginal differences, the

shirt with a flap over the breast pocket (J. Press), the shirt
with no breast pocket (Brooks), the pants with military pockets, the polo coat with welted seams—and so on and on,
through study and disastrous miscalculations, until they learn,
at last, the business of marginal differentiations almost as perfectly as those teen-agers who make their mothers buy them
button-down shirts and then make the poor old weepies sit up
all night punching a buttonhole and sewing on a button in the
back of the collar because they bought the wrong damn shirt,
one of those hinkty ones without the button in the back.

And after four years of Daddy bleeding to pay the tabs,
Yale, Harvard, and the rest of these schools turn out young
gentlemen who are confident that they have at last mastered
the secret vice, marginal differentiations, and they go right
down to Wall Street or wherever and—blam!—they get it like
old Ross, right between the eyes. A whole new universe to
learn! Buttonholes! A whole new set of clothing firms to know
about—places like Bernard Weatherill, probably the New York
custom tailor with the biggest reputation, very English, Frank
Brothers and Dunhill's, Dunhill's the tailor, which are slightly
more—how can one say it?—flamboyant?—places like that, or
the even more esoteric world of London tailors, Poole, Hicks,
Wells, and God knows how many more, and people knock
themselves out to get to London to get to these places, or else
they order straight from the men these firms send through
New York on regular circuits and put up in hotels, like the
Biltmore, with big books of swatches, samples of cloths, piled
up on the desk-table.

The secret vice! A whole new universe! Buttonholes! The
manufacturers can't make ready-made suits with permanent
buttonholes on the sleeves. The principle of ready-made
clothes is that each suit on the rack can be made to fit about
four different shapes of men. They make the sleeves long and
then the store has a tailor, an unintelligible little man who does

alterations, chop them off to fit men with shorter arms and move the buttons up.

And suddenly Ross found that as soon as you noticed this much, you started noticing the rest of it. Yes! The scyes, for example. The scyes! Imagine somebody like Ross knowing all this esoteric terminology. Ross is a good old boy, for godsake. The scyes! The scyes are the armholes in a coat. In ready-made clothes, they make the armholes about the size of the Holland Tunnel. Anybody can get in these coats. Jim Bradford, the former heavyweight weight-lifting champion, who has arms the size of a Chapman Valve fire hydrant, can put on the same coat as some poor bastard who is mooning away the afternoon at IBM shuffling memos and dreaming of going home and having a drink and playing with the baby. Naturally, for everybody but Jim Bradford, this coat is loose and looks sloppy, as you can imagine. That's why custom-made suits have high armholes; because they fit them to a man's own particular shoulder and arm. And then all these other little details. In Ross's league, Wall Street, practically all of these details follow the lead of English tailoring. The waist: the suits go in at the waist, they're fitted, instead of having a straight line, like the Ivy League look. This Ivy League look was great for the ready-made manufacturers. They just turned out simple bags and everybody was wearing them. The lapels: in the custom-made suits they're wider and have more "belly," meaning more of a curve or flared-out look along the outer edge. The collar: the collar of the coat fits close to the neck—half the time in ready-made suits it sits away from the neck, because it was made big to fit all kinds. The tailor-made suit fits closer and the collar itself will have a curve in it where it comes up to the notch. The sleeves: the sleeves are narrower and are slightly tapered down to the wrists. Usually, there are four buttons, sometimes three, and they really button and unbutton. The shoulders are padded to give the coat shape; "natural shoulders" are for turkeys and wet smacks. The vents: often the coat will have side vents or no vents, instead of center vents, and the vents will be deeper than in a ready-made suit. Well, hell, Ross could go on about all this—but there, you can already see what the whole thing is like.

Ross even knows what somebody is likely to say to this. You walk into a room and you can't tell whether somebody has real buttonholes on his sleeves or not. All of these marginal differences are like that. They're so small, they're practically invisible. All right! That's what's so maniacal about it. In women's clothes, whole styles change from year to year. They have new "silhouettes," waists and hems go up and down, collars go in and out, breasts blossom out and disappear; you can follow it. But in men's clothes there have been only two style changes in this century, and one of them was so esoteric, it's hard for a tailor to explain it without a diagram. It had to do with eliminating a breast seam and substituting something called a "dart." That happened about 1913. The other was the introduction of pleats in pants about 1922. Lapels and pants leg widths have been cut down some, but most of the flashy stuff in lapels and pants goes on in ready-made suits, because the manufacturers are naturally hustling to promote style changes and make a buck. In custom-made suits, at least among tailors in the English tradition, there have really been no changes for fifty years. The whole thing is in the marginal differences— things that show that you spent more money and had servitors in there cutting and sewing like madmen and working away just for you. Status! Yes!

Yes, and how can these so-called Big men really get obsessed with something like this? God only knows. Maybe these things happen the way they happened to Lyndon Johnson, Our President. Mr. Johnson was campaigning with John Kennedy in 1960, and he had to look at Kennedy's clothes and then look at his own clothes, and then he must have said to himself, in his winning, pastoral way, Great Hairy Ned on the mountaintop, my clothes look like Iron Boy overalls. Yus, muh cluths look luk Irun Bouy uvverulls. Now, this Kennedy, he had most of his clothes made by tailors in England. Anyway, however it came about, one day in December, 1960, after the election, if one need edit, Lyndon Johnson, the salt of the good earth of Austin, Texas, turned up on Savile Row in London, England, and walked into the firm of Carr, Son & Woor. He said he wanted six suits, and the instructions he gave were: "I want to look like a British diplomat." Lyndon Johnson! Like a British diplomat! You can look it up. Lyndon Johnson, President of the United States, Benefactor of the Po', Lion of NATO, Defender of the Faith of Our Fathers, Steward of Peace in Our Times, Falconer of Our Sly Asiatic Enemies, Leader of the Free World—is soft on real buttonholes! And I had wondered about Ross.

16

The Nanny Mafia

All right, Charlotte, you gorgeous White Anglo-Saxon Protestant socialite, all you are doing is giving a birthday party for your little boy with the E. S. A. (Eastern Socially Attractive) little-boy bangs in his eyes and all his little friends. So why are you sitting there by the telephone and your old malachite-top coffee table gnashing on one thumbnail? Why are you staring out the Thermo-Plate glass toward the other towers on East 72nd Street with such vacant torture in your eyes?

"Damn. I knew I'd forget something," says Charlotte. "I forgot the champagne."

So gorgeous Charlotte twists around in the chair with her alabaster legs and lamb-chop shanks still crossed and locked together in hard, slippery, glistening skins of nylon and silk and starts going through the note pad by the telephone, causing her Leslie II Prince Valiant coiffure to hang in her eyes so that she has to keep blowing the strands away, snorting and leafing through the note pad.

O.K., Charlotte. Champagne for your little boy's birthday party?

"You're damned right," she says. "For all the nannies. I'm not kidding! If we ever tried to give a party for Bobby and his little friends without champagne for the nannies, we might as well, you know, forget about it.

"Bobby's nanny is mad enough as it is. All she can do is drop what are supposed to be very subtle hints about the V————'s party for little Sarah. Do you know what Van gave each kid as a *party favor?* An electric truck. I'm talking about a *real electric truck.* Of course, they're nothing much really. They're *smaller* than a Jaguar. By a little bit. The kid can get inside of it and drive it! They cost five hundred dollars, five *hundred* dollars! Can you imagine that? We had to carry the damn thing home. You should have seen us trying to get it in the cab. Of course, Van is absolutely petrified of the nannies.

"Well, I was damned if we were going to do anything like that. Robert had to take the whole afternoon off Tuesday to go to Schwarz. This was precisely the afternoon the Swedes came in with some bond thing, of course. The Swedes wear the *worst* clothes. They all look like striped cardboard. They think they're very *Eu*ropean. Anyway, Robert got some kind of bird with a tape recorder in it, I don't know. The kids can talk into it and it records it and says it back. Something like that. You know. Well, I don't care, I think it's a perfectly cute party favor, but our Mrs. G———— is not going to be happy with it, I'm sure of that.

"She wanted us to have the party in Robert's father's house on 70th Street in the first place. I'm serious! She doesn't *like* this apartment! It em*bar*rasses her! Do you know what it is? Do you know who runs the East Side of New York? The nanny mafia. There's a nanny mafia!"

The nanny mafia! At this moment, the nannies, the leading nannies, are all gathered down in Central Park, in the playground just over the stone wall next to Fifth Avenue, at the foot of East 77th Street. Down there, through the pin oak, birch, beech and sweetgum leaves, in the sun and dappled shadows, on this green-and-gold, bluebottle-fly afternoon, you can see the nannies sitting on the benches around the oval that the playground fence forms. In the middle of the oval are their charges. All these little boys and girls are either in English Brabingham baby carriages or else they are playing about the swings and the seesaws in Cerutti shorts and jumpers with only the most delightful verandah-in-Newport, Sundays-in-North Egremont sort of gaiety. The oval fence has high and rather graceful spikes and stands as a kind of genteel stockade against the customary terrors of New York life. In fact, the playground at the foot of 77th Street is the kind of place all the New Yorkers who feel like hopeless DPs from the genteel style of life can walk by and look at and recharge their gentility cells and walk on. Down there in the sun and dappled shadows, after all, are the nannies, fillers of these little vessels of the Protestant ethic, angels in starched white, gleaming in God's daylight.

Nannies are generally middle-aged women, or old women, whom upper-class families in Europe have hired over the last 125 years to look after the children up through age six or seven. Nannies have a higher standing than a nursemaid, since they have the power to impose discipline and manners on the child. But they have a lower standing than a governess, in that they undertake no real education. But, mainly, in Europe and in the United States, they have become a symbol of the parents' status. First of all, parents who have nannies to look after the children have to have money. That is one thing. And parents who have nannies lead their own lives. This gives them more status even in front of their own children. They don't have to appear in the ridiculous role of martyred, harried creatures, forever ill-kempt and ill-humored, waiting on the children like servants. They don't have to clean up after their tantrums, go fetch them crayons, mollify their stupid fears or otherwise cast themselves in some demeaning role. They can come on, say, a couple of times a day, as figures of authority, charm, largesse, awe, smelling languorously of grape and tonic.

Upper-class New York and Boston families, still living within a European tradition, have adopted the nanny system as their own. They hire English nannies, if possible, always nice middling women with sensible hairdos, sensible clothes and sensible shoes. Or, if not English nannies, French nannies, which is just about as good, especially as it enables a woman to report in an amused and tolerant way how many French words her daughter has picked up.

The only funny thing is, the nannies are the most complete and unabashed snobs in America. The rich themselves have abandoned many of the symbols of status. They really botch dinner now. They don't dress. They don't use the finger bowls and all that great business at the end. The nannies note and deplore it all. They are the products, the creations, of an older, sterner status system and style of life and they bring all of its conventions into the modern age.

"Do you know what she says about this apartment? Well, you know, they get on the phone to each other, it's like a network. The phone rings *all* the time around here, and it's always the nannies. They call up and say that little Sarah wants to say hello to little Bobby, and so the kids whine at each other in those little cretin voices they have for about 15 seconds and after that the nannies go on and on."

Anyway, one day after little Sarah V——— had been over here for something, Charlotte forgets what it was, Miss S———, the V———'s nanny, she's an absolute tyrant, Miss S——— was telling Mrs. G———, and the thing is, poor Mrs. G——— believes absolutely 100 per cent of every pronouncement that woman makes, Miss S——— was telling her, of course Charlotte could only hear Mrs. G———'s end of the conversation, but you could *tell* what she was saying, she was saying that Charlotte and Robert have the kind of apartment where everything looks cheap except what they got as wedding presents. She thought she would *die!* "Don't they have the most fantastic frame of mind you ever heard of?" Charlotte says. "We call Mrs. G——— the Black Widow, very much behind her back, I might add. But don't you just know the kind of apartment the nannies are talking about?"

You know, you're invited to dinner, says Charlotte, and this poor couple, as soon as you walk in, you can see they've gone to a *lot of trouble*, flowers and indirect lighting, yellow glows, city lights, and they've hired a butler. The girl always has on some kind of Ravish-Me hostess outfit and looks like Little Heidi of Switzerland conscripted into a seraglio. *So* pathetic. And the furniture is always sort of Department Store Louis, if you know the kind Charlotte means. Then you sit down to dinner at this *aw*ful table and then suddenly here is this *fa*bulous silver and china, Winslow table settings, apparently the real thing—fabulous! The comparison is just too crushing. It's always obvious where it came from. Their parents and their parents' friends shelled out and gave it to them when they got married. Haven't you ever been in that kind of apartment? It's *too*—Charlotte doesn't know—it's not even pathetic. Well, Charlotte didn't mean to go on about that. But that's exactly how the nannies think!

"I know that's what the Black Widow thinks about *this* apartment," says Charlotte, and her eyes start drifting over her own mountainscape of chaises, commodes, pier tables, settees and the wall-to-wall. "But what she's really against is that this is a new building. She thinks it's awful. That's why she wants to have the party over at Robert's father's. She says Robert's father will *love* it. He'll hate it. The Taylors actually did that. They actually gave the children a party at her parents', on Ninety-something Street, a lovely old place. Just so their nannies wouldn't be embarrassed in front of the other nannies!"

The nanny mafia! Nannies are rarely brilliant, shrewd or conniving people. They come out of the British low-heel, twist-weave suit, Kind Lady tradition. But they are very firm on all social matters. The nannies' hold on the East Side comes first from the fact that they keep holding up status values to their masters. If left alone, people can ignore status symbols to some extent. But if somebody keeps thrusting them in their face, and the claims seem to be at all valid, people wilt. They start getting nervous. They do what the nannies, the little old status pharisees, say about children's clothes, children's parties and the size and decor of a fit parents' apartment in New York. Second, there is the nannies' network. They all seem to know each other. They all seem to live in the same section of the Bronx, around Mosholu Parkway up near the Zoo. They all seem to have supper together on Wednesday, their day off. They all seem to send each other cards, supposedly from one child to another but all written by the nannies and really just part of the nannies' network. They all spend half their working day with one another by telephone or else out in the stockade in Central Park. All this time they are trading information. Such information! Never mind politics, industry and culture. The nannies deal in intelligence that lies close to the soul. Who was seen insinuating his trembly knee between whose silky shanks in the crush at whose party. The nannies are most explicit, for Kind Ladies in hob heels. There are people who count on hearing what went on at their own parties from their nanny, who heard it from other nannies, who overheard it from the mouths of the principals themselves. And finances! They can smell the stalking of poverty in high places so thoroughly they must have been bred to sniff it out. So naturally everyone puts on the best possible face, the best possible performance, for the nannies, because everything is going to be broadcast all over the East Side via the nanny network.

"I wasn't planning on having a nanny at first," Charlotte says. "Robert's father offered to pay for it so we could have one—you know—but I didn't want to do that, and I didn't want to have anybody else around the house all the time, and I was going to be independent about this and that, blah-blah-blah. Then there was this very funny day, right after we moved here, and I decided to take Bobby down to the playground in Central Park, down at 77th Street."

So she just put Bobby in the baby carriage and wheeled him on down. You go in the entrance at 76th Street. It was a Monday, Charlotte believes, because they had just finished moving in on the weekend. And here was this nice playground, and all these nice little children, and all these nice ladies sitting around those benches around the edge. She knew most of them were nannies because they had on white uniforms, but others just looked like sort of these aging women at a country weekend or those women who stay back in the living room and they are just sitting there talking when you go out to go sailing. Anyway, she came rolling in with Bobby in the baby carriage and bygod she had never been so frosted out in her life! They stopped talking when she came by, they started whispering, nudging, giving her the most ma*lign* looks, it was unbe*liev*able!

"Well, now I know why, but then I just didn't know what was going on," Charlotte is saying. "You see, the nannies have this very set social hierarchy. The English nannies rank highest and maybe the French, all depending, but anyway, they are very cliqueish. Irish nannies try to act British. The German nannies are accepted if they're old enough or confident enough. But the poor Negro nannies, they haven't got a prayer, I don't care what they're like. There is just an absolute color bar, and the poor Negro nannies just have to sit off by themselves. But there is somebody—and I can tell you this from first-hand experience—there is somebody lower than the Negro nannies, and that is a mother who brings her own baby into the 77th Street playground. I mean it! At least the Negro nanny has probably been hired by a reasonably good family. But a mother who has to bring her own baby into the playground is absolutely *nothing!*"

The only time a mother can go in there is on Wednesday, the nannies' day off. So all the mothers go in on Wednesday and talk about the nannies. It's the uppermost thought in their brains. So there Charlotte was that time in a pen full of nannies. And that was not nearly the end of it. She had the wrong kind of baby carriage. It was white. It was too shiny. The wheels were too heavy-looking. It was made in America. They looked at the thing the way people look at Cadillacs or something.

"The only acceptable one is this Brabingham," says Charlotte. "It's a very old make. They have to be shipped in from England. It costs a fortune. They're dark blue with all sorts of fine hand work, you know, and, oh, I don't know, all these little touches here and there. I don't know what we did with ours or I'd show it to you."

Lord, the nannies are absolutely dictatorial about what you have to buy. Charlotte remembers that first day, when ie went into the playground by herself, there was this poor little girl, about six, who came in with her nurse. The nurse was a colored girl. Neither of them knew a thing, poor dears. The little girl saw these other little girls her age, and, oh, she

wanted to go play with them. Her little eyes lit up like birthday candles in her little buttery face and her little legs started
churning, and there she was, the original *tabula rasa* of joy and
friendship. Did they let *her* have it! Rather! The first girl she
came up to, Carey K———'s little girl, a real budding little
bitch named Jennifer, if you wanted Charlotte's frank opinion,
just stared at her, no smile at all, and said, "My shoes are
Indian Walk T-strap." Then another little girl came up and
said the same thing, "My shoes are Indian Walk T-strap." Then
Jennifer says it again, "My shoes are Indian Walk T-strap,"
and then they both start whining this at the poor little thing,
"My-shoes-are-Indian-Walk-T-strap!" And the little girl—all
she had done was come into the playground, to try to make
friends, with the wrong shoes on—she's about to cry, and she
says, "Mine are, too," and little Jennifer starts saying in that
awful sarcastic sing-song kids pick up as one of their early
instruments of torture: "Oh-no-they're-not—your shoes are *gar*-
bage!" So the other little girl starts saying it, and they start
chanting again, and the little girl is bawling, and the colored
girl can't figure out what's going on—and the other nannies,
Jennifer's nanny, all of them, they're just *beau*tiful, as Charlotte remembers it.

"They just sat there through the whole performance with
these masks on, until their little terrors had absolutely annihi-
lated this poor kid, and *then* they were so concerned.

" 'Now, Jennifer, you mustn't tease, you know. Mustn't tease.'
The whole time, of course, she was just delighted over how
well Jennifer had learned her lessons."

The nannies dictate that kids have to have Indian Walk
shoes. They have to get their hair cut at this and that hotel.
And clothes! Charlotte gives up on clothes. There is no such
thing as knockabout clothes in the nanny's entire rubric of life.
There is all this business about herringbones, Shetland weaves,
light flannel, heavy flannel, raw silk even, Danish sweaters.

The only thing that saves even the wealthiest family from total bankruptcy is that the kids start going to school and watching television, after which they demand dungarees and their tastes in general deteriorate medievally. Until then, however, the nannies have all picked Cerutti on Madison Avenue, and so all the kids go trooping off to Cerutti for clothes.

"Of course," says Charlotte, "there's this place in England the nannies really prize. They get practically emotional over it. There's a photograph of the Duke of Windsor as a baby, on the wall, and it's signed, something like, 'Best of luck to my dear friends, Sincerely, Edward, Duke of Windsor.' Do you see why they love the place? The message, naturally, was written by his nanny. So here is the nanny mafia speaking through the throne of England!"

A nanny will do anything to get you to go to England, just so you can get to this damned store.

"Robert, you know, is always handling these bond transfers, for the Swedes, and he goes off to Stockholm, for the Belgians, and he is off to Brussels—everywhere, for some reason, except England. If the Black Widow doesn't let up, I swear he is going to crawl in there on his hands and knees one day and ask to be sent to London. I'm only kidding about that. Actually, Robert is rather level-headed about Mrs. G———. It's me who—well, these are formidable people. They have power. I'm sure some of these people, like the party caterers, for example, wine them and dine them. They ought to, if they don't. . . ."

The phone rings and Charlotte wheels around again, those alabaster shanks still crossed, locked, silken, glistening. She twists around in the chair to pick up the phone.

"Hello, Robert . . . Well, all right . . . I suppose so . . . that's fine . . . I guess that's fine . . . All right . . . Good-bye."

She untwists and faces me again, looking kind of blank.

"That was Robert. He's been talking to his father about the party . . ."

And out in Central Park, in the 77th Street playground, within the leafy stockade, amid a thousand little places where the sun peeps through, the nanny mafia rises and stretches and the Black Widow tucks little Bobby's bangs—one thing in that family has gone right, anyway—up under his eight-piece Shetland herringbone cap, matching his four-button coat, to be sure, takes him by the hand and heads for home, the white brick tower, the tacky Louis chaises and the gathering good news.

5

LOVE AND HATE
NEW YORK STYLE

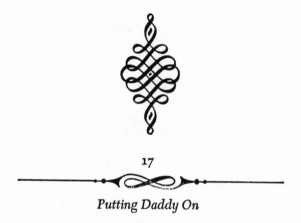

17

Putting Daddy On

Parker wants me to go down to the Lower East Side and help him retrieve his son from the hemp-smoking flipniks. He believes all newspaper reporters know their way around in the lower depths. "Come on down and ride shotgun for me," he says. Parker has a funny way of speaking, using a lot of ironic metonymy and metaphor. He picked it up at Yale twenty-five years ago and has nurtured it through many lunches in the East 50's. On the other hand, he doesn't want to appear to be too uneasy. "I just want you to size it up for me," he says. "The whole thing is ridiculous, except that it is just as pathetic as hell. I feel like I'm on my back with all four feet up in the air." Parker says his son, Ben, suddenly left Columbia in his junior year, without saying anything, and moved to the Lower East Side. Parker speaks of the Lower East Side as the caravansary for flipniks. Flipniks is his word for beatniks. As Parker pictures it, his son, Ben, now lies around on the floor in lofts and four-story walkups on the Lower East Side, eaten by lice and aphids, smoking pot and having visions of the Oneness of the hip life.

I think Parker is a casualty of the Information Crisis. The world has had a good seventy-five years of Freud, Darwin, Pavlov, Max Weber, Sir James Frazer, Dr. Spock, Vance Packard and Rose Franzblau, and everything they have had to say about human motivation has filtered through Parker and all of Parker's friends in college, at parties, at lunch, in the magazines and novels they read and the conversations they have at home with wives who share the same esoterica. As a result, Parker understands everybody's motives, including his own, which he has a tendency to talk about and revile.

He understands, for example, that he is now forty-six years old and close to becoming a vice-president of the agency and that at this particular age and status he now actually feels the *need* to go to the kind of barbershop where one makes an appointment and has the same barber each time and the jowls are anointed with tropical oils. It is as if Parker were looking through a microscope at a convulsive amoeba, himself, Parker. "I can't go into any other kind of barbershop," he says. "It has gotten so I have an *actual, physical* need to have my hair cut in that kind of barbershop." He can go on like this about the clothes he buys, about the clubs he joins, the music he listens to, the way he feels about Negroes, anything.

He understands why pot-smoking is sort of a religion. He understands Oneness, lofts, visions, the Lower East Side. He understands why Ben has given up everything. He understands why his wife, Regina, says he is a ---- ---- ---- and has to *do* something. Her flannel mouth is supposed to goad him into action. He understands everything, the whole thing, and he is in a hopeless funk.

So here are Parker and I walking along Avenue B on the Lower East Side. Parker is wearing a brown Chesterfield and a Madison Avenue crash helmet. Madison Avenue crash helmet is another of Parker's terms. It refers to the kind of felt hat that is worn with a crease down the center and no dents in the sides, a sort of homburg without a flanged brim. He calls it a Madison Avenue crash helmet and then wears one. Inevitably, Parker is looking over his own shoulder, following his own progress down Avenue B. Here is Parker with his uptown clothes and his anointed jowls, walking past the old Avenue B Cinema, a great rotting building with lions' heads and shattered lepers' windows. Here is Parker walking past corner stores with posters for Kassel, Kaplan, Aldrich and the others, plastered, torn, one on top of the other, like scales. Here is Parker walking along narrow streets with buildings all overhung with fire escapes on both sides. Here is this ripening, forty-six-year-old agency executive walking along amid the melted store fronts. There are whole streets on the Lower East Side where it looks as if the place had been under intense heat and started melting and then was suddenly frozen in amber. Half the storefronts are empty and there is a gray film inside the windows. Pipes, bins, shafts of wood and paper are all sort of sliding down the walls. The ceilings are always covered with squares of sheet metal with quaint moldings on them to make an all-over design, and they are all buckling. The signs have all flaked down to metal the color of weathered creosote, even the ones that say *Bodega y Carneceria.* Everything is collapsing under New York moss, which is a combination of lint and soot. In a print shop window, under the soot and lint, is a sample of a wedding announcement. Mr. and Mrs. Benjamin Arnschmidt announce the marriage of their daughter, Lillian, to Mr. Aaron Kornilov, on October 20, 1951. This seems to deepen Parker's funk. He is no doubt asking himself what sort of hopeless amber fix Lillian Arnschmidt and Aaron Kornilov are frozen in today.

Parker sticks his head inside a doorway. Then he walks in. Then he turns around and says, "Are you sure?"

"You said 488," I tell him, "this is 488."

"Nifty," Parker says.

Here is Parker in the entryway of a slum tenement. Slum tenements are worse than they sound. The hallway is painted with a paint that looks exactly the color, thickness and lumpiness of real mud. Parker and I walk in, and there are three big cans of garbage by the stairway. Behind them are two doors, one to the basement apartment, one to the first-floor apartment, out of which two or three children have overflowed when the mother rises in the doorway like a moon reflecting a 25-watt light and yells something in Spanish. The children squeeze back, leaving us with the garbage and the interesting mud tableau. At some point they painted the mud color over everything, even over the doorbell-buzzer box. They didn't bother to pull the wiring out. They just cut the wires and painted over the stubs. And there they have it, the color called Landlord's Brown, immune to time, flood, tropic heat, arctic chill, punk rumbles, slops, blood, leprotic bugs, cockroaches the size of mice, mice the size of rats, rats the size of Airedales, and lumpenprole tenants.

On the way up there are so many turns amid the muddy gloom, I can't tell what floor we stop at. But Parker finds the door up there and knocks.

For a while we don't hear anything, but there is a light through the door. Then somebody inside says, "Who is it?"

"Ben!" says Parker. "It's me."

There is another long pause, and then the door opens. There in the doorway, lit up from behind by an ochre light, is a boy with a very thick head of hair and a kind of Rasputin beard. It is a strange combination, the hair and the beard. The hair is golden, a little red, but mostly golden and very thick, thatchy, matted down over his ears and his forehead. But the beard is one of those beards that come out a different color. It is red and stiff like a nylon brush.

"Ah," says Parker, "the whole scene."

Ben says nothing. He just stands there in a pair of white ducks and rubber Zorrie sandals. He has no shirt on. He looks as robust as a rice pudding.

"The whole scene," Parker says again and motions toward Ben's Rasputin beard.

Ben is obviously pained to hear his old man using hip talk. He gives a peeved twist to his mouth. He is rather startling to look at, a little chunk of rice pudding with all this ferocious hair. Parker, the understanding, understands, but he is embarrassed, which is his problem.

"When did all this happen?" says Parker. "The beaver. When did you grow the beaver?"

Ben still just stands there. Then he narrows his eyes and clamps his upper teeth over his lower lip in the Italian tough guy manner, after the fashion of Jack Palance in *Panic in the Streets*.

"Beaver is a very old expression," says Parker. "Before you were born. About 1803. I was using a very old expression, from my childhood. Did you ever hear a song that goes 'Alpha, beta, delta handa poker?' That was a very hip song."

Then he says, "I didn't mean that, Ben. I just want to talk to you a minute."

"All right," says Ben, and he opens the door wider and we walk in.

We walk into a sort of kitchen. There is a stove with all four gas burners turned up, apparently for heat. The apartment is all one room, of the sort that might be termed extremely crummy. The walls actually have big slags of plaster missing and the lathing showing, as in a caricature of an extremely crummy place. The floor is impacted with dirt and looks as if it has been chewed up by something. And off to one side is more of the day's gathering gaffe: two more kids.

They are both up against the wall as if they have been squashed there. One of them is slouched up against the wall in an upright position. He is a chubby boy with receding blond hair and a walrus mustache. The other, a thin, Latin-looking boy with miles of black hair, is right next to him, only he is sitting down on the floor, with his back propped against the wall. They are both looking at us like the tar baby or a couple of those hard-cheese mestizos on the road to Acapulco. There is a sweet smell in the room. The understanding Parker isn't going to start in on that, however. Parker looks a little as if he has just been pole-axed and the sympathetic nervous system is trying to decide whether to twitch or fold up. Here is Parker in the net of the flipniks, in the caravansary.

Nobody is saying a word. Finally Ben nods toward the chubby boy and says, "This is Jaywak." Then he nods toward the boy on the floor and says, "This is Aywak."

Jaywak stares at Parker a little longer with the tar-baby look, and then he fans his lips out very slowly, very archly, into a smile. After what seems about eight or ten seconds, he holds out his hand. Parker shakes his hand, and as soon as he starts to do that, the boy on the floor, Aywak, sticks his hand straight up in the air. He doesn't get up or even look at Parker. He just sticks his hand straight up in the air and waits for Parker. Parker is so flustered he shakes it. Then Parker introduces me. All this time Ben never introduces Parker. He never says this is my father. One's old man does not show up in a brown Chesterfield with ratchety pleas in his poor old voice, such as he wants to talk to you.

"Well, take off your coat," says Ben. But when he says something to Parker, he looks at Jaywak and Aywak.

Parker keeps his coat wrapped around him like a flag and a

shield. Parker can't take his eyes off the place. Between the kitchen and the other part of the apartment is a low divider, like a half-wall, with two funny pillars between it and the ceiling. God knows what the room was for originally. In the back part there is another big craggy space on the wall, apparently where a mantelpiece has been ripped off. Some kind of ratty cloth is over the windows. It is not the decor that gets you. It is this kind of special flipnik litter. Practically every Lower East Side pad has it. Little objects are littered all over the floor, a sock, a Zorrie sandal, a T shirt, a leaflet from the Gospel Teachers, some kind of wool stuffing, a rubber door wedge, a toothbrush, cigarette butts, an old pair of blue wool bathing trunks with a white belt, a used Band-aid, all littered around the chewed-up floor. There is almost no furniture, just a mattress in the corner with a very lumpy-looking blanket over it. There is also a table top, with no legs, propped up on some boxes. Parker keeps gawking.

"Very colorful," he says.

"It's not very colorful," Ben says. "It's a place."

Ben's voice tends to groan with pretentious simplicity.

Suddenly Aywak, the tar baby on the floor, speaks up.

"It has a lot of potential," he says. "It really has a lot of potential. Doesn't it? Or doesn't it?"

He looks straight at Parker with his eyes rolled up sadly.

"We're helping Bewak," he says. "We're helping Bewak put down the tiles. Bewak's going to do a lot with this place because it has a lot of potential. We talked it over. We're going to put all these tiles over he-e-e-ere, and then, over he-e-e-ere, on this wall, all these bricks. White bricks. We're going to paint them white. I kind of like the idea, all these white bricks and the tiles. I mean, it's not *much*. I'm not saying it's a *lot*. But the important thing is to know what you've got to do and then do something about it and *improve* on it, you know?"

"Cool it," says Ben.

This is all very bad for Parker. Suddenly Parker turns to Jaywak and says, "He's an interior decorator. What do you do?"

"I'm not an interior decorator," says Aywak, "I've got a trade."

"I'm a social worker," says Jaywak. Jaywak spreads his face out into the smile again.

"Who do you social work for?" says Parker.

"Well, it's sort of like the Big Brothers," says Jaywak. "You know the Big Brothers?"

Jaywak says this very seriously, looking at Parker with a very open look on his face, so that Parker has to nod.

"Yes," Parker says.

"Well, it's like them," says Jaywak, "only . . . only . . ."— his voice becomes very distant and he looks off to where the mantelpiece used to be—"only it's different. We work with older people. I can't tell you how different it is."

"I'm not an interior decorator," says Aywak. "I don't want you to think I'm an interior decorator. We're not going to do miracles in here. This is *not* the greatest building in the world. I mean, that's probably pretty obvious. But I mean, like I was going on about it—but that just happens to be the way I *feel* about it."

"What are you if you're not an interior decorator?" says Jaywak.

"You mean, what do I *do*?" says Aywak.

"I mean, what do you *do*," says Jaywak.

"That's a very important question," says Aywak, "and I think he's right about it."

" 'What do you do?' "

"Yes."

"Someone ask Aywak what he does," Jaywak says.

"I have a trade," says Aywak. "I'm a cooper. I make barrels.

Barrels and barrels and barrels. You probably think I'm kidding."

So Parker turns on Ben. He speaks severely his only time. "Just what do *you* do?" he says to Ben. "I'd really like to know!"

"What do *you* do?" says Ben. "What are you doing right now?"

"Look," says Parker, "I don't care what you want to look like in front of these—"

Ben reaches into an old tin of tea and pulls out a string of dried figs. This is one of the Lower East Side's arty foods, along with Ukrainian sausages. Ben turns completely away from Parker and says to me, "Do you want a fig?"

I shake my head no, but even that much seems stupid.

"Are you going to listen?" says Parker.

"They're very good for you," says Aywak, "only they're filling. You know what I mean?"

"Yeah," Jaywak says to me, "sometimes you *want* to be hungry. You know? Suppose you want to be hungry, only you aren't hungry. Then you want to *get* hungry, you know? You're just waiting to get hungry again. You think about it. You want it. You want to get hungry again, but the time won't pass."

"A dried fig ruins it," says Aywak.

"Yeah!" says Jaywak.

I have the eerie feeling they're starting in on me.

"Are you going to listen?" Parker is saying to Ben.

"Sure," says Ben. "Let's have a talk. What's new? Is something new?"

Parker seems to be deflating inside his Chesterfield. Here is Parker amid the flipniks, adrift amid the litter while the gas jets burn.

Parker turns to me. "I'm sorry," he says. Then he turns to Ben. "O.K., we're going."

"O.K.," says Ben.

"Only one thing," says Parker. "What do you want me to . . ."

He doesn't finish. He turns around and walks toward the door. Then he wheels around again.

"What do you want me to tell your mother?"

"What do you mean?" Ben says.

"Do you have a message for her?"

"Such as what?"

"Well, she's been praying for you again."

"Are you being funny?"

"No, it's true," says Parker. "She has been praying for you again. I hear her in the bedroom. She has her eyes shut tight, like this, and she is on her knees. She says things like, 'O dear Lord, guide and protect my Ben wherever he may be tonight. Do you remember, O Lord, how my sweet Ben stood before me in the morning so that I might kiss him upon his forehead in the early brightness? Do you remember, O Lord, the golden promise of this child, my Ben?' Well, you know, Bewak, things like that. I don't want to embarrass you."

"That was extremely witty," Ben says.

"What do you want me to tell her?" says Parker.

"Why don't you just go?" Ben says.

"Well, we're all going to be on our knees praying tonight, Bewak," says Parker. "So long, Bewak."

Down in the hallway, in the muddy tableau, Parker begins chuckling.

"I know what I'm going to tell Regina," he says. "I'm going to tell her Ben has become a raving religious fanatic and was down on his knees in a catatonic trance when we got there."

"What is all this about kneeling in prayer?"

"I don't know," Parker says. "I just want everybody who is japping me to get down on their knees, locked in a battle of harmless zeal. I discovered something up there."

"Which was?"

"He's repulsive," says Parker. "The whole thing was repulsive. After a while I didn't see it from the inside. It wasn't me looking at my own son. I saw it from the outside. It repelled me, that was all. It repelled me."

At the corner of Avenue B and 2d Street Parker sticks out his hand and bygod there is a cab. It is amazing. There are no cabs cruising the Lower East Side. Parker looks all around before he gets in the cab. Up the street, up Avenue B, you can see the hulk of the Avenue B Cinema and the edge of the park.

"That is a good augury," he tells me. "If you can walk right out on the street and get a cab—any time, any place, just stick out your hand and a cab stops—if you can do that, that is the sign that you are on top of it in New York."

Parker doesn't say anything more until we're riding up Fourth Avenue, or Park Avenue South, as it now is, up around 23d Street, by the Metropolitan Life Insurance Building.

"You tell me," he says. "What could I say to him? I couldn't say anything to him. I threw out everything I had. I couldn't make anything skip across the pond. None of them. Not one."

18

A Sunday Kind of Love

Love! Attar of libido in the air! It is 8:45 A.M. Thursday morning in the IRT subway station at 50th Street and Broadway and already two kids are hung up in a kind of herringbone weave of arms and legs, which proves, one has to admit, that love is not *confined* to Sunday in New York. Still, the odds! All the faces come popping in clots out of the Seventh Avenue local, past the King Size Ice Cream machine, and the turnstiles start whacking away as if the world were breaking up on the reefs. Four steps past the turnstiles everybody is already backed up haunch to paunch for the climb up the ramp and the stairs to the surface, a great funnel of flesh, wool, felt, leather, rubber and steaming alumicron, with the blood squeezing through everybody's old sclerotic arteries in hopped-up spurts from too much coffee and the effort of surfacing from the subway at the rush hour. Yet there on the landing are a boy and a girl, both about eighteen, in one of those utter, My Sin, backbreaking embraces.

He envelops her not only with his arms but with his chest, which has the American teen-ager concave shape to it. She has her head cocked at a 90-degree angle and they both have their eyes pressed shut for all they are worth and some incredibly feverish action going with each other's mouths. All round them, ten, scores, it seems like hundreds, of faces and bodies are perspiring, trooping and bellying up the stairs with arterio-sclerotic grimaces past a showcase full of such novel items as Joy Buzzers, Squirting Nickels, Finger Rats, Scary Tarantulas and spoons with realistic dead flies on them, past Fred's barbershop, which is just off the landing and has glossy photographs of young men with the kind of baroque haircuts one can get in there, and up onto 50th Street into a madhouse of traffic and shops with weird lingerie and gray hair-dyeing displays in the windows, signs for free teacup readings and a pool-playing match between the Playboy Bunnies and Downey's Showgirls, and then everybody pounds on toward the Time-Life Building, the Brill Building or NBC.

The boy and the girl just keep on writhing in their embroilment. Her hand is sliding up the back of his neck, which he turns when her fingers wander into the intricate formal gardens of his Chicago Boxcar hairdo at the base of the skull. The turn causes his face to start to mash in the ciliated hull of her beehive hairdo, and so she rolls her head 180 degrees to the other side, using their mouths for the pivot. But aside from good hair grooming, they are oblivious to everything but each other. Everybody gives them a once-over. Disgusting! Amusing! How touching! A few kids pass by and say things like "Swing it, baby." But the great majority in that heaving funnel up the stairs seem to be as much astounded as anything else. The vision of love at rush hour cannot strike anyone exactly as romance. It is a feat, like a fat man crossing the English Channel in a barrel. It is an earnest accomplishment against the tide. It is a piece of slightly gross heroics, after the manner of those knobby, varicose old men who come out from some place in baggy shorts every year and run through the streets of Boston in the Marathon race. And somehow that is the gaffe against love all week long in New York, for everybody, not just two kids writhing under their coiffures in the 50th Street subway station; too hurried, too crowded, too hard, and no time for dalliance. Which explains why the real thing in New York is, as it says in the song, a Sunday kind of love.

There is Saturday, but Saturday is not much better than Monday through Friday. Saturday is the day for errands in New York. More millions of shoppers are pouring in to keep the place jammed up. Everybody is bobbing around, running up to Yorkville to pick up these arty cheeses for this evening, or down to Fourth Avenue to try to find this Van Vechten book, *Parties,* to complete the set for somebody, or off to the cleaner's, the dentist's, the hairdresser's, or some guy's who is going to loan you his station wagon to pick up two flush doors to make tables out of, or over to some place somebody mentioned that is supposed to have fabulous cuts of meat and the butcher wears a straw hat and arm garters and is colorfully rude.

True, there is Saturday night, and Friday night. They are fine for dates and good times in New York. But for the dalliance of love, they are just as stupefying and wound up as the rest of the week. On Friday and Saturday nights everybody is making some kind of scene. It may be a cellar cabaret in the Village where five guys from some place talk "Jamaican" and pound steel drums and the Connecticut teen-agers wear plaid ponchos and knee-high boots and drink such things as Passion Climax cocktails, which are made of apple cider with watermelon balls thrown in. Or it may be some cellar in the East 50's, a discotheque, where the alabaster kids come on in sleeveless minksides jackets, tweed evening dresses and cool-it Modernismus hairdos. But either way, it's a scene, a production, and soon the evening begins to whirl, like the whole world with the bed-spins, in a montage of taxis, slithery legs slithering in, slithery legs slithering out, worsted, piqué, grins, eye teeth, glissandos, buffoondos, tips, par lamps, doormen, lines, magenta ropes, white dickies, mirrors and bar bottles, pink men and shawl-collared coats, hatcheck girls and neon peach fingernails, taxis, keys, broken lamps and no coat hangers. . . .

And, then, an unbelievable dawning; Sunday, in New York.

George G., who writes "Z" ads for a department store, keeps saying that all it takes for him is to smell coffee being made at a certain point in the percolation. It doesn't matter where. It could be the worst death-ball hamburger dive. All he has to do is smell it, and suddenly he finds himself swimming, drowning dissolving in his own reverie of New York's Sunday kind of love.

Anne A.'s apartment was nothing, he keeps saying, and that was the funny thing. She lived in Chelsea. It was this one room with a cameo-style carving of a bored Medusa on the facing of the mantelpiece, this one room plus a kitchen, in a brownstone sunk down behind a lot of loft buildings and truck terminals and so forth. Beautiful Chelsea. But on Sunday morning by 10:30 the sun would be hitting cleanly between two rearview buildings and making it through the old no man's land of gas effluvia ducts, restaurant vents, aerials, fire escapes, stairwell doors, clotheslines, chimneys, skylights, vestigial lightning rods, Mansard slopes, and those peculiarly bleak, filthy and misshapen backsides of New York buildings, into Anne's kitchen.

George would be sitting at this rickety little table with an oilcloth over it. How he goes on about it! The place was grimy.

You couldn't keep the soot out. The place was beautiful. Anne is at the stove making coffee. The smell of the coffee being made, just the smell . . . already he is turned on. She had on a great terrycloth bathrobe with a sash belt. The way she moved around inside that bathrobe with the sun shining in the window always got him. It was the *at*mosphere of the thing. There she was, moving around in that great fluffy bathrobe with the sun hitting her hair, and they had all the time in the world. There wasn't even one flatulent truck horn out on Eighth Avenue. Nobody was clobbering their way down the stairs in high heels out in the hall at 10 minutes to 9.

Anne would make scrambled eggs, plain scrambled eggs, but it was a feast. It was incredible. She would bring out a couple of these little smoked fish with golden skin and some smoked oysters that always came in a little can with ornate lettering and royal colors and flourishes and some Kissebrot bread and black cherry preserves, and then the coffee. They had about a million cups of coffee apiece, until the warmth seemed to seep through your whole viscera. And then cigarettes. The cigarettes were like some soothing incense. The radiator was always making a hissing sound and then a clunk. The sun was shining in and the fire escapes and effluvia ducts were just silhouettes out there someplace. George would tear off another slice of Kissebrot and pile on some black cherry preserves and drink some more coffee and have another cigarette, and Anne crossed her legs under her terrycloth bathrobe and crossed her arms and drew on her cigarette, and that was the way it went.

"It was the *torpor,* boy," he says. "It was beautiful. Torpor is a beautiful, underrated thing. Torpor is a luxury. Especially in this stupid town. There in that kitchen it was like being in a perfect cocoon of love. Everything was beautiful, a perfect cocoon."

By and by they would get dressed, always in as shiftless a

getup as possible. She would put on a big heavy sweater, a raincoat and a pair of faded slacks that gripped her like neopreme rubber. He would put on a pair of corduroy pants, a crew sweater with moth holes and a raincoat. Then they would go out and walk down to 14th Street for the Sunday paper.

All of a sudden it was great out there on the street in New York. All those damnable millions who come careening into Manhattan all week weren't there. The town was empty. To a man and woman shuffling along there, torpid, in the cocoon of love, it was as if all of rotten Gotham had improved overnight. Even the people looked better. There would be one of those old dolls with little flabby arms all hunched up in a coat of pastel oatmeal texture, the kind whose lumpy old legs you keep seeing as she heaves her way up the subway stairs ahead of you and holds everybody up because she is so flabby and decrepit . . . and today, Sunday, on good, clean, empty 14th Street, she just looked like a nice old lady. There was no one around to make her look slow, stupid, unfit, unhip, expendable. That was the thing about Sunday. The weasel millions were absent. And Anne walking along beside him with a thready old pair of slacks gripping her like neopreme rubber looked like possibly the most marvelous vision the world had ever come up with, and the cocoon of love was perfect. It was like having your cake and eating it, too. On the one hand, here it was, boy, the prize: New York. All the buildings, the Gotham spires, were sitting up all over the landscape in silhouette like ikons representing all that was great, glorious and triumphant in New York. And, on the other hand, there were no weasel millions bellying past you and eating crullers on the run with the crumbs flaking off the corners of their mouths as a reminder of how much *Angst* and *Welthustle* you had to put into the town to get any of that out of it for yourself. All there was was the cocoon of love, which was complete. It was like being inside a scenic Easter Egg where you look in and the Gotham spires are just standing there like a little gemlike backdrop.

By and by the two of them would be back in the apartment sprawled out on the floor rustling through the Sunday paper, all that even black ink appliquéd on big fat fronds of paper. Anne would put an E. Power Biggs organ record on the hi-fi, and pretty soon the old trammeler's bass chords would be vibrating through you as if he had clamped a diathermy machine on your solar plexus. So there they would be, sprawled out on the floor, rustling through the Sunday paper, getting bathed and massaged by E. Power Biggs' sonic waves. It was like taking peyote or something. This marvelously high feeling would come over them, as though they were psychedelic, and the most commonplace objects took on this great radiance and significance. It was like old Aldous Huxley in his drug experiments, sitting there hooking down peyote buttons and staring at a clay geranium pot on a table, which gradually became the most fabulous geranium pot in God's world. The way it curved . . . why, it curved 360 d-e-g-r-e-e-s! And the clay . . . why, it was the color of the earth itself! And the top . . . It had a r-i-m on it! George had the same feeling. Anne's apartment . . . it was hung all over the place with the usual New York working girl's modern prints, the Picasso scrawls, the Mondrians curling at the corners . . . somehow nobody ever gets even a mat for a Mondrian print . . . the Toulouse-Lautrecs with that guy with the chin kicking his silhouette leg, the Klees, that Paul Klee is cute . . . why, all of a sudden these were the most beautiful things in the whole hagiology of art . . . the way that guy with the chin k-i-c-k-s t-h-a-t l-e-g, the way that Paul Klee h-i-t-s t-h-a-t b-a-l-l . . . the way that apartment just wrapped around them like a cocoon, with lint under the couch like angel's hair, and the plum cover on the bed lying halfway on the floor in folds like the folds in a Tiepolo cherub's silks, and the bored Medusa on the mantelpiece looking like the most splendidly, gloriously b-o-r-e-d Medusa in the face of time!

"Now, that was love," says George, "and there has never been anything like it. I don't know what happens to it. Unless it's Monday. Monday sort of happens to it in New York."

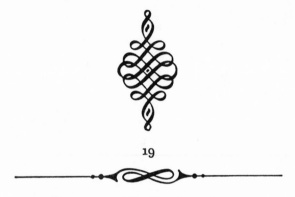

19

The Woman Who Has Everything

It is a very odd, nice, fey thing. Helene can sit over here with her nylon shanks sunk in the sofa, the downy billows, and watch Jamie over there on one knee, with his back turned, fooling with a paw-foot chair. It's *only Jamie*, an interior decorator. But all right! he has a beautiful *small of the back*. Helene has an urge to pick him up by the waist like a . . . vase. This is a marvelous apartment, on 57th Street practically on Sutton Place. In fact, Helene—well, Helene is a girl who, except for a husband, has everything.

Helene was divorced three years ago. Even so! she is only twenty-five. She went to Smith. She has money, both a great deal of alimony and her own trust fund. She is beautiful. Her face—sort of a hood of thick black hair cut Sassoon fashion with two huge eyes opened within like . . . morning glories— her face is seen in *Vogue, Town & Country,* practically all the New York newspapers, modeling fashions, but with her name always in the caption, which is known as "social" modeling. She is trim, strong, lithe, she exercises. She has only one child. *Only one child*—she doesn't even mean to think that way, Kurt Jr. is three years old and *beautiful.*

Helene also has Jamie, who is her interior decorator. Here is Jamie down on one knee adjusting the detachable ebony ball under the paw-foot of one of his own chairs. He designed it. Everyone *sees* Jamie's furniture. *Oh, did Jamie do your apartment?* It is exotic but simple. You know? Black and white, a modern paw-foot, if you can imagine that, removable ebony balls——

Oh, what the hell is going on? Suddenly she feels hopeless. There are at least ten girls in New York whom she knows who are just like her: divorced, and young; divorced, and beautiful; divorced, and quite well off, really; divorced, and invited to every party and every this and that that one cares to be invited to; divorced, and written about in the columns by Joe Dever and everyone; divorced, a woman who has everything and, like the other ten, whose names she can tick off just like that, because she knows their cases forward and backward, great American *baronial* names, some of them, and she, and all of them, are utterly . . . utterly, utterly unable to get another husband in New York.

Of course she has tried! A great deal of good will has gone into it, hers and her friends'. The J——s invited her to dinner and set the whole thing up for no other reason than for her to meet their favorite among all the eligible young men of New York. He was beautiful, he was one of the youngest bank vice-presidents in New York, a bona-fide vice-president in this case, and a great Bermuda Racer. They talked about his strenuous life among the Wall Street studs. They talked about the things her friends had been pumping her conversation full of—Jasper Johns, *nouvelle vague*, the bogus esthetics of fashion photographers. They grimaced, mugged, smiled, picked over crab meat—and there was no "chemistry" about it all. And he took her back to East 57th Street and they stepped into an elevator with a lot of scrolly wood and a little elevator man with piping all over his uniform and the moment the door closed on them, there was practically a sound like steam in the brain that told them both, this is, yes, rather impossible; let me out.

Two weeks later the D——s invited her to dinner and Mrs. D—— met her practically as she stepped off the elevator and told her very excitedly, very confidentially, "Helene, we've put you next to absolutely our *favorite* young man in New York"—who, of course, was Bermuda Racer. Everybody's favorite. This time they just smiled, grimaced, mugged, turned the other way answering imaginary questions from the other side and picked over the melon prosciutto.

Maddening! These so-called men in New York! After a while Bermuda Racer began to look good, in retrospect. One could forget "chemistry" in time. Helene's liaisons kept falling into the same pattern; all these pampered, cautious, finicky, timid . . . vague, maddening men who wind their watches before they make love. Suddenly it would have almost been better not to be the woman who had everything. Then she could have married the stable boy, who, in New York, is usually an actor. Helene is in a . . . set whose single men are not boys. They are absorbed in careers. They don't hang around the Limelight Café with nothing more on their minds than getting New York lovelies down onto the downy billows. Somehow they don't *need* wives. They can find women when they need them, for decoration, for company, or for the downy billows, for whatever, for they are everywhere, in lavish, high-buffed plenitude.

Very ironic! It is as if Helene can see herself and all the

other divorced women-with-everything in New York this afternoon, at this very moment, frozen, congealed, this afternoon, every afternoon, in a little belt of territory that runs from
east to west between 46th and 72nd Streets in Manhattan.
They are all there with absolutely nothing to do but make
themselves irresistibly attractive to the men of New York. They
are in Mr. Kenneth's, the hairdresser's, on East 54th Street, in a
room hung with cloth like a huge Paisley tent or something,
and a somehow Oriental woman pads in and announces, "Now
let us go to the shampoo room," in the most hushed and reverent voice, as if to say, "We are doing something very *creative*
here." Yet coiffures, even four hours' worth at Mr. Kenneth's,
begin to seem like merely the basic process for the Woman
Who Has Everything. There is so much more that must be
done today, so much more has been learned. The eternal
search for better eyelashes! Off to Deirdre's or some such place,
on Madison Avenue—moth-cut eyelashes? square-cut eyelashes? mink eyelashes? really, mink eyelashes are a joke, too
heavy, and one's lids . . . sweat; pure sweet saline eyelid
perspiration. Or off to somewhere for the perfect Patti-nail
application, $25 for both hands, $2.50 a finger, false fingernails
—but where? Saks? Bergdorf's? Or is one to listen to some girl
who comes back and says the only perfect Patti-nail place is
the Beverly Hills Hotel. Or off to Kounovsky's Gym for Exercise—one means, this is 1965 and one must face, now, the fact
that chocolate base and chalk can only do so much for the
skin; namely, nothing; *cover* it. The important thing is what
happens to the skin, that purple light business at Don Lee's
Hair Specialist Studio, well, that is what it is about. And at
Kounovsky's Gym one goes into the cloak room and checks
clothes labels for a while and, eventually, runs into some girl
who has found a *new* place, saying, this is my last time here,
I've found a place where you *really have to take a shower*
afterwords. Still—Kounovsky's. And Bene's, breaking down the

water globules in the skin—and here they are all out doing nothing every day but making themselves incomparably, esoterically, smashingly lovely—for men who don't seem to *look* anyway. Incredible! Arrogant! impossible men of this city, career-clutched, selfish and drained.

So Helene sits morosely in the downy billows watching *Mr. Jamie* adjust an ebony ball on a paw-foot chair. Jamie is her interior decorator, but even before that, he had become her Token Fag, three years ago, as soon as she was divorced. She needed him. A woman is divorced in New York and for a certain period she is *radioactive* or something. No man wants to go near. She has to cool off from all that psychic toxin of the divorce. Eventually, people begin asking her for dinner or whatever, but *who* is going to escort her? She is radioactive. The Token Fag will escort her. He is a token man, a *counter* to let the game go on and everything. She can walk in with him, into anybody's coy-elegant, beveled-mirror great hall on East 73rd Street, and no one is going to start talking about her new *liaison*. There is no *liaison* except for a sort no one seems to understand. Jamie is comfortable, he is no threat. The *old business* is not going to start up again. This has nothing to do with sex. Sex! The sexual aggression was the only kind that didn't really have that *old business,* the eternal antagonisms, clashes of ego, fights for "freedom" from marriage one day and for supremacy the next, the eternal piling the load on the scapegoat. Helene's last *scene* with Kurt—Helene can tell one about that, all this improbable, ridiculous stuff in front of the movers. They had just been separated. This was long before the afternoon plane ride to El Paso and the taxi ride across the line to Juarez and the old black Mexican judge who flipped, very interested, through a new and quite ornate—arty—deck of Tarot cards under his desk the whole time. They had just separated—they were separating this particular evening. One *does* separate. One stands out in the living room in the midst of incredible heaps of cartons and duffle bags, and Kurt stands there telling *his* movers what to pick up.

"I don't mean to be picayune, Helene, but it *isn't* exactly picayune. You didn't put the Simpson tureen out here," and he starts fluttering his hand.

"The Morgetsons gave that to—they're friends of my parents."

"That isn't even the point, Helene. This is something we *agreed* on."

"You know as well as I do—"

Kurt makes a circle with his thumb and forefinger, the "O.K." sign, and thrusts it toward Helene as if he is about to say, Right, and in that very moment he says:

"Wrong!"

Oh, for godsake. Sal Mineo, or whoever it was. Somebody told Kurt once that "Sal Mineo and his set" are always putting each other on with his O.K. sign—then saying, "Wrong!"— and Kurt was so *impressed* with the Sal Mineo humor of it. Just like right now, standing out amid the packing cartons, with a couple of fat movers . . . lounging, watching. Kurt has to stand there with his hands on his hips and his thatchy head soaking up perspiration, wearing a cable-stitch tennis sweater and Topsiders. His *moving clothes*. He has to wear this corny thing, a cable-knit tennis sweater, about $42, because he is going to pick up a couple of boxes and his precious hi-fi tubes or whatever it is. They do something to these tall ironsides at Hotchkiss or some place and they never get over it. Glowering in his $42 White Shoe physical exertion sweater—the *old business*.

Kurt Jr. is out of bed, waddling into the living room and all he sees is *Daddy*, wonderful, thatchy Daddy. Children, to be honest, have *no* intuition, no insight.

"These men don't want to sit there and listen to you recite your parents' friends," says Kurt.

But they *do*, Kurt. They *are* seated, as you say yourself. Placid, reedy fat rises up around their chins like mashed potatoes. They sit on the arms of Helene's chairs and *enjoy* it, watching two wealthy young fools coming apart at the seams. Kurt Jr. apparently thinks everything Daddy says is *so funny;* he comes on, waddling in, chuckling, giggling, *Daddy!* The movers think Kurt Jr. is *so funny—a Baby!—*and they slosh around, chuckling in their jowls. Good spirits, and so obscene, all of it.

Jamie was at least an end to the *old business.* Most of them, Helene, all these divorcees who have everything, soon move into a second stage. Old friends of theirs, of Helene and Kurt— you know? Helene and Kurt, the Young Couple? Helene and Kurt here, Helene and Kurt there—old friends of theirs, of Kurt's, really, start taking Helene out. Fine, fat simple-minded waste of time. What do they want? It is not sex. It is nothing like that old *Redbook* warning to divorcees, that he, Mr. Not Quite Right, will say, She was married, so it is a safe bet she will play on the downy billows. In fact, practically nothing is sex madness with men in Helene's set in New York. Would that the Lord God of Hotchkiss, St. Paul's and Woodberry Forest would *let* them go mad as randy old goats—one wishes He would. Not for the sex but the madness. One longs to see them go berserk just once, sweating, puling, writhing, rolling the eyeballs around, bloating up the tongue like a black roast gizzard—anything but this . . . *vague* coolness, super-cool interest. Anyway, these old friends come around and their eyes breathe at her like gills out of the aquarium, such as that dear dappled terrier from Sullivan & Cromwell whom Kurt used to wangle invitations for, over and over. He did something on the Cotton Exchange. The Cotton Exchange! He came around with his gilly eyes breathing at her, *wondering,* beside himself with this strange delight of *Kurt's Wife* being now available for him to speculate over and breathe his gilly look at. Sweet! One day Douglas, well, Douglas is another story, but one day Douglas invited everyone to a champagne picnic in Central Park for Memorial Day, all these bottles of champagne in Skotch Koolers, huge blue and yellow woven baskets full of salmon and smoked turkey and Southside Virginia ham sandwiches prepared by André Surmain of Lutéce. Kurt's poor old dappled terrier friend from the Cotton Exchange arrived in a correct, "informal," one understands, long-sleeved polo shirt from someplace, Chipp or something, with the creases popped up in straight lines and a sheen on it. Obviously he had gone out and bought the correct thing for this champagne picnic. Poor thing! But Helene kept on going out with him. Old Terrier never made a pass. Never! He always left at 1 A.M., or whenever, with a great, wet look of rice-pudding adoration. But he was *easy*, none of the *old business*.

A terrible lesson! Soon Helene was *identified* with this placid Cotton Exchange lawyer, who still breathed unsaid longings at her through his gills. She didn't care about that. The problem was with other men. In New York there *are* no Other Men. Men in New York have no . . . confidence, whatsoever. They see a girl with a man four or five times, and she is *his*. They will not move in. Happy ever after! Helene and Terrier! Stupid! New York men would not dream of trying to break up a romance or even a relationship. That would take confidence. It would take interest. Interest—mygod, some kind of sustained interest is too much to ask.

That is why it was so absolutely marvelous when Helene saw Porfirio Rubirosa again at C———'s. She hadn't seen him for a year, but he immediately remembered and began pouring absolutely marvelous hot labial looks all over her from across the room and then came over, threading through the rubber jowls, and said:

"Helene, how do you do it! Last year, the white lace. This

year, the yellow—you are . . . wonderful, what is the expression? One hundred per cent wonderful!"

And the crazy thing is, one—Helene—knows he means it because he doesn't mean it. Is that too crazy? You are a woman, he is a man. He would break up this stupid Cotton Exchange Terrier universe just to *have* you. Well, he didn't, but he would. Does one know what Helene means?

Why should Helene have to end up in these ridiculous drunk evenings with Davenport? Davenport is not a serious person. Davenport practically enters with orange banners waving, announcing that he will never get married. He is like a tepezquintle boar who runs, rut-boar, all night, and if they put him in the pen, he dies, of pure childish pique. He stops breathing until the middle of his face turns blue. Dear Davenport! One morning—too much!—they overslept and Helene woke to Kurt's Nanny rattling in through the drop lock and had to make Davenport get up, skulk around, get dressed and sneak out when Nanny was in the kitchen. But little Kurt, with his idiot grin, saw him, coming out of the room. Davenport was, of course, still mugging, *pantomiming* great stealth, tiptoeing and rubber-legging around, but Kurt Jr.—incredible! what do three-year-old children think about?—he cries out, "Daddy!" Davenport is slightly shocked himself, for once, but Helene has this horrible mixed agony. She realizes right away that what has really hit her is not the cry—Daddy!—but the fact that it might bring Nanny running to see Davenport sidewinding across the wall-to-wall like a trench-coat gigolo or something.

No more Davenport! Short nights with Pierre. Pierre was a Frenchman who had come to the United States and grown wealthy from the mining industry in South America or some such thing. South America! he used to say. The slums of the United States! Helene used to rather like that. But Pierre used to wind his watch before he went to bed. A very beautiful watch. At parties, at dinner, anywhere, Pierre always grew suddenly . . . *vague,* switching off, floating away like a glider plane. He even grew vague in the downy billows. Now he is there, now he isn't. Pierre may be French but now he is thoroughly New York. In New York a man does not have to devote himself to a woman, or think about her or even pay attention to her. He can . . . glide at will. It is a man's town, because there are not fifty, not one hundred, not one thousand, beautiful, attractive, available women in New York, but *thousands* of these nubile wonders, honed, lacquered, buffed, polished—Good Lord, the spoiled, pampered worthlessness of New York men in this situation. Helene can even see the process and understand it. Why should a talented, a wealthy, even a reasonably good-looking and congenial, cultivated man in New York even feel the *need* for marriage? Unlike Cleveland, Pittsburgh, Cincinnati or practically anywhere else in America, single men are not shut out of social life in New York. Just the opposite. They are *terribly* desirable. They are invited everywhere. A mature man's social life inevitably flags a bit in New York after his marriage. A single man, if he has anything going for him, is not going to get *lonely* in New York. What does he need a wife for? What does a man need children for in New York? Well, Helene doesn't mean to even *think* that. Of course, every man has a natural desire for a son, just as she has a natural desire for a son, she *loves* Kurt Jr., he is a *beautiful* boy.

Well, this is the last straw about Pierre. Pierre winding his watch. There was enough about Pierre without this final night when he got just euphorically high enough on wine and began expanding on the metaphysics of man and woman. Some metaphysics. Some brain. It turned out Pierre had decided about ten years ago, when he was thirty-two, that he ought to get married. This was more or less a theoretical decision, one understands. It would be *fitting*. So he set out with a list of specifications for finding a wife. About so tall, with this type of figure, he even wanted a certain gently bellied look, but firm, one understands, a certain education, a certain age, not over twenty-five, a certain personality, a certain taste for decor, and on and on. It was all quite specific. He never found her, but, then, one gets the impression that he did not look all that hard and was never very disappointed about that. And so, finally, this night, with his watch wound, Pierre announced that, well, now he was forty-two years old, and he had mellowed, and life is a complex drama, and blah-blah-blah, and now he is amending his specifications to include *one child*. Not two, one understands. Two are *underfoot*. But one is all right. And what gets to Helene when she thinks about it is that for a moment there her heart leapt! Her spirits rose! She could see a breakthrough! For a second she no longer thought about the Horror number for New York divorcees—forty, age forty, after which the packing under the skin begins to dry up, wither away, Don Lee can't do a thing about it, Mr. Kenneth and Kounovsky are helpless, all that packing under the skin is drying up, withering away, until one day, they make an autopsy of the most beautiful woman in New York, in her seventy-seventh year, and they find her brain looking like a mass of dried seawood at Tokyo Sukiyaki. The packing is gone! For one moment she no longer had that vague, secret dread of the fate of the ten other divorcees she knows, all failing miserably in the only job they have, viz., finding a husband.

But—*sink*—the folded-napkin life with Pierre. Pierre's specification. Thank you for including me in your stem-winding *Weltanschauung*. So that was it with Pierre.

And now, in a few minutes, the new Buyer will be coming around, he's an editor at *Life*, not a *top* editor, one understands, but he *looks* good, he has none of that ironside Hotchkiss in him, he seems to *know* things. Helene—well, *journalists*

—but Helene met him at Freddie's and it *went* well, and now he is coming around for the first time.

So Jamie is fitting the last ebony ball onto the paw feet—Jamie comes around like this at any time; it brings some kind of peace to Jamie to be down on his knees in the wall-to-wall. Or something. And, ultimately, the doorman calls up, the buzzer rings, Old Nanny fools around with the drop lock and brings him in. And—simple mind!—it happens again. Helene can almost feel her eyes rolling up and down him, inspecting him, his shoes, which are cordovan with heavy soles—how sad!—but she goes on, inspecting him, she can't stop it, sizing up every man who comes through that door as . . . Mr. Potential.

The nanny had to leave Kurt Jr.'s room to go to the door and now—oh, wonderful!—the little—boy—comes waddling out—and, like someone frozen, Helene sees that simple, widening grin on his face and knows precisely what it means and can say nothing to ward off what she knows she is going to hear. Big *Lifey* stands a little nervously, sloshing around in his cordovans, grinning stupidly at this little waddling Child in the Plot, while Jamie keeps coming and—pow!—throws his arms around big *Lifey's* leg and looks up—idiot appeal!—and says, "Are you going to be my new Daddy?"

Ah—one thing has not changed. Helene has wheeled about, can't think up a thing to say, it doesn't really matter—and Jamie is still bent over on one knee, fooling with the chair. What would it be like with Jamie? And why not? She *can* size up Jamie. Perhaps she has been sizing up Jamie since the first time he walked through the door. There is something about Jamie. There is . . . *beauty*. It is . . . very odd, nice, fey, sick, but Jamie—never mind!—has a beautiful *small of the back*, poised, pumiced, lacquered, and it remains only for her to walk over, travel just a few feet, and put her hands upon him like a . . . vase.

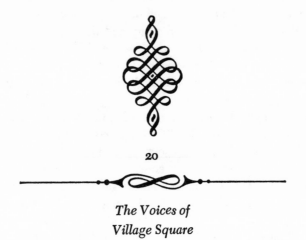

20

The Voices of
Village Square

"Hai-ai-ai-ai-ai-ai-ai-ai-ai-ai-ai-ai-ai-ai-ai-ai-ai-ai-ai-ai-ai-ai-ai-ai
-ai-ai-ai-ai-ai-ai-ai-ai-ai-ai-ai-ai-ai-ai-ai-ai-ai-ai-ai-ai-ai-ai
-reeeeeeeeeeeeeeeeeeee!"

O, dear, sweet Harry, with your French gangster-movie
bangs, your Ski Shop turtleneck sweater and your Army-Navy
Store blue denim shirt over it, with your Bloomsbury corduroy
pants you saw in the *Manchester Guardian* airmail edition and
sent away for and your sly intellectual pigeon-toed libido
roaming in Greenwich Village—that siren call really for you?

"Hai-ai-ai-ai-ai-ai-ai-ai-ai-ai-ai-ai-ai-aireeeeeeeeeeee!"

Obviously Harry thinks so. There, in the dusk, on the south

side of Greenwich Avenue, near Nut Heaven, which is the intersection of Greenwich Avenue, Sixth Avenue, Eighth Street and Christopher Street, also known as Village Square, Harry stops and looks up at the great umber tower at 10 Greenwich Avenue. He can see windows but he can't see through them. He gives a shy wave and thereby becomes the eighth man in half an hour to get conned by The Voices.

Half of them, like Harry, look like the sort of kids who graduated in 1961 from Haverford, Hamilton or some other college of the genre known as Threadneedle Ivy and went to live in New York City. Here they participate in discussions denouncing our IBM civilization, the existing narcotics laws, tailfins and suburban housing developments, and announce to girls that they are Searching. Frankly, they are all lonesome and hung up on the subject of girls in New York. They all have a vision of how one day they are going to walk into some place, usually a second-hand bookstore on Bleecker Street west of Sixth Avenue, and there is going to be a girl in there with pre-Raphaelite hair, black leotards and a lambskin coat. Their eyes will meet, their minds will meet—you know, Searching, IBM civilization and all that, and then——

"Hai-ai-ai-ai-ai-ai-ai-ai-ai-ai-ai-ai-ai-ai-reeeeeeeee!"

All of a sudden old Harry is waving away from down there on Greenwich Avenue, out front of the Casual-Aire shop and yelling back: "Hey! who is it?"

"Hey, Harry!" the girl yells.

"Hey, Harry!" another girl yells.

"Hey, Harry!" still another girl yells.

Four girls, five girls, six girls yell, "Hey, Harry!"

Then one of them yells, "Hai-ai-ai-ai-ai-ai-ai-ai-aireeeee! Have you got a —— —— for me?"

Then another one yells, "Hey, Harry, come on up and —— —— ——!"

Harry looks like a poleaxed lamb in that wobbly moment

just before the cerebral cortex shuts off for good. Old Harry has been searching all right, and he has had some lubricous thoughts about what would happen after his and Dream Girl's eyes and mind met, but this laying it on the line like that, right out in the middle of Nut Heaven—it was too *gamey* or something.

So Harry walks away, west on Greenwich Avenue, with the cellblock horselaughs following him, and by now, of course, he knows he has been had.

So the girls take up new names to see if anybody will bite:

"John-n-n-n-n-n-ny!"

"Hey, Bil-l-l-l-l-l-l!"

"Frankie!"

"Hi, Honey!"

"Sammy!"

"Max!"

For some reason, a name like Max breaks everybody up, and all the girls start the cellblock horselaugh even before they find out if there is anybody down there named Max who is going to look up with the old yearning gawk.

The girls, these Sirens, these Voices, are all up in the cellblocks of the Women's House of Detention, 10 Greenwich Avenue, overlooking Village Square, and, well, what the ———, as the girls like to say, these yelling games are something to do. The percentages are in their favor. There are thousands of kids trooping through the intersection all the time, and eventually a girl is going to get somebody named Harry, Johnny, Bill, Frankie, Sammy or, affectionately, Honey.

The Women's House of Detention is, no doubt, a "hellhole," as even the Corrections Department people speak of it every time they ask for an appropriation to build a bigger one. It is a mess: 600 women in a space meant for 400. Teen-age girls, first offenders, some of them merely awaiting trial, are heaped in with "institutionalized" old puggies who feel like bigger shots inside than out. The place is filthy. It is so bad that a convicted prostitute, narcotics user and peddler, Kim Parker, combining, at age 35, the sins that land 80 per cent of the girls inside 10 Greenwich Avenue, pleaded guilty to a felony rather than a misdemeanor last October. The felony sentence might be five years at the state prison farm, which to her was a happier prospect than one year in the Women's House of Detention.

Yet there is probably not another large prison in the country that is in such intimate contact with the outside world. The building, twelve stories high, was built in 1932 as a monument to Modern Penology. The idea was to make it look not like a jail at all but like a new apartment building. There are copper facings with 1930's modern arch designs on them between the floors. In the place of bars there are windows with a heavy grillwork holding minute square panes. The panes are clouded, like cataracts. Actually, the effect is more like that of the power plant at Yale University, which was designed to resemble a Gothic cathedral, but, in any case, it does not look like a jail.

So here is a jail that looks like a Yale power plant with cataracts standing out in the middle of a community that has become a paradise for kids in New York, Greenwich Village. The girls in the House of Detention can stand up on the toilet bowl or something and look out the couple of hinged window panes they have out onto all that Life among the free kids. Right down there, off the intersection, are all the signs, Trude Heller's, the twist and bossa nova place, Burger Village, Hamburger Train, Luigi's, Lamanna Liquors, Foam Rubber City, the Captain's Table, Nedick's and the swingingest Rexall drug store in New York City. Skipping across Sixth Avenue and screaming every time the lights change are all the bouffant bohemians, with bouffants up top and stretch pants and elf shoes down below, and live guys in Slim Jims and Desert boots, and aging bohemians in Avenger boots and matching plaid poncho and slacks sets, and Modern Churchmen, painted lulus, A-trainers and twenty-eight-year-old winos who say, "All right, you don't have a quarter, but if you had a quarter would you give it to me?"

Also junkies. The same night they conned Harry—"Hey! Who is it?"—the girls could see a kid known as Fester stumbling out of the Rexall wringing one hand and holding his stomach with the other. For a while Fester had folded his sweater up into a square and knelt down in the entrance to the Rexall with his head on the sweater, moaning. Everybody just stepped around him. But then Fester jumped up and ran to the cigarette counter and with a stifled shriek clouted a total stranger in the back of the neck with his open palm. The guy just wheeled around, still holding onto his Marlboros, shocked, and Fester started wringing his hand, saying in his elfy voice, "My hand stings!" and then stumbled out, holding his gut with the other. Fester is a junky; a lot of the girls know him. There was a time when a girl could hoist a fix up into the House of Detention on a "fishing line" with the help of a guy like Fester.

Well, Fester is in bad shape, but there he is, at least, out there on the loose in Greenwich Village, where everybody goes skipping and screaming across Sixth Avenue. The girls have to yell to all that life down there. The girls in one cellblock will all start yelling down there until the girl who is the lookout gives the warning signal, sometimes "Dum-da-dum-dum" from the old Jack Webb TV show, meaning that the turnkeys are coming. The girls will even yell to somebody they have just been talking to in the visitors room on the first floor on visiting night. It is one thing to talk to somebody inside the jail. It is a better thing to know you can still talk to them when they are back out there on the street in the middle of things.

"Willie!"

It is not long after Harry has disappeared west on Greenwich Village, and Willie has just come out of the front door at 10 Greenwich Avenue after visiting a girl whose name one never learns. One only hears her shrieking across Greenwich Avenue from somewhere up there in the great cataracted building.

"Willie! Are you gonna sell the pants!"

There are trucks bouncing along Greenwich Avenue and Sixth Avenue and cutting across into Greenwich from Ninth Street, but she can make herself heard. Willie, on the other hand, is the last of the great shoe buyers. He has on a pair of tan triple-A's that won't quit. He is not ready for yelling across Greenwich Avenue up at the Women's House of Detention. He gives a look at all the people walking his way past Tucker's Cut Rate Florist, Hamburger Train and the Village Bake Shop.

"Are you, Willie!"

Willie tries. "I don't know where they are, I told yuh!"

"What!"

Willie puts a little lung into it this time. "I told yuh! I don't know where they are!"

"You know where they are, Willie! You gonna sell 'em or not?"

Willie wants to get out of there. He doesn't want to be yelling across Greenwich Avenue to some unseen gal in the Women's House of Detention about selling a pair of pants. So he gives the first guy who comes by a weak, smiley, conspiratorial look, as if to say, Women! But the guy just stares at him and walks slow, so he can hear more. This makes Willie mad, and so he gives the next few people the death ray look—What you looking at!—which starts his adrenalin flowing, which in turn puts him in fuller, better voice.

"Aw, I don't know where the pants are! What you bother with the pants for!"

"You gonna sell 'em, Willie!"

"All right!"

" '*All right!* ' " she yells it very sarcastically. "All right, Willie, all right, you do what you want!"

"Aw, come on, honey!"

Willie wishes he hadn't yelled that. Now it seems like about a thousand nuts are scuttling through Nut Heaven laughing at him and sidling looks at him standing in his tan Triple-A's yelling at a blank building.

"Naw, you do me like you did Maureen! Go on!"

"Listen—"

"Naw, you so fine, Willie!"

There is a lot of laughing from the cellblocks after that. Willie wants to vanish. All these damned faces around here gawking at him.

"All right!" Willie yells.

"You mean it!" she yells from somewhere up there. "You gonna sell the pants!"

"I told yuh!" Willie yells, right over the garbage trucks, the Vespas, the Volkswagens, the people, over the whole lumbering, flatulent mess.

"And then you coming back!"

"All right!"

"When!"

"Soon's I sell 'em!"

"They in the closet, Willie!"

"All right!" Willie yells, and then he turns and walks fast down Christopher Street.

"Willie!" she yells. "Goodbye!"

There is a kid down there wearing a big black Borsalino hat and a George Raft-style 1930's double-breasted black overcoat who has got to find out what it is all about. He runs after Willie and just asks him, straight out, and Willie blows up and suggests by means of a homey colloquialism how he can dispose of the whole subject, and selling the pants remains a private affair.

And inside the Women's House of Detention, the girls are gathering spirit. It is eventide in a holiday season. On the Sixth

Avenue side, about four girls begin the old song, and then, gradually, more join in:

I'm dreaming of a white Christmas!
Just like the ones I used to know!
Where the treetops glisten!
And children listen!
To hear sleigh bells in the snow . . .

How touching are these words as they drift over Sixth Avenue from the cataracts of the Women's House of Detention! Villagers, laden with bundles, stop over there in front of the Kaiser clothing store and look up and listen, silently.

". . . *with every Christmas card I write!*"

By now maybe twenty or thirty people have stopped on the avenue in a bunch, and they all have their heads cocked, rheumy eyes turned up in the attitude that says, I am already deeply moved and ready for more.

. . . *may your days be mer-reeee and bright!* . . .

How the sound rises! Every girl on the east side of the Women's House of Detention, it seems like, has joined in and taken a gulletful of air for the final line, which comes out:

. . . *And may all your Christ-mases be bla-a-a-a-a-a-a-ack!*

Only some of the girls don't even say black, they use adjectives such as ——, ——, —— and ——. Others have already given themselves up wholly to cellblock horselaughs, and soon they all have, and now the horselaughs come shrieking out across old Sixth Avenue to where all the obedient epopts of old-sampler sentiment are bunched in front of Kaiser's. That was a good hit! Twenty or thirty of them, free squares of New York, bunched together and all conned! gulled! faked out! put on! had! by The Voices of Village Square.

21

Why Doormen Hate Volkswagens

Please do not get the idea from what our hustling boy, Roy, is going to say that he is one of those doormen who seize upon you with their low-floating eyeballs and make you listen to some sort of prole *Weltanschauung* about what a big operator you have to be to get by in New York. Actually, *I* approached *him*, and he admits that as East Side doormen go, he is nothing but a pocketful of change. He controls only one-third of his street in the Sixties. There are only 18 cars in his stable. He grosses barely $450 a month parking them on this little "tree-lined block," as the classified ads say. And that is before the payoffs, the fee-splitting with Rudy, the chap in the garage, and the investments in good will, like the superintendent's.

"It is a small operation, but more relaxed," Roy said. "I don't miss Park Avenue any more. I really don't. Oh, you might clear $600 a month, but that thing wrung me out. You know what I mean?"

So Roy is standing out front of the apartment house with its facing of nice diet-size white lavatory brick, Early Sixties Post-Mondrian Chic, with which fine new apartment houses are built. Mrs. Jansen, a matron who is just beginning to get that hummocky, rusty-jointed look about the hips, comes out walking three Welsh Corgies. Roy swings around like a grenadier and beams his 80-watt smile.

"Good evening, Mrs. Jansen," Roy says. "Was the—uh—operation a success?"

"Good Lord, no," says Mrs. Jansen. "Well, look at them; they're so little. That man was mad; *they* can't stand enemas. But they *look* so much better, don't you think so, Roy?"

Yes, yes, yes, says Roy, and Mrs. Jansen fades up the street with her rusting gams and her three Welsh Corgies, toward the trees on his tree-lined block.

Roy, on the other hand, from seven years as a doorman in the East Side car-parking dodge, remains youthful in appearance, lively, alert, springy. He relaxes, like a middleweight boxer in training, on the balls of his feet, looking both ways, bobbing up and down in his frogging, his white dickey and his visored cap.

"As I said," says Roy, "this is quiet. On Park Avenue I had 50 cars, both sides of the block. Figuring an average of $6 a week for each car, and that's conservative, *conservative,* you could gross $1,200 a month. That's with the transients, too, though.

"A lot of that you have to pay out. Most of the guys don't mind the cops, or even the cops' friends—other cops, you know; I mean, well, hell, O.K. But in my case the super wanted 50 per cent—50 *per cent.* He just walked up one day and said he wanted 50 per cent.

" 'Look,' I told him, 'be *reasonable*. Enough is enough. Without me you would get *nothing* from this. You couldn't run this operation. You've got to be fast. Even with the 12 M.D.'s you couldn't do it. . . .' "

A doctor, with his M.D. license plate, is the most sought-after client in the whole East Side doorman-parking operation. The doorman can stash the M.D. cars in no parking spaces while he shifts other cars around. A doorman will give an M.D. a rate as low as $3 a week, just to get him. Suppose all his spaces are filled—some with transients at 50 cents per—and one of his regulars pulls up. He *must* find room for him. So he takes his floater—the M.D. car—out of the line and moves it over to the other side of the street where there is no parking that day. Or he double parks it. The police will not tag the M.D. car. Of course, one does not want to abuse that fact. The first time someone else pulls out, he brings the floater back into a legal spot.

". . . and you have to know by the way they're walking and looking that they're going to get into that car and pull out. So I told the super, 'Look, you can't even wait for them to reach for the keys or you're going to lose the spot. You've got to know *people*,' I told him. But this super, he doesn't budge—'50 per cent.'

"This thing isn't easy. You've got to look after your door, take packages, open this door for them, open the cab door for them, get them a cab—and, boy, some rainy night about 8 P.M. when you're standing out in the middle of the avenue trying to get a cab for somebody and you see one of your cars pulling out from the curb, well, you get pulled apart right here"—he put his hand on his midsection—"you can actually feel it inside. Of course, you're going to lose some spots, but. . . ."

But not this time. Without saying a word, Roy bolts from my side and sprints 40 yards up his tree-lined block, past Mrs.

Jansen and the Corgies, who appear quite startled, jumps in a car and revs it up.

Roy has seen what I had not; a man in one of those $42 East Side Bohemian bulky-knit sweaters is leading his two children toward his Pontiac; now he is opening the front door for them. There is a motion picture theater nearby; cars are coursing through the block, Roy roars up in his M.D. floater, a black Ford Galaxie, and stops right alongside the Pontiac.

The man in the sweater looks out, nonplussed, but Roy motions him to go ahead and start pulling out. Roy backs up slowly to give him room. A man in a Rambler sees the Pontiac is getting ready to pull out and pulls up ahead so he can back in. So Roy takes off his visor hat and moves up right behind him, blowing his horn. The Rambler takes off. Roy backs up again, just behind the Pontiac once more. A Ford from New Jersey with four kids in it, double-dating, pulls up ahead to back in. Roy puts his visor hat back on, roars up behind it, blows the horn, chases it off, then backs up again as the Pontiac leaves the curb. Roy whips in there and the space is saved. Two spaces, actually.

Roy bounds back in front of the door.

"See how I parked it?" he says. "It takes up two spaces. That's what you've got to do when you have too many vacant spaces. You stretch 'em. You have to move all these cars back and forth like an accordion. You can always spot a set-up like this. On an ordinary street the cars are all crammed up. Here they're stretched out. See these keys"—he pulled a vast ring out from under the frogging of his uniform—"a duplicate for every regular. You couldn't run this thing without 'em. For the alternate side parking—you know—I have to shift the whole bunch of them around 11 at night.

"I'll tell you something else. You have to know *people*. When a guy brings his kid out to the car, he's not just going to reach inside and get something out of the glove compartment. He's *leaving*. That's the time you have to run for the floater.

"Also you notice how I blocked off that spot. You can't pull up *ahead* of somebody pulling out, because one of these Volks-wagens or something—boy, you ask any doorman, they *hate* these Volkswagens—they'll pull right in there while you're up ahead with your chin hanging.

"And did you notice this business I do with the hats? This, if you don't mind me saying it, is finesse. If you want to chase off an older guy—you know, an adult—you take the hat off, be-cause an older guy, he'll see this doorman trying to bluff him out of the spot, and he'll say to himself, 'Well, that clown isn't shoving me around. I'm not ninety-seven years old for noth-ing.' But for the kids, you put the hat *on*. A kid in a car, he feels guilty a little, you know, even if he hasn't done anything. Don't ask me why, but it's true. So he sees this hat, and even if he knows it isn't a cop, he's not sure what it is, you know? So he scrams off. You saw how that kid scrammed off? That's what I mean, you have to know *people*."

A little while while later Roy says, "Wait a minute, I got to go over to the garage."

I had wondered about the garage. It is barely three-fourths of a block away. It rents space to apartment dwellers at $70 a month, and to transients at $2.50 a day, and Roy's business must be costing them about $10,000 a year. They should be screaming murder. I follow Roy up the block, and I hear him hollering at the entrance, "Hey, Rudy, I got three out here."

"Sure, the owner would ruin me if he knew about it," Roy says, "but the guys in the garage, we work together. Suppose they're filled up, like tonight with everybody coming to the movie. I tell Rudy, 'Rudy, I got three out here.' That means I can take three cars where I got my cars stretched out. Okay. Some guy pulls up to the garage. Without me, Rudy would have to tell the guy, 'We're filled up.' Instead, he takes the guy's car, and after the guy walks off, he turns it over to me. I park it, and we split the $1.50. Everybody's happy.

"Hell, you *got* to play the angles. I have a wife and two kids in Queens, and you know what my take-home pay as a doorman is? $62.50 a week. I kid you not—sixty-two dollars and fifty cents. So what can you do?

"Practically every doorman on the East Side has this operation going for him. It runs from about 60th Street to 86th and anywhere from Fifth Avenue all the way over to the river in some parts. In this town, my friend, you play the angles. That's New York."

An old guy in a great chalk-stripe blue suit, English cut, four buttons at the cuff, growing old gracefully the fine worsted way, comes out of the apartment building with three aging *belles dames,* all linked, lacquered, sprayed, and collared in foxheaded fur.

"Roy," he says, "can you get us a cab?"

And there goes Roy, giving a sweep of his 20-20 eyes over his curbline domain, then streaking out onto the Avenue, blowing his whistle, summoning the hacks. He snares one and here he comes back, cantering down the middle of the street beside the cab and opening the door for the four old parties.

"There were *eight* people out there waiting for cabs, Mr. Thornton," says Roy, the most likely sounding but thoroughly preposterous figure he could think of bubbling up into his brain. He is panting like a Method actor finishing a 3:56 mile. "It's a lucky thing I know this cab driver. Take good care of them, Raymond. See you around, boy," he says earnestly and quite familiarly and pockets the dollar bill Mr. Thornton gives him. "Thank you, sir," he says to that.

The cabbie stares at Roy and then he looks at me with that quizzical, sempiternal New York cab driver look that asks the impartial judge, "Who the hell is this nut?"

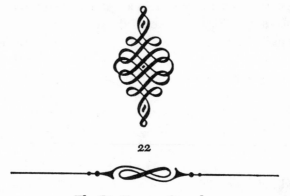

22

The Big League Complex

Hey! It's Jason! Star of stage, screen and true romance. Right now I could live without other people's spectacular arrivals. Today one of my ships didn't come in. I forget which one. Fame, Love, Last Week's Rent, one of them sank without a bubble. So naturally this is the night I start running into half the successful hotshots in New York, none of whom I have ever laid eyes on before in my life. Out of a cab in front of an apartment house where the servitors haul iron lilies out of the cellar and into the courtyard and paint them green, white and gold every spring, namely, The Dakota, No. 1 West 72nd Street, here comes Jason Robards, dressed up like what the Beatles call a "rocker."

A rocker, as opposed to the Beatles, who are fops, is a teen-ager who wears tight levis and leather jackets and says things like "Cool it." Only Jason Robards, easing himself out of a cab in front of the Dakota, sighing, drooping his eyeballs, is at this moment the best-known actor in New York. He is just coming home after doing his three-hour stint for the second time, the second night of the most publicized play in New York, Arthur Miller's play about Arthur Miller and Marilyn Monroe, *After the Fall.* He wears a gray suit in the play, but now he has his skinny shanks encased in a pair of buff-colored levis. He has on a leather jacket and a Tyrolean hat with feathers in it. He is dragging himself up the driveway of the most iron-lilied, sentry-boxed, wood-paneled, maid's-roomy apartment house in New York City, with his eye pouches sliding down over his cheekbones. Here is a gray-haired, long-faced man protruding from the collar of his teen-age rocker outfit.

Two rather grand couples have just walked out of the Dakota, and one of the women says, "Hey! It's Jason!"

"He looks exhausted," says the other one.

"Jason!" says the first one, "You look exhausted!"

"Aaaaagggggh!" says Jason. "I *feel* exhausted. I'm beat."

"My God," says one of the men, in a wonderful bassoon voice, "it must be *bru*tal. I mean, I'm no judge, but how long are you on *stage,* Jason? It must be *three hours!*"

The newspapers have been full of that very intelligence, how Jason Robards is on stage three hours in *After the Fall.* Robards stares for a moment. Then he shrugs his eyebrows and rolls his eyes back into his optic chiasma and thrashes his mandibles around a little.

"I'm sorry," he says, "I am absolutely beat."

So a servitor comes out of the sentry box and opens the scrolly iron gate and Jason Robards goes sloughing into the Dakota in his rocker levis of the uptown bohemian Actors Studio genre, and the wide cravats and double-breasted waistcoats lie under glass in muggy memorabilia of Edwin Booth, John Barrymore and the Players Club.

O.K., there goes Jason Robards. The next thing I remember, I am on West 52nd Street, a block from Broadway. The theatres have let out. Some kids are playing Zonk Ball and shooting the cowboy in the Sports Palace at the corner of Broadway. Down the street women are hunkering in and out of cabs like arteriosclerotic flamingoes and bobbing through the electric pastel shadows of Junior's Lounge, Roseland and the Confucius Bar, underneath the neon bamboo at Ruby Foo's and the roadside Dairy Queen marquee of Jilly's, local throne room for Frank Sinatra and his friends, or just scuffing around the corner by the Republic Auto Parts store, which leads from Broadway back to plain cost-accountable Eighth Avenue again. Across the street at the ANTA Theater, where *Marathon '33* is playing, the show has let out, but there is a little blonde in a great fluffy silver-fox stole standing by the stage door. She has a soft face, very placid. I think I recognize it, but I can't place it. Then I realize that it is a young movie actress, Tuesday Weld. I have no idea what she doing there. I don't know if she is waiting for somebody to come out of the stage door or just standing around on Broadway, out amongst them, like Cassius Clay, who used to promenade down Seventh Avenue near the Metropole Café, just to see how long it took to pull a crowd. People come out of the stage door from time to time, and she gives them the once-over, and they head down 52nd Street. Then a funny thing happens.

An old man wearing an ulster coat and a homburg is walking west on 52nd Street. As he walks past Tuesday Weld, standing outside the stage door, he looks over and says, "Young lady, you were perfectly marvelous tonight. You were perfectly marvelous."

He seems altogether sincere, even though Tuesday Weld has never been in a Broadway play in her life. Tuesday Weld just sort of rolls around in her furs and laughs in a nonplussed way and looks around at the people on the sidewalk as if to ask whether anybody knows if this old guy is trying to put her on. He keeps right on talking. His voice has that upbeat, throbbing note in it, the note that says, "Courage, courage."

"You keep it up," he says. "You'll be in the movies some day."

Then he nods in a very nice way and walks on down 52nd Street.

Tuesday Weld rolls around a little inside her fur. What else can she do? Is this guy putting her on? He is a nice old man, for Christ's sake.

I never do find out what Tuesday Weld is up to. For some reason, I forget exactly why, I head on over to the East Seventies. I am with some people, and we are heading into their apartment when the fellow looks down at the floor by the door next to theirs and says, "What the devil is A——— doing with all those boots?"

A——— turns out to be a singer everybody has heard of. There is a big, gamey pile of old boots, telephone linesman's rubber boots, hunter's boots, all kinds of boots, lying in a promiscuous heap outside her door. It has been snowing.

"Well, I guess they're all in tonight," the guy's wife says. "And keep your voice down."

"*All* in?" says the guy. "Who's there besides F———?"

"K———," she says. "They're both there."

"Since when?" he says.

"I don't know," she says. "I don't know her that well. I don't know until it snows."

"That's lovely," he says. "A *ménage de ménages*."

F——— and K——— are two men anybody who follows popular music would have heard of. F———, the fellow's wife tells me, lives with A———. You will have to excuse all these initials. K——— is an old boyfriend. As the fellow says, it is a

funny *ménage*. It is funny to see the whole algebra of A———,
F——— and K———, the night life of these gods of the entertainment world, whom one often reads about or sees in dark
and arty photographs, summed up in a pile of boots in the hall
outside somebody's apartment in the East Seventies.

I think of that pile of boots every time I get on the subject of
what it is like to live in New York. I also think of Jason Robards in his rocker suit and Tuesday Weld rolling around nonplussed inside her silver fox, wondering if a courtly old man on
52nd Street is trying to make some esoteric, hermetic, hermitic,
geriatric sport of her. Naturally, everybody refuses to be impressed by the fact that New York is full of the rich, the great,
the glamorous, the glorious. If you have any kind of luck at all,
they exist chiefly as celebrities, stars, mandarins, magnates,
which is to say, types, abstractions. And yet here they are, in
the flesh. They keep turning up. This, after all, is where they
come to dance for a while in quest of the big honeydew melon.
This is where they pile up their boots and turn out the lights.
And this fact—the fact that New York is the status capital of
the United States, if not the whole hulking world—has curious
effects on everybody who lives here. And by that I mean
everybody, even people who are not in the game.

The way to become a glamorous jewel thief in New York,
for example, is to steal enough nickels from the honor-system
cigar box on the newspaper stand outside the delicatessen to
buy yourself four-fifths of a pint of half-and-half. Half-and-
half is a drink bottled for the benefit of the winos, made of half
sherry and half port, both of which are twenty per cent alcohol. After a bottle of half-and-half even some poor old muzzle-
head who has been sitting on the sidewalk swabbing the le-
sions around his ankles with spit and a paper towel from the
subway men's room can work up the *esprit* to go into the Hotel
Pierre, or some similarly elegant place, and go to work with
the esoteric technique of jewel thievery. In most cases, this

esoteric technique amounts to two pieces of information that a few twelve-year-olds on the street corner in Bedford-Stuyvesant may not be familiar with yet. One is how to open a snap lock with a strip of celluloid, like a pocket calendar from a bank, which takes about fifteen minutes to learn. The second is the knowledge that the wealthiest people in places like the Pierre live in corner suites on high floors. The rest is the dumb luck of urban demography.

"There are so many rich big shots living in New York," Imrov is telling me, "that what happens is, the guy goes to one of these corner suites on a high floor, he don't know who is living there, he's got no idea at all, and he opens the door with the celluloid, takes the stuff and buys the paper in the morning and finds out he is a glamorous jewel thief. The place he hit turns out to be Jack Benny's, Jerry Lewis's, Xavier Cugat's, Linda Christian's, Rosalind Russell's or somebody like that."

Imrov is a puffy, adrenal little man I run into every now and then in Greenwich Village who bills himself as a professional jewel thief, only he is a realistic professional jewel thief, he tells me. I gather he likes to talk to me mainly because he knows I am a newspaper reporter. This means that Imrov is not only a typical New York jewel thief, which is to say, an egomaniac, but he also enjoys being a bona-fide New York cynic as well—a realist—looking out at the world with his cap tilted over one eye.

Imrov's analysis, however, is correct, I am informed by Inspector Raymond Maguire, who heads the Police Department's anti-robbery work in Manhattan. In fact, by nightfall of the day the papers came out telling how a jewel thief robbed Jack Benny's wife of $200,000, or something of the sort, the jewel thief not only believes that he is a glamorous jewel thief but also believes that he must have planned the job, as the newspapers insinuate, from beginning to end, calculating their every movement and picking the lock on their door with esoteric tools and the dulcet, long-practiced talents of a harp player. And let's forget about the celluloid.

"The trouble with a jewel thief," the Inspector tells me, "is that he is dying to let somebody know that he is the genius who hit Jack Benny or Dolores Del Rio, or whoever it was, and sooner or later he is at a bar some night letting it be known that he is a much bigger man than everybody realizes. Their own ego is the best thing we've got going for us against them."

Once a jewel thief is brought into Maguire's headquarters, at 400 Broome Street, there is usually no shutting the guy up. He is so grateful to be in the presence, at last, of a thoroughly understanding audience, with the fully technical knowledge of his problems, that he will replay his life in crime hour by hour, with bursts of rhetoric and every piece of jargon he can think of. The job of hearing them out usually falls to Lt. Robert McDermott. The high point comes if McDermott lets them demonstrate something on a set of mock-up locks he has. There in the ancient wood and plaster gloom of 400 Broome Street, it is like getting a concert hall at last for a fellow who is the glamorous jewel thief who hit a rich big shot in New York City.

The story of the jewel thieves is really the parable of life in New York. New York more than any other city in the world probably is the city full of rich big shots—the rich, the powerful, the celebrated, the glamorous. That is only half the story, however. There, at the top, are the *glamorosi* locked in the battle for the big prizes and the status. And there, at the bottom, are millions of people, like the jewel thieves, through whom the status feeling is racing like a rogue hormone. Much of what is chalked off as New York's rudeness, aggressiveness or impersonal treatment is in fact nothing more than some poor bastard convinced that he is in the "big-league" town, trying to put a little extra spin on his delivery.

A boy in a tweed coat and a rep tie who is in New York for

the weekend from Hotchkiss, the prep school, is down in the
men's room of the Biltmore Hotel washing his hands at the
basin, and an attendant in a gray orderly's coat comes over and
sticks a towel out toward him.

The boy gives him a level look and says, "Will it cost me
money?"

The attendant gives him a level look and says, "No, I'm
a —— jerk. I work for nothing."

And so down there amid the button tiles, the white enamel,
the perfume discs, the dime slots and the cascading flush, boy,
this is the big-league men's room with no —— jerks working
for nothing.

New York also has big-league bums. I remember the first
two bums who ever approached me in New York. It was down
at Broadway and 18th Street one night. The first one, a stocky
lout who didn't look more than thirty-eight, came up and
mumbled something, and I shook my head no, the usual, but
he wouldn't let up. He kept on coming and said, "I ain't asking
you for eighteen hundred dollars, for chrissake. I ain't going
off to Acapulco for the winter." I started outwalking him, mull-
ing over the way he had thrown in these specific details, the
eighteen hundred dollars and Acapulco, after the manner of
Wordsworth, who would be off in the middle of some lyric
passage about the woods and the glades, God, Freedom and
Immortality, when his glorious delicatessen owner's love of
minute inventory would overwhelm him and he could not help
recording that the little girl who appeared on the bridge over
the brook, a vision of love's own nostalgia, was exactly seven
and a half years old, or like Dickens, who—when this train of
thought was broken by the second bum, and old scrime with a
flaky face, who came up and asked me for something or other.
This time I tried something that had always worked in Washington, D.C., when the winos climbed Meridian Hill, I threw
my hands up and started talking in a gibberish approximation

of French, like Danny Kaye in the old git-gat-gittle days, the idea being that I didn't speak English and therefore didn't know what he was saying. So the guy just stares at me for a moment and says, "O.K., since you're a —— foreigner who don't speak English, then why don't you go — — — — — — hat, you — — — —."

Well, he had me there. What could I do? Announce that I only understood the swear words? A real big-league bum who had to let me know this town has the kind of bums you don't put anything over on.

The big-league complex is also responsible for a lot of what strikes visitors to New York as gratuitous rudeness. I remember one day in the spring I was walking around Gramercy Park, which is an elaborate formal garden, one city block in size, surrounded by a tall, ornate iron fence, where Lexington Avenue hits 21st Street, and here was a young couple, very nice-looking, standing in front of Gramercy Park's east gate. He had a camera around his neck and a big map in his hands, and she had a camera around her neck and a baby in her arms, and they were both trying to figure out Gramercy Park. Apparently here was this nice-looking park and they had tried to get in but none of the gates was open. What they didn't know was that Gramercy Park is a private park, owned by the Gramercy Park Association and open only to certain people who live around it. Its usual population is nurses, nannies, mothers in Casual Shoppe tweeds who can't afford nurses and nannies because of the $25,000 cash, raised by a personal loan at a cool 10 per cent that daddy had to lay down for the co-op, and children, the children they wanted to be on Gramercy Park for, so they could play in it, surrounded by an iron spear fence, and convalescing dowagers taking the rays with lap robes from the old La Salle sedan days over their atrophying shanks. That is the place the young couple is puzzling over. As for them, they look like the kind of Swedish couple that turns up in the airline ads—good, wholesome, tan and windblown, except that she offers every promise of owning a pair of stretch slacks that live in all the secret fissures the Z-ad writers cannot offer a vocabulary for.

From across the street a doorman at one of the big apartment houses on the park sees the man and his wife puzzling over the map and the park and walks across the street and says, "Can I help you folks?"

This seems like a nice enough gesture, so the young man says, "Well, thank you. We just happened to notice this park, it's a very lovely park, but the gates don't seem to be open."

"Of course they're not open," says the doorman, as if he has not heard many more obvious remarks in his entire life.

"What do you mean?" says the young man. "How do you get in?"

"You get in if you have a key," says the doorman.

"A key?" says the young man.

"It's a pri-vate park," says the doorman, in the tone of voice you spell out inane instructions to a child in.

"I see," says the young man. "Well, couldn't we just step inside for a minute and look around. We just happened to be walking by and it's such a lovely park—"

"What do you think we have *rules* for!" yells the doorman, suddenly opening up, as if a weakling young daddy with a large mortgage and no common sense has dragged him all the way out of his home and across the street to ask him a lot of simple-minded questions. "If we let everybody 'just step inside for a minute,' we might as well not have any rules! Right?"

"Well, now, just a minute!" begins the young man, because after all, he is standing here in front of his wife and his child, being bullied around by a doorman.

"Just a minute yourself!" says the doorman.

So the poor guy's baby starts to cry, and his wife is looking to him to for God's sake solve this stupid situation, and he is trying to be firm and say, "Look—," while the doorman says,

"As a matter of fact, this is a good example of why we *have* rules!" And the baby is crying louder, and the girl is trying to quiet down the baby and some of the arteriosclerotic old denizens of Gramercy Park are shuffling their shanks and staring out through the iron fence with that look on the face intended to kill instantly all young people who can't control their squalling children, or for that matter, all children, on a kind of lap-robe-genteel Herodian principle. The young guy, of course, is humiliated and he will spend the rest of the day taking it out in secret ways on his wife and his damnable kid for every comeback he didn't think of to put the doorman in his place, and all the while, as the day goes up in smoke, he will not realize that the doorman was only doing the usual, being the big-leaguer and walking a block, if that is what it takes, to set the outlanders straight.

The secret vice of New York cab drivers is the same thing. They all secretly relish New York traffic. They consider it the most big-league traffic in the world. By god, we navigate big-league traffic. That is behind half the yelling they do. It explains their unflagging, unbeatable boorishness. They all believe that this is real big-league traffic and everyone but big leaguers should stay the hell out of it, they have no *bus*iness there. I can remember a cab driver who had a couple of people in his cab, who were presumably going some place, pulling up right behind a woman who was stranded in the middle of traffic at Fifth Avenue and Forty-second Street, a very well-dressed, elderly woman, rather frightened, naturally, and leaning out and yelling at her, right behind her aging mastoids:

"Hey! Jackass!"

The woman ignored him, but he didn't pull off. He yelled it again: "Hey! Jackass!"

She still didn't flinch, so he yelled it again, just sitting there in the middle of traffic himself: "Hey! Jackass!"

She didn't turn around so he said it again: "Hey! Jackass!"

And she didn't turn around, so he kept on saying it: "Hey! Jackass! Hey! Jackass! Hey! Jackass! Hey! Jackass!" all the time in the loudest voice you can imagine, the kind of voice cab drivers develop from yelling from way back in the throat and enriching and compacting the sound with phlegm, rheum, tobacco scum, guinea grinders, cheese Danishes, grease-soaked knishes, tooth decay, flat beer, constipation and sinus snufflings: "Hey! Jackass!"

Finally, the woman can't stand it anymore, and she wheels around, furious, she doesn't care which way cars are coming from at this point, and as soon as she does, the cabbie sticks his face squarely in hers and yells, "Hey! Jackass! Look where you're going! Jackass!" and then guns off in first gear, letting her have a good, soggy, liquid spray of exhaust across the knees. This is big-league traffic, lady.

The curious thing is, however, that there is still a genre of intellectuals, serious writers even, who talk about New York's cab drivers and dirt, the foul air, the overcrowding, the noise, the rudeness, and all the rest of it, and say that, you know, in spite of all that it all adds up to "magic." They really still use words like "magic" and tell how stimulating it all is. The "magic" and the similar euphemisms that crop up in this connection, like 19th century perennials, are really unconscious translations of the word "status." There is a hell of a lot of magic in New York as long as you're riding high and can drink two Scotches-on-the-rocks before dinner and look out at the city lights while your blood rises up into your nice, pellucid 1930's Manhattan Tower brain like charged-water bubbles. It is Pavlov and not Freud who has had something to say about New York City. It is as if New York were operating on a pleasure principle like that which was discovered, darkly, when they imbedded an electrode in the dog's brain and it hit some unknown pleasure center. He could turn on the impulse and feel the mysterious sensation by hitting a pedal with his foot, which he began doing over and over again. This brain center had nothing to do with any of the conventional senses. They could place bowls full of food before him and lead bitches in heat before him, and he never showed the slightest inclination to budge from the pedal. He just kept hitting it, over and over, not sleeping, not eating, until the strain of exhaustion and starvation became too much and he keeled over, his last gesture being a feeble push with his paw toward the pedal, which stirred up the mysterious pleasure beyond the senses by a simple, direct impulse to the brain.

The pleasures of status, the impulses of status striving, seem almost to have that sort of physical basis in New York.

For example, there are people who do not ride the subways, or do not want it known that they ride the subways and develop twitches and cringes on the subject. It is a point of social standing with them. There are men in New York who ride the subways but do not want it generally known and cringe when they pull out a pocketful of change and other people can see that along with the other change, there are subway tokens. There is no one around who ever heard of them, but they cringe anyway. The impulse is that the subways are for proles, and people of status travel only by cab, or perhaps once in a great while by bus.

I can remember a scene in the Artist & Writers Restaurant, on West 40th Street, when one of the fashion magazines sent a team in to shoot a fashion shot. "Team" is only the convenient word; it was really more like a cast. There were about twelve people. The photographer was a little guy in a hairy gray kimono-style overcoat, no buttons and a sash belt, chalk-stripe pants, orange stripes on blue, like a Gulf Station attendant's, only cut "continental." He had two helpers, both zombie-like men in black who carried his equipment or something. There was the model, who lounged back against the bar, and she had what seemed to be two ladies-in-waiting and one keeper. In addition there was a major editor from the magazine, a fashion editor and two or three satraps, little girls from Sarah Lawrence, still in sweaters, skirts and buttercup blouses. It had been snowing that day and they were all late. The photographer looked around the premises, then closed his eyes and said in a kind of huge stage whisper: "No!"

"What do you mean?" somebody else said.

"What do you mean?" somebody else said.

"It won't do!" said the photographer, looking straight ahead.

"Why not?" somebody said.

"It won't do," said the photographer.

"What do you mean?" Somebody else said.

"I said it won't do," said the photographer. "The decision is up to me and I say it won't do."

Meantime, I was standing around and I introduced myself to the model. She just nodded.

"What is your name?" I said.

"Ravena," she said.

"Ravena what?" I said.

"Ravena," she said.

"Ravena what?" I said.

"Ravena's enough," she said.

"Ravena Zenuf," I said, on the grounds that that was quite a name.

She just turned up her lips in that bored way some girls have, then let them drop.

Just then the decision was announced, the decision that the place wouldn't do.

"How am I gonna get back?" said Ravena. "It took us an hour to get over here."

"Why don't you take the subway?" I said. And then, just that one time, I got an answer out of Ravena.

"The subway! Are you kidding?"

"You can catch it right up the street, the shuttle, and it'll take you across town in no time.

"I don't ride no subways!" said Ravena.

"Why not?"

"Down deh wid dose Puerto Ricans and creeps?" said Ravena. "Are you kidding!"

In a way, of course, the subway is the living symbol of all that adds up to lack of status in New York. There is a sense of madness and disorientation at almost every express stop. The ceilings are low, the vistas are long, there are no landmarks, the lighting is an eerie blend of fluorescent tubing, electric light bulbs and neon advertising. The whole place is a gross assault in the senses. The noise of the trains stopping or rounding curves has a high-pitched harshness that is difficult to describe. People feel no qualms about pushing whenever it becomes crowded. Your tactile sense takes a crucifying you never dreamed possible. The odors become unbearable when the weather is warm. Between platforms, record shops broadcast 45 r.p.m. records with metallic tones and lunch counters serve the kind of hot dogs in which you bite through a tensile, rubbery surface and then hit a soft, oleaginous center like cottonseed meal, and the customers sit there with pastry and bread flakes caked around their mouths, belching to themselves so that their cheeks pop out flatulently now and then.

The underground spaces seem to attract every eccentric passion. A small and ancient man with a Bible, an American flag and a megaphone haunts the subways of Manhattan. He opens the Bible and quotes from it in a strong but old and monotonous voice. He uses the megaphone at express stops, where the noise is too great for his voice to be heard ordinarily, and calls for redemption.

334

Also beggars. And among the beggars New York's status competition is renewed, there in the much-despised subway. On the Seventh Avenue IRT line the competition is maniacal. Some evenings the beggars ricochet off one another between stops, calling one another ———s and ———s and telling each other to go find their own ——— car. A mere blind man with a cane and a cup is mediocre business. What is demanded is entertainment. Two boys, one of them with a bongo drum, get on and the big boy, with the drum, starts beating on it as soon as the train starts up, and the little boy goes into what passes for a native dance. Then, if there is room, he goes into a tumbling act. He runs from one end of the car, first in the direction the train is going, and does a complete somersault in the air, landing on his feet. Then he runs back the other way and does a somersault in the air, only this time against the motion of the train. He does this several times both ways, doing some native dancing in between. This act takes so long that it can be done properly only over a long stretch, such as the run between 42nd Street and 72nd Street. After the act is over, the boys pass along the car with Dixie cups, asking for contributions.

The Dixie cup is the conventional container. There is one young Negro on the Seventh Avenue line who used to get on at 42nd Street and start singing a song, "I Wish That I Were Married." He was young and looked perfectly healthy. But he would get on and sing this song, "I Wish That I Were Married," at the top of his lungs and then pull a Dixie cup out from under the windbreaker he always wore and walk up and down the car waiting for contributions. I never saw him get a cent. Lately, however, life has improved for him because he has begun to understand status competition. Now he gets on and sings "I Wish That I Were Married," only when he opens up his windbreaker, he not only takes out a Dixie cup but reveals a cardboard sign, on which is written: "MY MOTHER HAS

MULTIPLE SCHLERROSSIS AND I AM BLIND IN ONE EYE." His best touch is sclerosis, which he has added every conceivable consonant to, creating a good, intimidating German physiology-textbook solidity. So today he does much better. He seems to make a living. He is no idler, lollygagger or bum. He can look with condescension upon the states to which men fall.

On the East Side IRT subway line, for example, at 86th Street, the train stops and everyone comes squeezing out of the cars in clots and there on a bench in the gray-green gloom, under the girders and 1905 tiles, is an old man slouched back fast asleep, wearing a cotton windbreaker with the sleeves pulled off. That is all he is wearing. His skin is the color of congealed Wheatena laced with pocket lint. His legs are crossed in a gentlemanly fashion and his kindly juice-head face is slopped over on the back of the bench. Apparently, other winos, who are notorious thieves among one another, had stripped him of all his clothes except his windbreaker, which they had tried to pull off him, but only managed to rip the sleeves off, and left him there passed out on the bench and naked, but in a gentlemanly posture. Everyone stares at him briefly, at his congealed Wheatena-and-lint carcass, but no one breaks stride; and who knows how long it will be before finally two policemen have to come in and hold their breath and scrape him up out of the gloom and into the bosom of the law, from which he will emerge with a set of green fatigues, at least, and an honorable seat at night on the subway bench.

The unfortunate thing is that a nekkid old wino on a subway bench is not even a colorful sight, or magical. It is something worth missing altogether, and in fact much of the status symbolism of New York grows out of the ways the rich and the striving manage to insulate themselves, physically, from the lower depths. They live up high to escape the dirt and the noise. They live on the corners to get the air. And on Monday nights they go to the Metropolitan Opera in limousines.

Up to the Broadway and the 39th Street entrances roll the limousines and out debouch the linked and the lacquered, as Wallace Stevens used to say, and then, as no one ever notices, the limousines pull off. The chauffeurs have to go somewhere, after all, while their people, as they call them, go settling down, like animated Lalique, into the Parterre Boxes and the Dress Circle, for two, three, even four hours of opera. So the chauffeurs have developed an opera-night social life of their own. They drive across 39th Street, over to Eighth Avenue, and then turn back up 40th, between Eighth and Seventh. There may be as many as fifty limousines heading for the block. There is a mounted policeman with nothing to do but wait for them. At 7:30 he raises his right hand as the signal, and the chauffeurs can start lining up on either side. In a few minutes the neon signs of the London Tavern, a set-'em-up and hook-'em-down saloon near the corner, are flooding in splendid orange pools on the grilles, hoods, and Art Nouveau radiator caps of Rolls-Royces and Cadillacs, and the lineup of limousines begins to stretch all the way to Eighth Avenue.

The chauffeurs, after all, come to the opera as often as their employers, and so it is a social thing for them, too. By 8 P.M. in their black coats, black ties, black visored caps, they are already standing around in groups on the sidewalk, and by 8:30 the first groups head for Bickford's Cafeteria. Someone has to stay behind to watch the automobiles. They end up tooling in and out of Bickford's in shifts. They sit down at the formica tops and drink coffee and talk about opera, among other things.

"Germans!" Leland, who drives for Mrs. -——, tells me. "Richard Strauss. They won't let out until 11:45."

"Strauss isn't so bad," says a friend of Leland's, a very old and apoplectic-looking chauffeur who doesn't shave very well.

"It's only *Der Rosenkavalier*," Frank, Mr. P——'s man,

tells me. "The rest of the time"—he shrugs—"Strauss is O.K. Wagner is the holy terror."

"You're not kidding now."

"Wagner!"

"Give me the Italians," Leland says.

"Puccini!"

"Right!"

"*Tosca.*"

"*Tosca*?" I say.

"Yes," says Leland. "*Tosca* lets out about 10:30."

"I've been to *Tosca* when it lasted to 11:15," says a younger chauffeur, an earnest man with a great head of straight black hair, but no one pays any attention to him. He drives Carey Cadillacs, rented by opera-goers who do not have limousines of their own.

"The Italians I can live with," Leland announces, and they all nod over the heavy-duty ochre chinaware and the formica tops.

Jason Robards, Tuesday Weld, the *ménage à trois*, celebrity-style—and now chauffeurs who sit in Bickford's cafeteria discussing opera and cutting the Carey crowd. All that New York needs is simpler people.

Hugh Troy eased the situation a little. Hugh Troy, the artist and children's book author, got one of the cab drivers who has an exposition to make.

"It's a hot day for the middle of February!" says the cab driver.

"Yes, it is," Hugh Troy says.

"You know," the cab driver says, "they say the earth's skin is slipping, and right now New York is right over where Savannah, Georgia used to be. The whole skin is slipping."

Hugh Troy thinks that over a second and says, "It must be getting very baggy."

"Baggy?" says the cab driver.

"You know—baggy down around the South Pole."

The cab driver thinks that over a while and never does go on with his exposition of how the earth's skin is slipping.

"Baggy," Hugh Troy says to himself, "down around the South Pole."

Well, Hugh Troy has taken one big-leaguer out of the action—but there are so many millions to go.